HRM
in
Hotel and Tourism Industry

HRM
in
Hotel and Tourism Industry

Existing Trends and Practices

Percy K. Singh

KANISHKA PUBLISHERS, DISTRIBUTORS
NEW DELHI-110 002

KANISHKA PUBLISHERS, DISTRIBUTORS
4697/5-21A, Ansari Road, Daryaganj
New Delhi-110 002
Phones : 2327 0497, 2328 8285
Fax : 011-2328 8285
e-mail: kanishka_publishing@yahoo.co.in

First Published 2008

ISBN 978-81-8457-078-6

PRINTED IN INDIA

Published by Madan Sachdeva for Kanishka Publishers, Distributors, 4697/5-21A, Ansari Road, Daryaganj, New Delhi-110 002; Typeset by Sunshine Graphics, Delhi, and Printed at Nice Printing Press, Delhi.

Preface

This book deals with existing trends and practices in hotel and tourism industry with respect to human resource management. It provides an introductory overview of human resources, its management, management system, hospitality, tourism, and service aspects. Case study of selected hotel industry with reference to human resource management functions and strategies are provided. Also a diagnostic checklist is developed with respect to human resource management system in the said industry. Factors, such as, employees' education, training and education; their provision for services; industrial relations; employee evaluation; employee motivation; their recruitment and selection; manpower planning; etc. are discussed in detail vis-à-vis hotel industry in India and Abroad. Steps in developing HRM strategy and diagnostic checklists are outlined. Select case studies are also made regarding the aforementioned issues. Contemporary practices and areas of research in HRM management in hotel industry are also highlighted. Select case studies and educational syllabi are also provided here in for further understanding and reference. The training and development aspects in human resources management are described with respect to hotel, restaurant and hospitality agencies and institutions. Focus lies on developing strategy, innovation and performance aspects. Selected case studies are undertaken with focus on issues like, union certification elections; trainers chart; food service management; women chefs; associations; and group of hotels. This book further addresses the issue of human resource training in travel and tourism sectors. The elements which have got enough elaboration in this book include training's needs and assessment; tourism teachers and trainers; human resources council; model course on organizational behaviour; tourism research; and HR initiative in India and Abroad. Ways and means of integrating human resources management in tourism and hospitality industries are dealt in detail, with focus on both hard and soft approaches. Relevant case studies from the airlines industry and hotel industry are provided with quality enhancement as the central goal. Other case studies refer to related institutes and universities. In sum this book will serve the purpose of a sourcebook on the said subject in all-times to come. Detailed acronyms/abbreviations, glossary of terms, bibliography, websites/links and a user-friendly index makes this book special in terms of reference and future research.

Percy K. Singh

Contents

1

Introduction to Human Resource Management, Hospitality Service and Tourism

HUMAN RESOURCE

Human resources term in which many organizations describe the combination of traditionally administrative personnel functions with performance management, employee relations and resource planning. The field draws upon concepts developed in Industrial/ Organizational Psychology. Human resources has at least two related interpretations depending on context. The original usage derives from political economy and economics, where it was traditionally called labour, one of four factors of production. The more common usage within corporations and businesses refers to the individuals within the firm, and to the portion of the firm's organization that deals with hiring, firing, training, and other personnel issues. This article addresses both definitions.

The objective of Human Resources is to maximize the return on investment from the organization's human capital and minimize financial risk. It is the responsibility of human resource managers to conduct these activities in an effective, legal, fair and consistent manner. Human resource management serves these key functions:

1. Recruitment Strategy Planning.
2. Hiring Processes (recruitment).
3. Performance Evaluation and Management.
4. Promotions.
5. Redundancy.
6. Industrial and Employee Relations.
7. Record keeping of all personal data.

8. Compensation, pensions, bonuses etc., in liaison with Payroll.
9. Confidential advice to internal 'customers' in relation to problems at work.

Modern analysis emphasizes that human beings are not "commodities" or "resources", but are creative and social beings that make class contributions beyond 'labour' to a society and to civilization. The broad term human capital has evolved to contain some of this complexity, and in micro-economics the term "firm-specific human capital" has come to represent a meaning of the term "human resources."

Advocating the central role of "human resources" or human capital in enterprises and societies has been a traditional role of Human Resource socialist parties, who claim that value is primarily created by their activity, and accordingly justify a larger claim of profits or relief from these enterprises or societies. Critics say this is just a bargaining tactic which grew out of various practices of medieval European guilds into the modern trade union and collective bargaining unit.

A contrary view, common to capitalist parties, is that it is the infrastructural capital and (what they call) intellectual capital owned and fused by "management" that provides most value in financial capital terms. This likewise justifies a bargaining position and a general view that "human resources" are interchangeable.

A significant sign of consensus on this latter point is the ISO 9000 series of standards which requires a "job description" of every participant in a productive enterprise. In general, heavily unionized nations such as France and Germany have adopted and encouraged such descriptions especially within trade unions. One view of this trend is that a strong social consensus on political economy and a good social welfare system facilitates labour mobility and tends to make the entire economy more productive, as labour can move from one enterprise to another with little controversy or difficulty in adapting.

An important controversy regarding labour mobility illustrates the broader philosophical issue with usage of the phrase "human resources": governments of developing nations often regard developed nations that encourage immigration or "guest workers" as appropriating human capital that is rightfully part of the developing nation and required to further its growth as a civilization. They argue that this appropriation is similar to colonial commodity fiat wherein a colonizing European power would define an arbitrary price for natural resources, extracting which diminished national natural capital.

The debate regarding "human resources" versus human capital thus in many ways echoes the debate regarding natural resources versus natural capital. Over time the United Nations have come to more generally support the developing nations' point of view, and have requested significant offsetting "foreign aid" contributions so that a developing nation losing human capital does not lose the capacity to continue to train new people in trades, professions, and the arts.

An extreme version of this view is that historical inequities such as African slavery must be compensated by current developed nations, which benefited from stolen "human resources" as they were developing. This is an extremely controversial view, but it echoes the general theme of converting human capital to "human resources" and thus greatly diminishing its value to the host society, i.e. "Africa", as it is put to narrow imitative use as "labour" in the using society.

In a series of reports of the UN Secretary-General to the General Assembly over the last decade [e.g. A/56/162 (2001)], a broad inter sectoral approach to developing human resourcefulness has been outlined as a priority for socio-economic development and particularly anti-poverty strategies. This calls for strategic and integrated public policies, for example in education, health, and employment sectors that promote occupational skills, knowledge and performance enhancement.

In the very narrow context of corporate "human resources", there is a contrasting pull to reflect and require workplace diversity that echoes the diversity of a global customer base. Foreign language and culture skills, ingenuity, humor, and careful listening, are examples of traits that such programmes typically require. It would appear that these evidence a general shift to the human capital point of view, and an acknowledgment that human beings do contribute much more to a productive enterprise than "work": they bring their character, their ethics, their creativity, their social connections, and in some cases even their pets and children, and alter the character of a workplace. The term corporate culture is used to characterize such processes.

The traditional but extremely narrow context of hiring, firing, and job description is considered a 20th century anachronism. Most corporate organizations that compete in the modern global economy have adopted a view of human capital that mirrors the modern consensus as above. Some of these, in turn, deprecate the term "human resources" as useless.

As the term refers to predictable exploitations of human capital in one context or another, it can still be said to apply to manual labour, mass agriculture, low skill "McJobs" in service industries, military and other work that has clear job descriptions, and which generally do not encourage creative or social contributions.

In general the abstractions of macro-economics treat it this way—as it characterizes no mechanisms to represent choice or ingenuity. So one interpretation is that "firm-specific human capital" as defined in macro-economics is the modern and correct definition of "human resources"—and that this is inadequate to represent the contributions of "human resources" in any modern theory of political economy.

Human Resource Development

In terms of recruitment and selection it is important to consider carrying out a thorough job analysis to determine the level of skills/ technical abilities, competencies, flexibility of the employee required etc. At this point it is important to consider both the internal and external factors that can have an effect on the recruitment of employees. The external factors are those out-with the powers of the organization and include issues such as current and future trends of the labour market e.g. skills, education level, government investment into industries etc. On the other hand, internal influences are easier to control, predict and monitor, for example management styles or even the organizational culture.

In order to know the business environment in which any organization operates, three major trends should be considered:

- *Demographics*: The characteristics of a population/ workforce, for example, age, gender or social class. This type of trend may have an effect in relation to pension offerings, insurance packages etc.

- *Diversity*: The variation within the population/workplace. Changes in society now mean that a larger proportion of organizations are made up of "baby-boomers" or older employees in comparison to thirty years ago. Also, over recent years organizations have had to become more diverse in their employment practices to cope with the lower work ethic of the newer generations. The service industry, for example, has embraced those "baby-boomers" desiring to re-enter the workforce. Traditional advocates of "workplace diversity" simply advocate an employee base that is a mirror reflection of the make-up of society insofar as race, gender, sexual orientation, etc. These advocates focus on the social engineering theory without understanding the more important points: diversity of ideas to prevent stagnation of products and business development; expanding the customer base through "outreach"; and profit. Alarmists and advocates of social engineering theory cite a "rise in discrimination, unfair dismissal and sexual/racial harassment cases" as an indicator of the need for more diversity legislation. While such measures have a significant effect on the organization, they effect little or no real change in advancing diversity of ideas in the workplace. Anti-discrimination laws and regulations do require businesses to undertake a cost-benefit analysis. The result of this analysis is often to adopt an approach that generally recognizes gender, racial, and sexual orientation diversity as a cheaper alternative to fighting endless litigation. In summary, diversity, based on social engineering "is about creating a working culture that seeks, respects and values difference" without regard to how diversity increases productivity and unity of effort.
- *Skills and qualifications*: As industries move from manual to a more managerial professions so does the need for more highly skilled graduates. If the market is "tight" (i.e. not enough staff for the jobs), employers will have to compete for employees by offering financial rewards, community investment, etc.

In regard to how individuals respond to the changes in a labour market the following should be understood:

- *Geographical spread*: How far is the job from the individual? The distance to travel to work should be in line with the pay offered by the organization and the transportation and infrastructure of the area will also be an influencing factor in deciding who will apply for a post.
- *Occupational structure*: The norms and values of the different careers within an organization. Mahoney 1989 developed 3 different types of occupational structure namely craft (loyalty to the profession), organization career (promotion through the firm) and unstructured (lower/unskilled workers who work when needed).
- *Generational difference*: Different age categories of employees have certain characteristics, for example their behaviour and their expectations of the organization.

While recruitment methods are wide and varied, it is important that the job is described correctly and that any personal specifications are stated. Job recruitment methods can be through job centres, employment agencies/consultants, headhunting, and local/national newspapers. It is important that the correct media is chosen to ensure an appropriate response to the advertised post.

Modern Concept of Human Resources

Though human resources have been part of business and organizations since the first days of agriculture, the modern concept of human resources began in reaction to the efficiency focus of Taylorism in the early 1900s. By 1920, psychologists and employment experts in the United States started the human relations movement, which viewed workers in terms of their psychology and fit with companies, rather than as interchangeable parts. This movement grew throughout the middle of the 20th century, placing emphasis on how leadership, cohesion, and loyalty played important roles in organizational success. Although this view was increasingly challenged by more quantitatively rigorous and less "soft" management techniques in the 1960s and beyond, human resources had gained a permanent role within an organization.

HUMAN RESOURCE MANAGEMENT (HRM)

Human resource management is the strategic and coherent approach to the management of an organization's most valued assets—the people working there who individually and collectively contribute to the achievement of the objectives of the business. The terms "human resource management" and "human resources" have largely replaced the term "personnel management" as a description of the processes involved in managing people in organizations. Human resource management is evolving rapidly. Human resource management is both an academic theory and a business practice that addresses the theoretical and practical techniques of managing a workforce.

Synonyms

Its synonyms include:

- Personnel administration.
- Personnel management.
- Manpower management.
- Industrial management.

But these traditional expressions are becoming less common for the theoretical discipline. Sometimes even industrial relations and employee relations are confusingly listed as synonyms, although these normally refer to the relationship between management and workers and the behaviour of workers in companies.

The theoretical discipline is based primarily on the assumption that employees are individuals with varying goals and needs, and as such should not be thought of as basic business resources, such as trucks and filing cabinets. The field takes a positive view of workers, assuming that virtually all wish to contribute to the enterprise productively, and that the main obstacles to their endeavours are lack of knowledge, insufficient training, and failures of process.

HRM is seen by practitioners in the field as a more innovative view of workplace management than the traditional approach. Its techniques force the managers of an enterprise to express their goals with specificity so that they can be understood and undertaken by the workforce, and to provide the resources needed for them to successfully accomplish their assignments. As such, HRM techniques, when properly practiced, are expressive of the goals and operating practices of the enterprise overall. HRM is also seen by many to have a key role in risk reduction within organistions.

Synonyms such as *personnel management* are often used in a more restricted sense to describe activities that are necessary in the recruitment of a workforce, providing its members with payroll and benefits, and administrating their work-life needs. So if we move to actual defintions, Torrington and Hall (1987) define personnel management as being;

> "a series of activities which: first enable working people and their employing organisations to agree about the objectives and nature of their working relationship and, secondly, ensures that the agreement is fulfilled" (p. 49).

While Miller (1987) suggests that HRM relates to:

> "...those decisions and actions which concern the management of employees at all levels in the business and which are related to the implementation of strategies directed towards creating and sustaining competitive advantage" (p. 352).

Academic Theory

The goal of human resource management is to help an organization to meet strategic goals by attracting, and maintaining employees and also to manage them effectively. The key word here perhaps is "fit", i.e. an HRM approach seeks to ensure a fit between the management of an organisation's employees, and the overall strategic direction of the company (Miller, 1989).

The basic premise of the academic theory of HRM is that humans are not machines, therefore we need to have an inter-disciplinary examination of people in the workplace. Fields such as psychology, industrial engineering, industrial and organizational psychology, industrial relations, sociology, and critical theories: postmodernism, post-structuralism play a major role. Many colleges and universities offer bachelor and master degrees in Human Resources Management.

One widely used scheme to describe the role of HRM, developed by Dave Ulrich, defines 4 fields for the HRM function:

- Strategic business partner.
- Change agent.
- Employee champion.
- Administration.

However, many HR functions these days struggle to get beyond the roles of administration and employee champion, and are seen rather as reactive than strategically proactive partners for the top management. In addition, HR organizations also have the difficulty in proving how their activities and processes add value to the company. Only in the recent years HR scholars and HR professionals are focusing to develop models that can measure if HR adds value.

Critical Academic Theory

Post-modernism plays an important part in Academic Theory and particularly in Critical Theory. Indeed Karen Legge in 'Human Resource Management: Rhetorics and Realities' poses the debate of whether HRM is a modernist project or a post-modern discourse (Legge 2004)? In many ways, critically or not, many writers contend that HRM itself is a movement away from the modernist traditions of personnel (man as machine) towards a post-modernist view of HRM man as individuals. Critiques include the notion that because 'Human' is the subject we should recognise that people are complex and that it is only through various discourses that we understand the world. Man is not Machine, no matter what attempts are made to change it i.e. Fordism/Taylorism, McDonaldisation (Modernism).

Critical theory also questions whether HRM is the pursuit of "attitudinal shaping" (Wilkinson, 1998), particularly when considering empowerment, or perhaps more precisely pseudo-empowerment—as the critical perspective notes.

Business Practice

Human resources management comprises several processes. Together they are supposed to achieve the above mentioned goal. These processes can be performed in an HR department, but some tasks can also be outsourced or performed by line-managers or other departments.

- Workforce planning.
- Recruitment (sometimes separated into attraction and selection).
- Induction and Orientation.
- Skills management.
- Training and development.
- Personnel administration.
- Compensation in wage or salary.
- Time management.
- Travel management (sometimes assigned to accounting rather than HRM).
- Payroll (sometimes assigned to accounting rather than HRM).
- Employee benefits administration.
- Personnel cost planning.
- Performance appraisal.

Careers

The sort of careers available in HRM are varied. There are generalist HRM jobs such as human resource assistant. There are careers involved with employment, recruitment and placement and these are usually conducted by interviewers, EEO (Equal Opportunity Employment) specialists or college recruiters. Training and development specialism is often conducted by trainers and orientation specialists. Compensation and benefits tasks are handled by compensation analysts, salary administrators and benefits administrators.

Professional Organizations

Professional organizations in HRM include the Society for Human Resource Management, the Chartered Institute of Personnel and Development (CIPD), the International Public Management Association for HR (IPMA-HR) and the International Personnel Management Association of Canada (IPMA-Canada).

HUMAN RESOURCE MANAGEMENT SYSTEMS (HRMS)

Human Resource Management Systems, Human Resource Information Systems (HRIS), HR Technology or also called HR modules, shape an intersection in between Human Resource Management (HRM) and information technology. It merges HRM as a discipline and in particular its basic HR activities and processes with the information technology field, whereas the planning and programming of data processing systems evolved into standardised routines and packages of Enterprise Resource Planning (ERP) software. On the whole, these ERP systems have their origin on software that integrates information from different applications into one universal database. The linkage of its financial and human resource modules through one database is the most important distinction to the individually and proprietary developed predecessors, which makes this software application both rigid and flexible.

The HR Function's Reality

All in all, the HR function is still to a large degree administrative and common to all organizations. To varying degrees, most organizations have formalised selection, evaluation, and payroll processes. Efficient and effective management of the "Human Capital Pool" (HCP) has become an increasingly imperative and complex activity to all HR professionals. The HR function consists of tracking innumerable data points on each employee, from personal histories, data, skills, capabilities, experiences to payroll records. To reduce the manual workload of these administrative activities, organizations began to electronically automate many of these processes by introducing innovative HRMS/HCM technology. Due to complexity in programming, capabilities and limited technical resources, HR executives rely on internal or external IT professionals to develop and maintain their Human Resource Management Systems (HRMS). Before the "client-server" architecture evolved in the late 1980s, every single HR automation process came largely in form of mainframe computers that could handle large amounts of data transactions. In consequence of the high capital investment necessary to purchase or programme proprietary software, these internally developed HRMS were limited to medium to large organizations being able to afford internal IT capabilities. The advent of client-server HRMS authorised HR executives for the first time to take responsibility and ownership of their systems. These client-server HRMS are characteristically developed around four principal areas of HR functionalities:

1. "Payroll".
2. Time and labour management.
3. Benefits administration.
4. HR management.

The *Payroll module* automates the pay process by gathering data on employee time and attendance, calculating various deductions and taxes, and generating periodic paycheques and employee tax reports. Data is generally fed from the human resources and time keeping modules to calculate automatic deposit and manual cheque writing capabilities. Sophisticated HCM systems can set up accounts payable transactions from employee deduction or produce garnishment cheques. The payroll module sends accounting information to the general ledger for posting subsequent to a pay cycle.

The *time and labour management module* applies new technologies and methods (time collection devices) to cost effectively gather and evaluate employee time/work information. The most advanced modules provide broad flexibility in data collection methods, as well as labour distribution capabilities and data analysis features. This module is a key ingredient to establish organizational cost accounting capabilities.

The *benefits administration module* permits HR professionals to easily administer and track employee participation in benefits programmes ranging from health-care provider, insurance policy, and pension plan to profit sharing or stock option plans.

The *HR management module* is a component covering all other HR aspects from application to retirement. The system records basic demographic and address data, selection, training and development, capabilities and skills management, compensation planning records and other related activities. Leading edge systems provide the ability to "read" applications and enter relevant data to applicable database fields, notify employers and provide position management and position control. Human resource management function involves the recruitment, placement, evaluation, compensation and development of the employees of an organisation. Initially, business used computer based information system to:

- produce paychecks and payroll reports;
- maintain personnel records; and
- analyse the use of personnel in business operations.

Many organizations have gone beyond the traditional functions and developed human resource management information system, which supports recruitment, selection, hiring, job placement, performance appraisals, employee benefit analysis, training development, health, safety and security.

HOSPITALITY

Hospitality refers to the relationship process between a guest and a host, and it also refers to the act or practice of being hospitable, that is, the reception and entertainment of guests, visitors, or strangers, with liberality and goodwill. Hospitality frequently refers to the hospitality industry jobs for hotels, restaurants, casinos, catering, resorts, clubs and any other service position that deals with tourists.

Hospitality is also known as the act of generously providing care and kindness to whomsoever is in need.

For an indepth understanding of the term of hospitality, the starting point is the etymology of the word itself. The word hospitality derives from the Latinhospes, which is formed from hostis, which originally meant a 'stranger' and came to take on the meaning of the enemy or 'hostile stranger' (hostilis) + pets (polis, poles, potentia) to have power. Furthermore, the word hostire means equalize/compensate.

If you combined the above etymological analysis with the story of Telemachus and Nestor you can develop in your mind the concept and idea of hospitality.

First of all, Telemachus is a complete stranger for Nestor, however, he was hosted and treated more than warmly. In the Homeric ages, hospitality was under the protection of Zeus. The God of the Gods. For that reason Zeus was also attributed with the title 'Xenios Zeus' ('xenos' means stranger). The semantic behind this was to highlight the fact that hospitality for Ancient Greeks was of the utmost importance. A stranger passing outside a Greek house, could be invited inside the house by the family. The host washed the strangers feet, offered him/her food and wine and only after he/she was feeling at comfortably could be asked to tell his/her name.

After having welcomed Telemachus, Nestor asks his unknown guest to introduce himself to find out that he was the son of Odysseus. By that time, the man in front of him was a complete stranger, a hostis as described in the etymological analysis of hospitality at the beginning. Nonetheless, Telemachus was equilized with his host. Another meaning that is included in the etymology of hospitality. Note also that one of the Nestor's sons slept on a bed close by Telemachus to take care that he should not suffer any harm. This means that hospitality for Ancient Greeks include also the idea of protection. Lastly, Nestor put a chariot and horses at Telemachus' disposal so that he could travel the land route from Pylos to Sparta in two days, having as charioteer Nestor's son Pisistratus. The last element of hospitality as can be realized is guidance.

Based on the story above and its current meaning, hospitality is about compensating/equalizing a stranger to the host, making him feel protected and taken care of, and at the end of his hosting, guiding him to his next destination.

Contemporary Usage

Contemporary usage seems different from historical uses that lend it personal connotations. Today's hospitality conjures images of throwing good parties, gracious hosts entertaining, etiquette, Martha Stewart or even talk shows, or, the hospitality services industry as it relates to the entertainment and tourism business. On the other hand, hospitality used to be, and still is, a serious duty, responsibility, or ethic. Hospitality ethics is a discipline that studies this usage of hospitality.

In the western context, with its dynamic tension between Athens and Jerusalem, two phases can be distinguished with a very progressive transition: a hospitality based on an individually felt sense of duty, and one based on "official" institutions for organized but anonymous social services: special places for particular types of "strangers" such as the poor, orphan(s), ill, alien, criminal, etc. Perhaps this progressive institutionalization can be aligned to the transition between Middle Ages and Renaissance (Ivan Illich, *The Rivers North of the Future*).

Biblical and Middle Eastern

In Middle Eastern Culture, it was considered a cultural norm to take care of the strangers and foreigners living among you. These norms are reflected in many Biblical commands and examples.

Perhaps the most extreme example is provided in Genesis. Lot provides hospitality to a group of angels (who he thinks are only men); when a mob tries to rape them. Lot goes so far as to offer his own daughters as a substitute, saying "Don't do anything to these men, for they have come under the protection of my roof." (Genesis 19:8, NIV).

The obligations of both guests are stern. The bond is formed by eating salt under the roof, and is so strict that an Arab story tells of a thief who tasted something to see if it was sugar, and on realizing it was salt, put back all that he had taken and left.

Cultural Value or Norm

Hospitality as a cultural norm or value is an established sociological phenomenon that people study and write papers about.

HOSPITALITY SERVICE

The concept of Hospitality Services, also known as "accommodation sharing", "hospitality exchange" and "home stay networks", refers to centrally organized social networks of individuals who trade accommodation without monetary exchange. While this concept could also include house swapping or even time share plans, it has come to be associated mostly with travellers and tourists staying with one another free of charge. Since the 1990s, these services have increasingly moved away from using printed catalogues and phone frees to connect users towards Internet websites. These have grown exponentially since 2000 and as of March, 2007 over 500,000 people are registered users of these networks. These vary in operational structure, place different emphasis on graphical vs. textual formatting, and cater disproportionately to specific geographic regions.

History

In 1949, Bob Luitweiler founded the first hospitality service called Servas Open Doors as a cross national, non-profit, volunteer run organization advocating interracial and international peace. The next earliest began in 1965 when John Wilcock set-up the Traveller's Directory, originally as a listing of his mutual friends willing to host each other when travelling. This later became the Hospitality Exchange in 1988 when Joy Lily rescued the organization from imminent demise. Hospitality Club is the direct successor Hospex, the first Internet-based service, operating out of Germany since 2000. CouchSurfing is a newer hospitality exchange organization founded in 2004. Just as all the individual services have their own individual creation stories and organizational histories (often including demise and resurrection), many also have specific niche markets that they cater to including students, activists, religious pilgrims, and even occupational groups like police officers. However, the trend in recent years points to a greater consolidation of users in networks without a specific group, value, or lifestyle affiliation.

How They Work?

In essence, these systems employ reciprocity-users gain access to other users' information only by posting their own. Required fields normally include name and contact information, though newer services encourage users to include more detailed personal material, including likes and dislikes, hopes and dreams, and even photographs. Of course, more information included tends to improve the chances that someone will find them trustworthy enough to host or stay with while travelling. It is very much akin to social networking sites.

Benefits

Monetary Savings

Staying in private homes means that travellers can save lots of money on accommodation that they would usually be spending on hotels or hostels. Used over a long period of time (2 to 4 weeks), this strategy can cut overall travel budgets in half, or even more combined with hitchhiking. These savings can then be passed on towards more generously patronizing local establishments or simply staying abroad for longer periods of time.

Local Economic Sustainability

Many tourist vacations today are sold in package form, often including flights, hotels, rental cars, sightseeing tours, and coupons for chain restaurants and bars. While this makes purchasing more convenient, it also puts more money in the hands of large multinational corporations exploiting the synergy strategy of marketing their products in the context of their subsidiary companies operating in other markets. Many years ago, this might have been termed *collusion*; today, however, it is the norm. This comes at the expense of locally owned independent businesses. Accommodation sharing helps to break apart this monopoly and hopefully redirects some of the tourist revenue back to the local or national economy.

Ecological Sustainability

While this is especially important in more rural travel venues where hotels are often built in very picturesque, though fragile environments, every night stayed at a local's home means that much less demand for such hotel rooms. Also, if accommodation sharing does in fact increase the length of average stays, it may reduce the amount of trips to and from different locations and back home again, thus reducing the overall fuel expenditures in the process.

Local Contact

Ostensibly, one of the primary reasons we travel is to experience what life is like for people living in other countries. Making interpersonal connections and fostering understanding of different cultures may in the long run also be important to international relations. However, even in our increasingly globalized world supposedly rife with diversity, in many popular travel destinations we find tourists milling around "tourist enclaves" where the companies they patronize back home have set up shop to cater to their desires while they are abroad. Sociologist George Ritzer has referred to this phenomenon as the "McDonaldisation of society" and the more recently, the "globalization of nothing". The location of hotels near these centres only fosters more convenient envelopment of the tourist dollar. During hospitality exchanges, hosts want to show off their local knowledge and exciting "off the map" venues. Not only may travellers get a distinctly different experience, but they will also get a feel for the everyday lives of local residents.

Reciprocity

These systems foster richer and more convenient travel experiences not so much on the premise of altruism, but on the basis of social exchange theory. Implicit in the agreement to host travellers is the ability to ask to be hosted by them in the future. If one enjoys having interesting guests in their home, this works out well for both parties. It works comparatively better if you are visited by travellers from a locale you find particularly attractive. Thus, hosting someone from New York City in Gainesville, FL seems to be an unbelievable opportunity. Moreover, if you are a Westerner visiting someone in a developing nation, your stay might be the only way that this individual or family could afford a trip to a rich nation. This may mean more than just a relaxing vacation for such disadvantaged parties.

Authenticity and Adventure

Tourism has always searched for these two qualities, but much like *Midas* and his golden touch, the reach of tourism has to a large extent destroyed the opportunity to encounter them in most places. Unluckily, the experience has been thoroughly commodified by everyone who wanted to secure their opportunity to make a buck in the process. Accommodation sharing offers a way out of this bind and a viable alternative to having one's desires manipulated by corporate conglomerates who never had the best interests of the place or the people foremost in their minds.

Drawbacks

Lack of Guarantee

There is no contractual agreement between users in these systems. Reservations are made, but if they are for some reason broken, there is no higher authority to which one could plead for a refund or other compensation. The only repercussion will be the poor rating you give that user and your only consolation will be that your warning will deter others from visiting or hosting them. For those who feel insecure unless their travel arrangements are written in stone before departure, this system will not be comforting.

Potential Interpersonal Conflict or Awkwardness

There is a chance that guest and host will not get along. Perhaps there will be scheduling or ideological conflicts. Maybe you will find that hosts or visitors have misrepresented themselves. Perhaps the experience will not live up to your expectations. Intense interpersonal communications in advance and a flexibility once you have arrived is your best bet. These experiences require additional planning and courtesy towards the demands of your host. Thus, your living conditions, length of stay, and overall experience will be circumscribed by the living conditions you enter into.

Digital Divide and Demographic Segregation

The average user is a young white person who speaks English and lives in a developed nation. While there are many users who do not fit this description, the more different they are, the less likely they will be involved. This is especially true for persons living in the developing world who likely do not have easy access to the fundamental prerequisite for using these services: computers and the Internet. Thus, the sample population found in searches of these databases are really much less diverse than a geographical representation of worldwide users might suggest.

Security

There is a distinct possibility that someone will abuse the system and that innocent users (especially women) will get hurt. All services include disclaimers that require users to waive their rights to hold anyone but themselves responsible for any harm that may come to them in using the system. They advise that the best defense mechanism is to only involve oneself with users that have extensive personal information and interpersonal networks within the system that have been verified by others. It does seem entirely plausible that someone clever and patient enough might be able to invent an entire group of complex user identities and build histories convincing enough to fool even more cautious patrons. Still, the difference between these systems and the other social networking platforms popular now-a-days on the web (such as MySpace, Tribe, Orkut, LiveJournal and Ebay) is that any agreement reached through the accommodation sharing medium is contingent on actually meeting other people face-to-face. Other web scams are easier because interpersonal interactions rely so much on putative identities that are never actually verified in the real world. However, this does not diminish the greater risk to physical well-being that this kind of travelling by definition must entertain. The best advice is to meet unknown persons in public spaces first, and try to meet some of their acquaintances in person before agreeing to a hospitality exchange.

Example Networks

General Networks

- *Hospitality Club*—one of the largest networks with over 300 thousand members in more than 200 countries.
- *Couch Surfing*—one of the largest networks with over 300 thousand members in more than 200 countries.

- *Servas International*—human rights and global peace oriented since 1949.
- *Global Free Loaders*—another active community.

Specialized Networks

- Lesbian and Gay Hospitality Exchange International.
- Warm Showers List —world-wide, internet based organisation for travelling pedal cyclists. Free registration.
- Pasporta Servo—for Esperanto speakers.
- WWOOF—"Worldwide Opportunities on Organic Farms", help on the property is exchanged for food, accommodation, education and cultural interaction.
- Homeshare International—charity organisation providing exchange of housing for help in the home.

GLOSSARY: HOSPITALITY

Sous Chef/Kitchen Manager

Primary Function: The operation and organisation of a designated part of the kitchen.

Duties and Responsibilities

- To take charge in the Head Chef's absence.
- Plan and organise prep lists and workflows.
- Assist with menu development and follow recipes.
- Produce all items related to the designated part of the menu to the establishment's standards in order to satisfy guest's expectations.
- Impart knowledge and train cooks to encourage high standards.
- Ensure equipment and work environment are operational.
- Control quality and costs.
- Manage staff roster in conjunction with Head Chef.

Pastry Chef/Chef De Partie

Primary Function: To manage the operation and organisation of the pastry section of the kitchen.

Duties and Responsibilities

- Liase with Head/Executive Chef to develop dessert menus.
- Plan and organise work flows, order food items where required.
- Produce all items related to the menus and functions to the establishment's standard, to satisfy guest's expectations.
- Impart knowledge and train staff to encourage high standards.
- Cost all pastry recipes and develop menu items for the establishment.
- Keep recipe book up to date.
- Ensure equipment and work environment are operational.
- Attend all kitchen meetings.

Breakfast Chef (Chef De Partie Level)

Primary Function: Produce all items relating to the menu to the establishment standards to satisfy customers' expectations.

Duties and Responsibilities

- Produce breakfast menu.
- Prepare mise-en-place for day shifts if required.
- Communicate with support and peers.
- Produce items for functions as required.

Chef De Partie

Primary Function: Produce all items relating to the menu to the establishment standards to satisfy customers' expectations.

Duties and Responsibilities

- Take charge in the absence of the Sous Chef.
- Work unsupervised to establishment standard.
- Order food items when required.
- Communicate with and support peers.
- Train new staff.
- Maximise quality whilst containing food and labour costs.

Commis Chef

Primary Function: Produce stipulated items relating to the menu to establishment standards to satisfy customer expectations.

Duties and Responsibilities

- Communicate with and support peers.

Steward/Kitchen Assistant

Primary Function: Assisting Chefs and cooks and cleaning all areas.

Duties and Responsibilities

- Wash dishes and equipment to establishment standards.
- Keep kitchen environment and equipment clean and tidy.
- Ensure dishwasher is functioning correctly.
- Keep all cleaning equipment orderly.

Food and Beverage Waiter

Primary Function: Ensure, under the guidance of the Maitre d' that a high and correct standard of service is maintained.

Duties and Responsibilities

- Ensure that customers receive good and courteous service at all times.
- Have a good knowledge of local and international food and beverage.
- Be flexible in relation to working late night hours or additional hours other than standard opening times.
- Follow establishment policies—particularly in regard to wastage, breakage and personal grooming.
- Carry out any requests by the Maitre d' or supervisors.
- Maintain a high standard of establishments equipment, crockery, cutlery and utensils etc.
- Maintain a high standard of table service.
- Keep the establishment clean and tidy.

Wine Waiter

Primary Function: Setting up, serving and clearing and cleaning for meals/events.

Duties and Responsibilities

- Ensure storage areas and back of house is kept tidy at all times.
- Attend to all customer queries and requests courteously and efficiently to establishment standards. Report to the Supervisor on duty.
- Ensure that all property is handled with due care.
- Maintain good working relationships with fellow staff and supervisors.
- Be fully conversant with establishment standards, operations and services and carry out duties to these standards.
- Assist with inventories as required.

Bar Manager

Primary Function: Ensure that all beverages served to customers meet the establishment's standards.

Duties and Responsibilities

- Interview and select staff, and manage appropriate rosters.
- Ensure all equipment and work environments are operational.
- Responsible for imparting knowledge skills and training to all bar staff.
- Ensure appropriate stock levels are maintained.
- Maintain costs to establishment standards.
- Set and maintain standards for food safety in the bar area.
- Communicate with and support kitchen and wait staff.
- Follow establishment policies and procedures.
- Undertake staff appraisals and disciplinary action when required.

Bar Staff

Primary Function: Ensure the quality of drinks served to customers meets establishment standards.

Duties and Responsibilities

- Receive, process and deliver all drink orders.
- Preparation of garnishes to establishment standards.
- Maintain service areas to establishment standards.
- Communicate with support and peers.
- Follow establishment policies—particularly in regard to wastage, breakage and personal grooming.
- Order supplies as required.
- Process payments for drink orders.

Barista

Primary Function: Ensure, under the guidance of the Maitre d' that a high standard of coffee service is maintained.

Duties and Responsibilities

- Ensure that customers receive good and courteous service at all times.
- Have a good knowledge of coffee and coffee beverage.
- Maintain a high standard of coffee service.
- Follow establishment policies—particularly in regard to wastage, breakage and personal grooming.
- Carry out requests by the Maitre d' or supervisors.
- Maintain a high standard of restaurant equipment, crockery, cutlery and utensils etc.
- Keep barista area clean and tidy.

Cashier

Primary Function: Ensure accurate accounting of all transactions.

Duties and Responsibilities

- Check cash drawer at beginning of shift.

- Code different menu items.
- Collect cash, cheque or credit card payment from customers.
- Reconcile cheques, cash receipts and charge sales with total sale.
- Optional: Greet customers, take food and beverage orders.

TOURISM

Tourism is travel for predominantly recreational or leisure purposes or the provision of services to support this leisure travel. The World Tourism Organization defines *tourists* as people who "travel to and stay in places outside their usual environment for not more than one consecutive year for leisure, business and other purposes not related to the exercise of an activity remunerated from within the place visited." Tourism has become a popular global leisure activity. In 2006, there were over 842 million international tourist arrivals.

Tourism is vital for many countries, due to the income generated by the consumption of goods and services by tourists, the taxes levied on businesses in the tourism industry, and the opportunity for employment in the service industries associated with tourism. These service industries include transportation services such as cruise ships and taxis, accommodation such as hotels, restaurants, bars, and entertainment venues, and other hospitality industry services such as spas and resorts.

Hunziker and Krapf in 1941, defined tourism as "the sum of the phenomena and relationships arising from the travel and stay of non-residents, insofar as they do not lead to permanent residence and are not connected with any earning activity." In 1976, Tourism Society of England defined it as "Tourism is the temporary, short-term movement of people to destination outside the places where they normally live and work and their activities during the stay at each destination. It includes movements for all purposes." In 1981, International Association of Scientific Experts in Tourism defined Tourism in terms of particular activities selected by choice and undertaken outside the home environment.

The United Nations classified three forms of tourism in 1994 in its Recommendations on Tourism Statistics: Domestic tourism, which involves residents of the given country travelling only within this country; Inbound tourism, involving non-residents travelling in the given country; and Outbound tourism, involving residents travelling in another country.

The UN also derived different categories of tourism by combining the 3 basic forms of tourism: Internal tourism, which comprises domestic tourism and inbound tourism; National tourism, which comprises domestic tourism and outbound tourism; and International tourism, which consists of inbound tourism and outbound tourism. *Intrabound tourism* is a term coined by the Korea Tourism Organization and widely accepted in Korea. Intrabound tourism differs from domestic tourism in that the former encompasses policy-making and implementation of national tourism policies.

Recently, the tourism industry has shifted from the promotion of inbound tourism to the promotion of intrabound tourism because many countries are experiencing tough competition for inbound tourists. Some national policy-makers have shifted their priority to the promotion of intrabound tourism to contribute to the local economy. Examples of such campaigns include "See America" in the United States, "Get Going Canada" in Canada, "Guseok Guseok" (corner to corner) in South Korea, and "Incredible India" in India.

Prerequisites

Before people are able to experience tourism they usually need disposable income (i.e., money to spend on non-essentials); time off from work or other responsibilities; leisure time tourism infrastructure, such as transport and accommodation; and legal clearance to travel.

Individually, sufficient health is also a condition, and of course the inclination to travel. Furthermore, in some countries there are legal restrictions on travelling, especially abroad. Certain states with strong governmental control over the lives of citizens (notably established Communist states) may restrict foreign travel only to trustworthy citizens. The United States prohibits its citizens from travelling to some countries, for example Cuba. Suitcases are also necessary for luggage.

History

Wealthy people have always travelled to distant parts of the world to see great buildings or other works of art, to learn new languages, to experience new cultures, or to taste new cuisine. As long ago as the time of the Roman Republic places such as Baiae were popular coastal resorts for the rich.

The terms *tourist* and *tourism* were first used as official terms in 1937 by the League of Nations. Tourism was defined as people travelling abroad for periods of over 24 hours.

Pilgrimage

The history of European tourism can perhaps be said to originate with the medieval pilgrimage. Although undertaken primarily for religious reasons, the pilgrims in the Canterbury Tales quite clearly saw the experience as a kind of holiday (the term itself being derived from the 'holy day' and its associated leisure activities). Pilgrimages created a variety of tourist aspects that still exist—bringing back souvenirs, obtaining credit with foreign banks (in medieval times utilizing international networks established by Jews and Lombards), and making use of space available on existing forms of transport (such as the use of medieval English wine ships bound for Vigo by pilgrims to Santiago De Compostela). Pilgrimages are still important in modern tourism—such as to Lourdes or Knock in Ireland. But there are secular equivalents—Graceland and the grave of Jim Morrison in Père Lachaise Cemetery.

During the seventeenth century, it became fashionable in England to undertake a Grand Tour. The sons of the nobility and gentry were sent upon an extended tour of Europe as an educational experience. The eighteenth century was the golden age of the Grand Tour, and many of the fashionable visitors were painted at Rome by Pompeo Batoni. A modern equivalent of the Grand Tour is the phenomenon of the backpacker, although cultural holidays, such as those offered by Swann-Hellenic, are also important.

Health Tourism

Health tourism has always existed, but it was not until the

eighteenth century that it became important. In England, it was associated with spas, places with supposedly health-giving mineral waters, treating diseases from gout to liver disorders and bronchitis. The most popular resorts were Bath, Cheltenham, Buxton, Harrogate, and Tunbridge Wells. Visits to take 'the waters' also allowed the visitors to attend balls and other entertainments. Continental Spas such as Carlsbad (Karlovy Vary) attracted many fashionable travellers by the nineteenth century.

Leisure Travel

Leisure travel was associated with the industrialisation of United Kingdom—the first European country to promote leisure time to the increasing industrial population. Initially, this applied to the owners of the machinery of production, the economic oligarchy, the factory owners, and the traders. These comprised the new middle class. Cox and Kings were the first official travel company to be formed in 1758. Later, the working class could take advantage of leisure time.

The British origin of this new industry is reflected in many place names. At Nice, one of the first and best-established holiday resorts on the French Riviera, the long esplanade along the seafront is known to this day as the *Promenade des Anglais*; in many other historic resorts in continental Europe, old well-established palace hotels have names like the *Hotel Bristol*, the *Hotel Carlton* or the *Hotel Majestic*—reflecting the dominance of English customers.

Winter Tourism

Winter sports were largely invented by the British leisured classes, initially at the Swiss village of Zermatt (Valais), and St Moritz in 1864. The first packaged winter sports holidays took place in 1902 at Adelboden, Switzerland. Winter sports were a natural answer for a leisured class looking for amusement during the coldest season.

The Fun Ski and Snow Festival, which has been organized annually by Korea tourism organization since 1998 and participated by about 10,000 tourists from Asia, is one of the most successful winter tourism products in Asia. The festival provides a variety of events such as ski and sled competitions, ski and snow board lessons, performances and recreational activities. Majority of the event participants are foreign visitors who come from countries with a warm climate that have no snow. The event offers them opportunities to enjoy winter and winter sports in Korea. In addition, southern South American countries making up the Patagonia region in Chile and Argentina attract thousands of tourists every year. Skiing is extremely popular in the mountainous areas.

Mass Tourism

Mass travel could only develop with improvements in technology allowed the transport of large numbers of people in a short space of time to places of leisure interest, and greater numbers of people began to enjoy the benefits of leisure time.

In the United States, the first great seaside resort, in the European style, was Atlantic City, New Jersey and Long Island.

In Continental Europe, early resorts included Ostend (for the people of Brussels), and Boulogne-sur-Mer (Pas-de-Calais) and Deauville (Calvados) (for Parisians).

In Britain

The pioneer of modern mass tourism was Thomas Cook who, on 5 July, 1841, organized the first package tour in history. He arranged for the rail company to charge one shilling per person for a group of 570 temperance campaigners from Leicester to a rally in Loughborough, eleven miles (18 km) away. Cook was paid a share of the fares actually charged to the passengers, as the railway tickets, being legal contracts between company and passenger, could not have been issued at his own price. There had been railway excursions before, but this one included entrance to an entertainment held in private grounds, rail tickets and food for the train journey. Cook immediately saw the potential of a convenient 'off the peg' holiday product in which everything was included in one cost. He organised packages inclusive of accommodation for the Great Exhibition, and afterwards pioneered package holidays in both Britain (particularly in Scotland) and on the European continent (where Paris and the Alps were the most popular destinations).

He was soon followed by others (the Polytechnic Touring Association, Dean and Dawson etc.), with the result that the tourist industry developed rapidly in late Victorian Britain. Initially it was supported by the growing middle classes, who had time off from their work, and who could afford the luxury of travel and possibly even staying for periods of time in boarding houses.

The Bank Holidays Act, 1871 introduced a statutory right for workers to take holidays, even if they were not paid at the time. By the last quarter of the nineteenth century, the tradition of the working class holiday had become firmly established in Britain. These were largely focussed upon the seaside resorts.

The spread of the railway network in the nineteenth century resulted in the growth of Britain's seaside towns by bringing them within easy distance of Britain's urban centres. Blackpool was created by the construction of a line to Fleetwood, and some resorts were promoted by the railway companies themselves—Morecambe by the Midland Railway and Cleethorpes by the Great Central Railway. Other resorts included Scarborough in Yorkshire, servicing Leeds and Bradford; Weston-super-Mare in Somerset, catering for the inhabitants of Bristol; and Skegness, patronised by the residents of the industrial East Midlands. The cockneys of London flocked to Southend-on-Sea, mainly by Thames Steamer, and the South Coast resorts such as Broadstairs, Brighton and Eastbourne were only a train ride away, with others further afield such as Bournemouth, Bognor Regis and Weymouth.

For a century, domestic tourism was the norm, with foreign travel being reserved for the rich or the culturally curious. A number of inland destinations, such as the English Lake District, and Snowdonia appealed to those who liked the countryside and fine scenery. The holiday camp began to appear in the 1930s, but this phenomenon really expanded in the post-war period. Butlins and Pontins set this trend, but their popularity waned with the rise of overseas package tours and the increasing comforts to which visitors became accustomed at home. Towards the end of the 20th century this market has been revived by the upmarket inland resorts of Dutch company Centre Parcs.

Cox and Co, the forebear of Cox and Kings were in existence from 1758 largely entwined with the travel arrangements for the British Army serving around the Empire. While acting as 'agents' for various regiments, they organised the payment, provision, clothing and travel arrangements for members of the armed forces. In the 19th century their network of offices contained a banking and also travel department. The company became heavily involved with affairs in India and its Shipping Agency had offices in France and the Middle East.

Other phenomena that helped develop the travel industry were paid holidays:

- 1.5 million manual workers in Britain had paid holidays by 1925.
- 11 million by 1939 (30% of the population in families with paid holidays).

NGOs and government agencies may sometimes promote a specific region as a tourist destination, and support the development of a tourism industry in that area. The contemporary phenomenon of mass tourism may sometimes result in over-development; alternative forms of tourism such as ecotourism seek to avoid such outcomes by pursuing tourism in a sustainable way.

International

Increasing speed on railways meant that the tourist industry could develop internationally. To this may be added the development of sea travel. By 1901, the number of people crossing the English Channel from England to France or Belgium had passed 0.5 million per year. Shipping companies were anxious to fill cabin space that was under-utilized.

For example, P&O found that the majority of their passengers for India and the Far East joined the ship at Marseilles. Consequently, they marketed holidays based upon sea trips from London to Lisbon and Gibraltar. Other companies diverted their older ships to operate cruises in the summer months.

However, the real age of international mass travel began with the growth of air travel after World War II. In the immediate post-war period, there was a surplus of transport aircraft, such as the popular and reliable Douglas Dakota, and a number of ex military pilots ready to fly them. They were available for charter flights, and tour operators began to use them for European destinations, such as Paris and Ostend.

Vladimir Raitz pioneered modern package tourism when on 20 May, 1950 his recently founded company, Horizon, provided arrangements for a two-week holiday in Corsica. For an all inclusive price of £32.10s.-, holiday makers could sleep under canvas, sample local wines and eat a meal containing meat twice a day—this was especially attractive due to the continuing austerity measures in post-war United Kingdom. Within ten years, his company had started mass tourism to Palma (1952), Lourdes (1953), Costa Brava (1954), Sardinia (1954), Minorca (1955), Porto (1956), Costa Blanca (1957) and Costa del Sol (1959).

These developments coincided with a significant increase in the standard of living in Britain. Further, the contribution of affordable air travel in combination with the package tour enabled international mass tourism to develop. The post-war introduction of an international system of airline regulation was another important factor. The bilateral agreements at the heart of the system fixed seat prices, and airlines could not fill blocks of empty seats on underused flights by discounting. But if they were purchased by a tour operator and hidden within the price of an inclusive holiday package, it would be difficult to prove that discounting had taken place—even though it was obvious that it had!

Another significant development also happened at the end of this decade. The devaluation of the Spanish peseta made Spain appear a particularly attractive destination. The cheapness of the cost of living attracted increasing numbers of visitors. Mass package tourism has at times been an exploitative process, in which tour operators in a country with a high standard of living make use of development opportunities and low operating costs in a country with a lower standard of living. However, as witness the development of many tourist areas in previously poor parts of the world, and the concomitant rise in standards of living, when there is equality of bargaining power, both parties can gain economic benefits from this arrangement.

Spain and the Balearic Islands became major tourist destinations, and development probably peaked in the 1980s. At the same time, British tour operators developed the Algarve in Portugal. The continuing search for new, cheaper, destinations spread mass tourism to the Greek Islands, Italy, Tunisia, Morocco, Turkey, and more recently Croatia.

For someone living in greater London, Venice today is almost as accessible as Brighton was 100 years ago. Consequently, the British seaside resort experienced a marked decline from the 1970s onwards. Some, such as New Brighton, Merseyside have disappeared. Others have reinvented themselves, and now cater to daytrippers, the weekend break market or business conferences.

Recent Developments

There has been an upmarket trend in the tourism over the last few decades, especially in Europe where international travel for short breaks is common. Tourists have higher levels of disposable income and greater leisure time and they are also better-educated and have more sophisticated tastes. There is now a demand for a better quality products, which has resulted in a fragmenting of the mass market for beach vacations; people want more specialised versions, such as 'Club 18-30', quieter resorts, family-oriented holidays, or niche market-targeted destination hotels. As well, people are taking second short break holidays.

The developments in technology and transport infrastructure such as jumbo jets and low-budget airlines have made many types of tourism more affordable. There have also been changes in life style, such as retiree-age people who living as a tourist all the year round. This is facilitated by internet purchasing of tourism products. Some sites have now started to offer dynamic packaging, in which an inclusive price is quoted for a tailor-made package requested by the customer upon impulse.

There have been a few setbacks in tourism, such as the September 11, 2001 attacks and terrorist threats to tourist destinations such as Bali and European cities. Some of the tourist destinations, including the beach resorts of Cancún have lost popularity due to shifting tastes. In this context, the excessive building and environmental destruction often associated with traditional "sun and beach" tourism may contribute to a destination's saturation and subsequent decline. Spain's Costa Brava, a popular 1960s and 1970s beach location is now facing a crisis in its tourist industry. On December 26, 2004 a tsunami, caused by the 2004 Indian Ocean earthquake hit Asian countries bordering the Indian Ocean, and also the Maldives. Tens of thousands of lives were lost, and many tourists died. This, together with the vast clean-up operation in place, has stopped or severely hampered tourism to the area.

The terms *tourism* and *travel* are sometimes used interchangeably. In this context travel has a similar definition to tourism, but implies a more purposeful journey. The terms *tourism* and *tourist* are sometimes used pejoratively, to imply a shallow interest in the cultures or locations visited by tourists.

Sustainable tourism is becoming more popular as people start to realize the devastating effects poorly planned tourism can have on communities. Receptive tourism is now growing at a very rapid rate in many developing countries, where it is often the most important economic activity in local GDP.

In recent years, second holidays or vacations have become more popular as people's discretionary income increases. Typical combinations are a package to the typical mass tourist resort, with a winter skiing holiday or weekend break to a city or national park.

Niche Tourism

Physical activity or sports-oriented niche tourism includes adventure tourism such as mountaineering and hiking (tramping); Backpacker Tourism. Sport travel to do skiing, golf and scuba diving or see a sports event (e.g., FIFA World Cup); and extreme tourism for people interested in risky activities.

Learning-oriented niche tourism includes *audio tourism* and *audio walking tours; bookstore tourism,* in which travellers visit independent bookstores; creative tourism workshops; educational tourism for classes; ancestry tourism, to visit birth places; *Hobby tourism* (such as garden tours, amateur radio DX-peditions, or square dance cruises).

- The cultural sub-type of learning-oriented niche tourism focuses on cultural and arts activities, including cultural tourism, music tourism, andheritage tourism. The nature and environment-oriented sub-types include Coastal tourism; Ecotourism *(e.g. sustainable tourism in Rainforests or national parks);* Garden tourism; and Rural tourism such as Agritourism.

Lifestyle-oriented niche tourism types include Gay tourism; Gourmet tourism; Wine tourism; Health tourism; Medical tourism; Inclusive tourism (or Accessible Tourism) for people with disabilities.

Other miscellaneous types of niche tourism include:

- *Armchair Tourism and Virtual Tourism*: Not traveling physically, but exploring the world through internet, books, or TV.
- *Dark Tourism* includes travel to sites associated with death and suffering, such as the scene of the Hindenburg airship disaster, or to the sites of disasters (Disaster tourism).
- *Drug Tourism*, (e.g., to use drugs in Amsterdam).
- *Free Independent Traveler*: A sector of the market in which the tourists select their own accommodation and transport, rather than going with a group or on a pre-arranged tour.
- *Pop-culture Tourism*: Tourism by those that visit a particular location after reading about it or seeing it used as a location in a film (e.g., the Lord of the Rings film sets in New Zealand).
- *Perpetual Tourism*: Individuals always on vacation; some of them, for tax purposes, to avoid being resident in any country.
- *Pilgrimage Tourism*: Pilgrimages to ancient holy places (Rome and Santiago de Compostela for Catholics, temples and stupas of Nepal for the Hindus and Buddhist, Mount Athos or Painted churches of northern Moldavia for the Orthodox), religious sites such as mosques and shrines.
- *Sacred Travel* or metaphysical tourism is a form of New Age travel where believers travel to and perform rituals at religious sites
- *Sex Tourism* (e.g., to have sex with prostitutes).
- *Shopping Tourism* promoting shopping festivals such as the Dubai Shopping Festival.
- *Space Tourism*: travelling in outer space or on spaceships.
- *Vacilando* is a special kind of wanderer for whom the process of travelling and discovery is more important than the destination.
- *Visiting Family and Relatives (VFR) Tourism*: Travelling to visit persons related by close family ties and combining

this with vacation-type activities; distinct from *ancestry tourism,* which involves genealogical research

Rural Areas

Many of the niche tourism programmes are located in Rural areas. From wine tourism, and ecotourism and seasonal events, tourism can be a viable economic component to rural community development. According the United States Department of Agriculture, Co-operative State Research, Education, and Extension Service, "Tourism is becoming increasingly important to the U.S. economy. A conservative estimate from the Federal Reserve Board in Kansas, based on 2000 data, shows that basic travel and tourism industries accounted for 3.6 per cent of all U.S. employment. Even more telling, data from the Travel Industry Association of America indicate that 1 out of every 18 people in the U.S. has a job directly resulting from travel expenditures."

The publication, *Promoting Tourism in Rural America,* explains the need for planning and marketing your rural community and weighing the pros and cons of tourism impacts. Local citizen participation is helpful and should be included in starting any kind of a tourism programme. Being prepared by planning tourism can assist in a successful programme that enhances the community.

Growth

The World Tourism Organization (UNWTO) forecasts that international tourism will continue growing at the average annual rate of 4 per cent. By 2020 Europe will remain the most popular destination, but its share will drop from 60 per cent in 1995 to 46 per cent. Long-haul will grow slightly faster than intraregional travel and by 2020 its share will increase from 18 per cent in 1995 to 24 per cent.

With the advent of e-commerce, tourism products have become one of the most traded items on the internet. Tourism products and services have been made available through intermediaries, although tourism providers (hotels, airlines, etc.) can sell their services directly. This has put pressure on intermediaries from both on-line and traditional shops.

It has been suggested there is a strong correlation between Tourism expenditure per capita and the degree to which countries play in the global context. Not only as a result of the important economic contribution of the tourism industry, but also as an indicator of the degree of confidence with which global citizens leverage the resources of the globe for the benefit of their local economies. This is why any projections of growth in tourism may serve as an indication of the relative influence that each country will exercise in the future.

Space tourism is expected to "take off" in the first quarter of the 21st century, although compared with traditional destinations the number of tourists in orbit will remain low until technologies such as a make space travel cheap.

Technological improvement is likely to make possible air-ship hotels, based either on solar-powered airplanes or large dirigibles. Underwater hotels, such as Hydropolis, expected to open in Dubai in 2009, will be built. On the ocean tourists will be welcomed by ever larger cruise ships and perhaps floating cities.

Some futurists expect that movable hotel "pods" will be created that could be temporarily erected anywhere on the planet, where building a permanent resort would be unacceptable politically, economically or environmentally.

Negative Impacts

Attracting a high volume of tourists can have negative impacts, such as the impact of 33 million tourists a year on the city of New York, or the potential to impact fragile environments, or the impact of the December 26, 2004 tsunami on the tourist themselves.

Tourism itself has been defined by the World Tourism Organization as "the activities of persons travelling to and staying in places outside their usual environment for not more than one consecutive year for leisure, business or other purposes."

Sustainable tourism is "tourism which actively fosters appreciation and stewardship of the natural, cultural and historic resources and special places by local residents, the tourism industry, governments and visitors. It is tourism which can be sustained over the long-term because it results in a net benefit for the social, economic, natural and cultural environments of the area in which it takes place." *(Definition used by Parks Canada)*

Three general types of travel have been identified, according to the motivation, purpose or reason for the trip, along with various sub-categories:

- *Pleasure/Leisure Travel*: Includes Group Travel and Fully Independent Travel (FIT).
- *Business Travel*: Includes Conventions and Meetings; Incentive Travel.
- *Personal Travel*: Includes Visiting Friends and Relatives (VFR).

Ecological integrity means, with respect to a park, "a condition that is determined to be characteristic of its natural region and likely to persist, including abiotic components (physical elements) and the composition and abundance of native species and biological communities, rates of change and supporting processes." *(Definition set forth in the Canada National Parks Act)*

Tourism Market Segments

The past decade or so has witnessed the segmenting of the tourism industry, globally, into a growing number of distinct markets in order to assist operators in developing targetted products and help consumers understand the product offerings. These market segments have been labelled in various ways.

Aboriginal tourism describes all tourism businesses that are owned or operated by First Nation, Métis and Inuit people. *(Definition used by Aboriginal Tourism Team Canada)*

- Adventure tourism.
- Agricultural tourism/Agri-tourism.
- Cultural/Culturally-based and heritage tourism.

Ecotourism is a segment of sustainable tourism that offers experiences that enable visitors to discover natural areas while preserving their integrity, and to understand, through interpretation and education, the natural and cultural sense of place. It fosters respect towards the environment, reflects sustainable business practices, creates socio-economic benefits for communities/regions, and recognizes and respects local and indigenous cultures, traditions and values. *(Definition developed by the Tourism Industry Association of Canada)*

Learning and enrichment travel refers to vacations with authentic, hands-on or interactive learning experiences featuring themes such as adventure, agriculture, anthropology, archeology, arts, culture, cuisine, education, forestry, gardening, language, maritime, mining, nature, science, spirituality, sports, wine, and wildlife to name a few! These are the travel experiences that broaden the mind and enrich the soul. *(Definition used by the Learning and Enrichment Travel Alliance)*

Nature-based Tourism

Sport Tourism

Wellness tourism is the sum of all the relationships and phenomena resulting from a journey and residence by people whose main motivation is to preserve or promote their health. They stay in a specialized hotel which provides the appropriate professional know how and individual care. They require a comprehensive service package comprising physical fitness/beauty care, healthy nutrition/diet, relaxation/meditation and mental activity/ education. *(Definition Developed by the Research Institute for Leisure and Tourism, University of Berne, Switzerland)*

Wine/Culinary tourism is tourism in which the opportunity for wine and/or culinary related experiences contributes significantly to the reason for travel to the destination or to itinerary planning while at the destination. *(Definition used by the Ontario Ministry of Tourism, Culture and Recreation and the Wine Council of Ontario)*

Winter Tourism

Spa Tourism

Tourism Marketing

In order to be considered export ready, an organization should:

- Have been in business for at least one year, with a proven track record of safe and professional operation.

- Provide contracted wholesale net rates to tour operators, travel wholesalers and retail travel agents. As a general guideline, requirements are 15 per cent off retail for activities and transportation and 20-30 per cent off retail for accommodation.
- Provide detailed pricing and programme information to tour operators, travel wholesalers and retail travel agents at least one year in advance of selling season, e.g. May 2004 for the summer/fall 2005 season.
- Communicate and accept reservations by telephone, fax or email. Provide same-day confirmation of booking arrangements.
- Set up billing arrangements with the operator, agency or receptive tour operator. Accept client vouchers as confirmation of booking arrangements.
- Carry adequate business liability insurance.
- Provide support (free or at reduced rates) for international media and FAM tours.
- Hold all appropriate operating licences. *(Definition used by Rendez-vous Canada).*

2

HRM Functions, Strategies and Diagnostic Checklists: Case Study of a Select Hotel Industry

HUMAN RESOURCE MANAGEMENT

Human resource (or personnel) management, in the sense of getting things done through people. It's an essential part of every manager's responsibilities, but many organizations find it advantageous to establish a specialist division to provide an expert service dedicated to ensuring that the human resource function is performed efficiently.

"People are our most valuable asset" is a cliché which no member of any senior management team would disagree with. Yet, the reality for many organizations is that their people remain

- under valued.
- under trained.
- under utilized.
- poorly motivated, and consequently.
- perform well below their true capability.

The rate of change facing organizations has never been greater and organizations must absorb and manage change at a much faster rate than in the past. In order to implement a successful business strategy to face this challenge, organizations, large or small, must ensure that they have the right people capable of delivering the strategy.

The market place for talented, skilled people is competitive and expensive. Taking on new staff can be disruptive to existing employees. Also, it takes time to develop 'cultural awareness', product/process/organization knowledge and experience for new staff members.

As organizations vary in size, aims, functions, complexity, construction, the physical nature of their product, and appeal as employers, so do the contributions of human resource management. But, in most the ultimate aim of the function is to: "ensure that at all times the business is correctly staffed by the right number of people with the skills relevant to the business needs," that is, neither overstaffed nor understaffed in total or in respect of any one discipline or work grade.

Functional Overview and Strategy for HRM

These issues motivate a well thought out human resource management strategy, with the precision and detail of say a marketing strategy. Failure in not having a carefully crafted human resources management strategy, can and probably will lead to failures in the business process itself.

This set of resources are offered to promote thought, stimulate discussion, diagnose the organizational environment and develop a sound human resource management strategy for your organization. We begin by looking at the seven distinguishable function human resource management provide to secure the achievement of the objective defined above.

Following on from this overview we look at defining a human resource strategy.

Finally, some questions are posed in the form of a HRM systems diagnostic checklist for you to consider, which may prove helpful for you to think about when planning your development programmes for the human resources in your organization, if they are truly "your most valuable asset."

HUMAN RESOURCE MANAGEMENT AND EMPLOYEE EDUCATION, TRAINING AND DEVELOPMENT

In general, education is 'mind preparation' and is carried out remote from the actual work area, training is the systematic development of the attitude, knowledge, skill pattern required by a person to perform a given task or job adequately and development is "the growth of the individual in terms of ability, understanding and awareness."

Within an organization all three are necessary in order to:

- Develop workers to undertake higher-grade tasks;
- Provide the conventional training of new and young workers (e.g. as apprentices, clerks, etc.);
- Raise efficiency and standards of performance;
- Meet legislative requirements (e.g. health and safety);
- Inform people (induction training, pre-retirement courses, etc.).

From time to time meet special needs arising from technical, legislative, and knowledge need changes. Meeting these needs is achieved via the 'training loop'. (Schematic available in PDF version.)

The diagnosis of other than conventional needs is complex and often depends upon the intuition or personal experience of managers and needs revealed by deficiencies. Sources of inspiration include:

- Common sense: it is often obvious that new machines, work systems, task requirements and changes in job content will require workers to be prepared.
- Shortcomings revealed by statistics of output per head, performance indices, unit costs, etc. and behavioural failures revealed by absentee figures, lateness, sickness etc. records.
- Recommendations of government and industry training organizations.
- Inspiration and innovations of individual managers and supervisors.
- Forecasts and predictions about staffing needs.
- Inspirations prompted by the technical press, training journals, reports of the experience of others.
- The suggestions made by specialist (e.g. education and training officers, safety engineers, work-study staff and management services personnel).

Designing training is far more than devising courses; it can include activities such as:

- Learning from observation of trained workers.
- Receiving coaching from seniors.
- Discovery as the result of working party, project team membership or attendance at meetings.
- Job swaps within and without the organization.
- Undertaking planned reading, or follow from the use of self-teaching texts and video tapes.
- Learning *via* involvement in research, report writing and visiting other works or organizations.

So far as group training is concerned in addition to formal courses there are:

- Lectures and talks by senior or specialist managers.
- Discussion group (conference and meeting) activities.
- Briefing by senior staffs.
- Role-playing exercises and simulation of actual conditions.
- Video and computer teaching activities.
- Case studies (and discussion) tests, quizzes, panel 'games', group forums, observation exercises and inspection and reporting techniques.

Evaluation of the effectiveness of training is done to ensure that it is cost effective, to identify needs to modify or extend what is being provided, to reveal new needs and redefine priorities and most of all to ensure that the objectives of the training are being met.

The latter may not be easy to ascertain where results cannot be measured mathematically. In the case of attitude and behavioural changes sought, leadership abilities, drive and ambition fostered, etc., achievement is a matter of the judgement of senior staffs. Exact validation might be impossible but unless on the whole the judgements are favourable the cooperation of managers in identifying needs, releasing personnel and assisting in training ventures will cease.

In making their judgements senior managers will question whether the efforts expended have produced:

- More effective, efficient, flexible employees.
- Faster results in making newcomers knowledgeable and effective than would follow from experience.
- More effective or efficient use of machinery, equipment and work procedures.
- Fewer requirements to implement redundancy (by retraining).
- Fewer accidents both personal and to property.
- Improvements in the qualifications of staff and their ability to take on tougher roles.
- Better employee loyalty to the organization with more willingness to innovate and accept change.

HUMAN RESOURCE MANAGEMENT AND PROVISION OF EMPLOYEE SERVICES

Attention to the mental and physical well-being of employees is normal in many organizations as a means of keeping good staff and attracting others.

The forms this welfare can take are many and varied, from loans to the needy to counselling in respect of personal problems.

Among the activities regarded as normal are:

- Schemes for occupational sick pay, extended sick leave and access to the firm's medical adviser.
- Schemes for bereavement or other special leave.
- The rehabilitation of injured/unfit/disabled employees and temporary or permanent move to lighter work.
- The maintenance of disablement statistics and registers (there are complicated legal requirements in respect of quotas of disabled workers and a need for 'certificates' where quota are not fulfilled and recruitment must take place).
- Provision of financial and other support for sports, social, hobbies, activities of many kinds which are work related.
- Provision of canteens and other catering facilities.
- Possibly assistance with financial and other aid to employees in difficulty (supervision, maybe, of an employee managed benevolent fund or scheme).

- Provision of information handbooks.
- Running of pre-retirement courses and similar fringe activities.
- Care for the welfare aspects of health and safety legislation and provision of first-aid training.

The location of the health and safety function within the organization varies. Commonly a split of responsibilities exists under which 'production' or 'engineering' management cares for the provision of safe systems of work and safe places and machines etc., but HRM is responsible for administration, training and education in awareness and understanding of the law, and for the alerting of all levels to new requirements.

HUMAN RESOURCE MANAGEMENT TO IMPROVE INDUSTRIAL RELATIONS

Good industrial relations, while a recognizable and legitimate objective for an organization, are difficult to define since a good system of industrial relations involves complex relationships between:

(*a*) Workers (and their informal and formal groups, i.e. trade union, organizations and their representatives);
(*b*) Employers (and their managers and formal organizations like trade and professional associations);
(*c*) The government and legislation and government agencies l and 'independent' agencies like the Advisory Couciliation and Arbitration Service.

Oversimplified, work is a matter of managers giving instructions and workers following them—but (and even under slavery we recognize that different 'managing' produces very different results) the variety of 'forms' which have evolved to regulate the conduct of parties (i.e. laws, custom and practice, observances, agreements) makes the giving and receipt of instructions far from simple. Two types of 'rule' have evolved:

- 'Substantive', determining basic pay and conditions of service (what rewards workers should receive);

- 'Procedural,' determining how workers should be treated and methods and procedures.

Determining these rules are many common-sense matters like:

- Financial, policy and market constraints on the parties (e.g. some unions do not have the finance to support industrial action, some have policies not to strike, some employers are more vulnerable than others to industrial action, some will not make changes unless worker agreement is made first, and rewards always ultimately reflect what the market will bear).
- The technology of production (the effect of a strike in newspaper production is immediate—it may be months before becoming effective in shipbuilding).
- The distribution of power within the community—that tends to vary over time and with economic conditions workers (or unions) dominating in times of full employment and employers in times of recession.

Broadly in the Western style economies the parties (workers and employers) are free to make their own agreements and rules. This is called 'voluntarism'. But it does not mean there is total non-interference by the Government. That is necessary to:

- Protect the weak (hence minimum wage).
- Outlaw discrimination (race or sex).
- Determine minimum standards of safety, health, hygiene and even important conditions of service.
- To try to prevent the abuse of power by either party.

HR Managers Responsibilities

The personnel manager's involvement in the system of industrial relations varies from organization to organization, but normally he or she is required to provide seven identifiable functions, thus:

1. To keep abreast of industrial law (legislation and precedents) and to advise managers about their responsibilities e.g., to observe requirements in respect of

employing disabled persons, not to discriminate, not to disclose 'spent' convictions of employees, to observe codes of practice etc., in relation to discipline and redundancy, and similarly to determine organizational policies (in conjunction with other managers) relevant to legal and moral requirements (see also 4.).

2. To conduct (or assist in the conduct) of either local negotiations (within the plant) or similarly to act as the employer's representative in national negotiations. This could be as a critic or advisor in respect of trade etc. association policies or as a member of a trade association negotiating team. Agreements could be in respect of substantive or procedural matters. Even if not directly involved the personnel manager will advise other managers and administrators of the outcome of negotiations.
3. To ensure that agreements reached are interpreted so as to make sense to those who must operate them at the appropriate level within the organization (this can involve a lot of new learning at supervisory level and new pay procedures and new recording requirements in administration and even the teaching of new employment concepts—like stagger systems of work—at management level).
4. To monitor the observance of agreements and to produce policies that ensure that agreements are followed within the organization. An example would be the policy to be followed on the appointment of a new but experienced recruit in relation to the offered salary where there is a choice of increments to be given for experience, ability or qualification.
5. To correct the situations which go wrong. 'Face' is of some importance in most organizations and operating at a 'remote' staff level personnel managers can correct industrial relations errors made at local level without occasioning any loss of dignity (face) at the working level. 'Human resource management' and the obscurity of its reasoning can be blamed for matters which go wrong at plant level and for unwelcome changes, variations of comfortable 'arrangements' and practices and unpopular interpretation of agreements.

6. To provide the impetus (and often devise the machinery) for the introduction of joint consultation and worker participation in decision-making in the organization. Formal agreement in respect of working conditions and behaviour could never cover every situation likely to arise. Moreover, the more demanding the task (in terms of the mental contribution by the worker to its completion) the more highly-educated the workers need to be and the more they will want to be consulted about and involved in the details of work life. Matters like the rules for a flexitime system or for determining the correction of absenteeism and the contents of jobs are three examples of the sort of matters that may be solely decided by management in some organizations but a matter for joint consultation (not negotiation) in others with a more twenty-first-century outlook and philosophy. Human resource management is very involved in promoting and originating ideas in this field.
7. To provide statistics and information about workforce numbers, costs, skills etc. as relevant to negotiations (i.e. the cost of pay rises or compromise proposals, effect on differentials and possible recruitment/retention consequences of this or whether agreement needs to be known instantly); to maintain personnel records of training, experience, achievements, qualifications, awards and possibly pension and other records; to produce data of interest to management in respect of personnel matters like absentee figures and costs, statistics of sickness absence, costs of welfare and other employee services, statements about development in policies by other organizations, ideas for innovations; to advise upon or operate directly, grievance, redundancy, disciplinary and other procedures.

HUMAN RESOURCE MANAGEMENT AND EMPLOYEE EVALUATION

An organization needs constantly to take stock of its workforce and to assess its performance in existing jobs for three reasons:

- To improve organizational performance *via* improving the

performance of individual contributors (should be an automatic process in the case of good managers, but (about annually) two key questions should be posed:
- what has been done to improve the performance of a person last year?
- and what can be done to improve his or her performance in the year to come?).

- To identify potential, i.e. to recognize existing talent and to use that to fill vacancies higher in the organization or to transfer individuals into jobs where better use can be made of their abilities or developing skills.
- To provide an equitable method of linking payment to performance where there are no numerical criteria (often this salary performance review takes place about three months later and is kept quite separate from 1. and 2. but is based on the same assessment).

On-the-spot managers and supervisors, not HR staffs, carry out evaluations. The personnel role is usually that of:

- Advising top management of the principles and objectives of an evaluation system and designing it for particular organizations and environments.
- Developing systems appropriately in consultation with managers, supervisors and staff representatives. Securing the involvement and co-operation of appraisers and those to be appraised.
- Assistance in the setting of objective standards of evaluation/assessment, for example:
  - Defining targets for achievement;
  - Explaining how to quantify and agree objectives;
  - Introducing self-assessment;
  - Eliminating complexity and duplication.
- Publicizing the purposes of the exercise and explaining to staff how the system will be used.
- Organizing and establishing the necessary training of managers and supervisors who will carry out the actual evaluations/appraisals. Not only training in principles and procedures but also in the human relations skills necessary.

(Lack of confidence in their own ability to handle situations of poor performance is the main weakness of assessors.)

- Monitoring the scheme—ensuring it does not fall into disuse, following up on training/job exchange etc. recommendations, reminding managers of their responsibilities.

Full-scale periodic reviews should be a standard feature of schemes since resistance to evaluation/appraisal schemes is common and the temptation to water down or render schemes ineffectual is ever present (managers resent the time taken if nothing else).

Basically an evaluation/appraisal scheme is a formalization of what is done in a more casual manner anyway (e.g. if there is a vacancy, discussion about internal moves and internal attempts to put square pegs into 'squarer holes' are both the results of casual evaluation). Most managers approve merit payment and that too calls for evaluation. Made a standard routine task, it aids the development of talent, warns the inefficient or uncaring and can be an effective form of motivation.

HUMAN RESOURCE MANAGEMENT TO IMPROVE EMPLOYEE MOTIVATION

To retain good staff and to encourage them to give of their best while at work requires attention to the financial and psychological and even physiological rewards offered by the organization as a continuous exercise.

Basic financial rewards and conditions of service (e.g. working hours per week) are determined externally (by national bargaining or government minimum wage legislation) in many occupations but as much as 50 per cent of the gross pay of manual workers is often the result of local negotiations and details (e.g. which particular hours shall be worked) of conditions of service are often more important than the basics. Hence, there is scope for financial and other motivations to be used at local levels.

As staffing needs will vary with the productivity of the workforce (and the industrial peace achieved) so good personnel policies are desirable. The latter can depend upon other factors (like environment, welfare, employee benefits, etc.) but unless the wage packet is accepted as 'fair and just' there will be no motivation.

Hence, while the technicalities of payment and other systems may be the concern of others, the outcome of them is a matter of great concern to human resource management.

Increasingly the influence of behavioural science discoveries are becoming important not merely because of the widely-acknowledged limitations of money as a motivator, but because of the changing mix and nature of tasks (e.g. more service and professional jobs and far fewer unskilled and repetitive production jobs).

The former demand better-educated, mobile and multi-skilled employees much more likely to be influenced by things like job satisfaction, involvement, participation, etc., than the economically dependent employees of yester-year.

Hence, human resource management must act as a source of information about and a source of inspiration for the application of the findings of behavioural science. It may be a matter of drawing the attention of senior managers to what is being achieved elsewhere and the gradual education of middle managers to new points of view on job design, work organization and worker autonomy.

HUMAN RESOURCE MANAGEMENT: RECRUITMENT AND SELECTION OF EMPLOYEES

Recruitment of staff should be preceded by an analysis of the job to be done (i.e. an analytical study of the tasks to be performed to determine their essential factors) written into a job description so that the selectors know what physical and mental characteristics applicants must possess, what qualities and attitudes are desirable and what characteristics are a decided disadvantage:

- In the case of replacement staff a critical questioning of the need to recruit at all (replacement should rarely be an automatic process).
- Effectively, selection is 'buying' an employee (the price being the wage or salary multiplied by probable years of

service) hence bad buys can be very expensive. For that reason some firms (and some firms for particular jobs) use external expert consultants for recruitment and selection.

- Equally some small organizations exist to 'head hunt', i.e. to attract staff with high reputations from existing employers to the recruiting employer. However, the 'cost' of poor selection is such that, even for the mundane day-to-day jobs, those who recruit and select should be well trained to judge the suitability of applicants.

The main sources of recruitment are:

- Internal promotion and internal introductions (at times desirable for morale purposes).
- Careers officers (and careers masters at schools).
- University appointment boards.
- Agencies for the unemployed.
- Advertising (often *via* agents for specialist posts) or the use of other local media (e.g. commercial radio).

Where the organization does its own printed advertising it is useful if it has some identifying logo as its trade mark for rapid attraction and it must take care not to offend the sex, race, etc. anti-discrimination legislation either directly or indirectly. The form on which the applicant is to apply (personal appearance, letter of application, completion of a form) will vary according to the posts vacant and numbers to be recruited.

It is very desirable in many jobs that claim about experience and statements about qualifications are thoroughly checked and that applicants unfailingly complete a health questionnaire (the latter is not necessarily injurious to the applicants chance of being appointed as firms are required to employ a percentage of disabled people).

Before letters of appointment are sent any doubts about medical fitness or capacity (in employments where hygiene considerations are dominant) should be resolved by requiring applicants to attend a medical examination. This is especially so where, as for example in the case of apprentices, the recruitment is for a contractual period or involves the firm in training costs.

Interviewing can be carried out by individuals (e.g. supervisor or departmental manager), by panels of interviewers or in the form of sequential interviews by different experts and can vary from a five minute 'chat' to a process of several days. Ultimately personal skills in judgement are probably the most important, but techniques to aid judgement include selection testing for:

- Aptitudes (particularly useful for school leavers).
- Attainments.
- General intelligence.

(All of these need skilled testing and assessment.) In more senior posts other techniques are:

- Leaderless groups.
- Command exercises.
- Group problem solving.

(These are some common techniques—professional selection organizations often use other techniques to aid in selection.)

Training in interviewing and in appraising candidates is clearly essential to good recruitment. Largely the former consists of teaching interviewers how to draw out the interviewee and the latter how to xratex the candidates. For consistency (and as an aid to checking that) rating often consists of scoring candidates for experience, knowledge, physical/mental capabilities, intellectual levels, motivation, prospective potential, leadership abilities etc. (according to the needs of the post). Application of the normal curve of distribution to scoring eliminates freak judgements.

HUMAN RESOURCE MANAGEMENT AND MANPOWER PLANNING

The penalties for not being correctly staffed are costly.

- Understaffing loses the business economies of scale and specialization, orders, customers and profits.
- Overstaffing is wasteful and expensive, if sustained, and it is costly to eliminate because of modern legislation in respect of redundancy payments, consultation, minimum

periods of notice, etc. Very importantly, overstaffing reduces the competitive efficiency of the business.

Planning staff levels requires that an assessment of present and future needs of the organization be compared with present resources and future predicted resources. Appropriate steps then be planned to bring demand and supply into balance.

Thus, the first step is to take a 'satellite picture' of the existing workforce profile (numbers, skills, ages, flexibility, gender, experience, forecast capabilities, character, potential, etc. of existing employees) and then to adjust this for 1, 3 and 10 years ahead by amendments for normal turnover, planned staff movements, retirements, etc., in line with the business plan for the corresponding time frames.

The result should be a series of crude supply situations as would be the outcome of present planning if left unmodified. (This, clearly, requires a great deal of information accretion, classification and statistical analysis as a subsidiary aspect of personnel management.)

What future demands will be is only influenced in part by the forecast of the personnel manager, whose main task may well be to scrutinize and modify the crude predictions of other managers. Future staffing needs will derive from:

- Sales and production forecasts.
- The effects of technological change on task needs.
- Variations in the efficiency, productivity, flexibility of labour as a result of training, work study, organizational change, new motivations, etc.
- Changes in employment practices (e.g. use of sub-contractors or agency staffs, hiving-off tasks, buying in, substitution, etc.)
- Variations, which respond to new legislation, e.g. payroll taxes or their abolition, new health and safety requirements.
- Changes in Government policies (investment incentives, regional or trade grants, etc.)

What should emerge from this 'blue sky gazing' is a 'thought out' and logical staffing demand schedule for varying dates in the future which can then be compared with the crude supply schedules. The comparisons will then indicate what steps must be taken to achieve a balance.

That, in turn, will involve the further planning of such recruitment, training, retraining, labour reductions (early retirement/redundancy) or changes in workforce utilization as will bring supply and demand into equilibrium, not just as a one-off but as a continuing workforce planning exercise the inputs to which will need constant varying to reflect 'actual' as against predicted experience on the supply side and changes in production actually achieved as against forecast on the demand side.

STEPS IN DEVELOPING A HRM STRATEGY

Step 1: Get the 'Big Picture'

Understand your business strategy.

- Highlight the key driving forces of your business. What are they? e.g. technology, distribution, competition, the markets.
- What are the implications of the driving forces for the people side of your business?
- What is the fundamental people contribution to bottom line business performance?

Step 2: Develop a Mission Statement or Statement of Intent

That relates to the people side of the business.

Do not be put off by negative reactions to the words or references to idealistic statements—it is the actual process of thinking through the issues in a formal and explicit manner that is important.

- What do your people contribute?

Step 3: Conduct a SWOT Analysis of the Organization

Focus on the internal strengths and weaknesses of the people side of the business.

- Consider the current skill and capability issues.

Vigorously research the external business and market environment. Highlight the opportunities and threats relating to the people side of the business.

- What impact will/might they have on business performance?
- Consider skill shortages?
- The impact of new technology on staffing levels?

From this analysis you then need to review the capability of your personnel department. Complete a SWOT analysis of the department—consider in detail the department's current areas of operation, the service levels and competences of your personnel staff.

Step 4: Conduct a Detailed Human Resources Analysis

Concentrate on the organization's COPS (culture, organization, people, HR systems)

- Consider: Where you are now? Where do you want to be?
- What gaps exists between the reality of where you are now and where you want to be?

Exhaust your analysis of the four dimensions.

Step 5: Determine Critical People Issues

Go back to the business strategy and examine it against your SWOT and COPS Analysis

- Identify the critical people issues namely those people issues that you must address. Those which have a key impact on the delivery of your business strategy.
- Prioritise the critical people issues. What will happen if you fail to address them?

Remember you are trying to identify where you should be focusing your efforts and resources.

Step 6: Develop Consequences and Solutions

For each critical issue highlight the options for managerial action generate, elaborate and create—don't go for the obvious. This is an important step as frequently people jump for the known rather than challenge existing assumptions about the way things have been done in the past. Think about the consequences of taking various courses of action.

Consider the mix of HR systems needed to address the issues. Do you need to improve communications, training or pay?

What are the implications for the business and the personnel function?

Once you have worked through the process it should then be possible to translate the action plan into broad objectives. These will need to be broken down into the specialist HR Systems areas of:

- employee training and development.
- management development.
- organization development.
- performance appraisal.
- employee reward.
- employee selection and recruitment.
- manpower planning.
- communication.

Develop your action plan around the critical issues. Set targets and dates for the accomplishment of the key objectives.

Step 7: Implementation and Evaluation of the Action Plans

The ultimate purpose of developing a human resource strategy is to ensure that the objectives set are mutually supportive so that the reward and payment systems are integrated with employee training and career development plans.

There is very little value or benefit in training people only to then frustrate them through a failure to provide ample career and development opportunities.

HRM SYSTEMS AND DIAGNOSTIC CHECKLISTS

The following check-lists present some questions which may prove helpful for you to think about when planning your development programmes for human resources (your people) in your organization.

Use them to provoke thought and to stimulate discussion. Consult with others in your organization. They will help you to identify the critical human resource issues facing your organization.

The aim is to begin to explore how a considered and planned approach to people management can improve business performance, to the benefit of all.

Use this checklist in conjunction with our team building diagnostic instrument. It will, via your team members responses identify critical issues they perceive as important. These issues may be at odds with your own perceptions and analysis and therefore any such discrepancy will need to be addressed.

Warning Indicators

Your organization is more than likely in trouble if any of the following holds true:

- chronic industrial relations problems.
- no means of resolving employee grievances.
- increasing/erratic employee turnover.
- increasing number of customer complaints.
- no pride in the organization.
- inter-group conflicts.
- no career paths for ambitious talented employees.
- dissatisfaction with pay and conditions.
- unclear job roles.
- no clear performance measures.
- quality is unimportant.
- bad product service/delivery records.
- poor recruitment standards/practices.
- no management development programmes.
- no induction training for new employees.
- critical skill shortages.

- inter-departmental conflict.
- you do not know if any of the above are applicable.
- you ignore any of the above.

Culture, Organization, People, Systems (COPS), Checklist

Culture

- Do your staff identify with the organization and 'the success of the organization' as being of direct benefit to themselves?
- Do your staff see themselves as having common interests with their work colleagues and group? Is there a strong team spirit?
- Is work allocated on the basis of individual expertise rather than position in the organization?
- Are there sufficient skills/power bases in the organization?
- Are there appropriate leadership skills within the organization?
- Are your staff encouraged to say what they think about the organization?
- Does your organization encourage innovation and creativity amongst staff?
- Do your staff feel a sense of personal responsibility for their work?
- Is quality emphasized in all aspects of the organization?

Organization

- Does the structure of your organization encourage effective performance?
- Is the organization structure flexible in the face of changing demands?
- Is the structure too complex? If so in what areas?
- Do your staff have clear roles and responsibilities?
- Does your organization structure tend to push problems up rather than resolve them at the point where they occur?
- Do your procedures and management practices facilitate the accomplishment of tasks?

- Do you constantly seek to challenge your organization structure?

People

- Do your staff have the necessary skills and knowledge to perform their jobs in the most effective manner?
- Do your staff understand their jobs and how they contribute to overall business performance i.e., have clear goals and objectives?
- Do your staff have a customer service orientation?
- Are people with potential spotted and developed for the future?
- Are your staff encouraged to perform well, through the giving of recognition, feedback, etc.?
- Do your people know what their expected performance standards are?

Systems

- Do your organization's systems (e.g. employee selection and recruitment, promotion, planning, management, information and control) encourage effective performance among your staff?
- Are these systems consistent across the organization?
- Are there clear rewards for effective performance within your work group?
- Does the organization review its systems frequently and ensure they mutually support each other?

You may now wish to consider and write down:

- What are the three critical people issues facing your business?
- What plans/actions can you take to address these issues?

EMPLOYEE EVALUATION AND SELECTION

This illustration will considerably help you improve the employee evaluation and selection processes. It will greatly assist in 'engineering' into the people you are charged with, the skills, experiences, knowledge and other attributes you deem important to success. The schematic below is an example of the outcome from the technique. It shows (in blue) the key dimensions of a job compared against the evaluated attributes (in red) of a suitable candidate. It is immediately apparent where the strengths and weaknesses of the candidate are, in relation to this one position. Actions and decisions can then be taken in respect of the strengths and weaknesses.

If you believe the these processes, employee evaluation and selection, are not key components in managing for success or you are looking for a better way to execute with a higher degree of measurable success these HR processes, this technique is for you. It will also enable you to conduct effective job interviews, focusing you on the interview questions you need to ask in order to ascertain candidate appropriateness for the important job dimensions you have analyzed as being important to success.

Some Uses

It can easily be applied inter alia other instances such as:

- Developing employees for internal promotion.
- Constructing training and development programmes for individuals and groups.
- Succession planning.
- You want to delegate more, to enable you to tackle the high payoff projects you have on the back burner, but cannot find away of developing a likely the chosen person.
- In team building, constructing a project team having key skill, knowledge and experience bases.
- Employee surveys, where you wish to compare an ideal situation, with the situation perceived by employees.

Also, one of the traits of an effective manager is his/her ability to extract information from informal conversations (management by wandering around) as he or she goes about daily routine. Such a manager would be able to use the technique of profile analysis to build a profile of key constructs in his/her area of responsibility (not covered by normal performance reporting, like say morale) and measure this over time.

When you browse this article, it is recommended that you keep in mind the question 'how else could I use this technique, outside of the job interview process?'

The following is an overview of each section. It is recommended that you first read the section on profile analysis, paying particular attention to the radar/spider charts. It should then be obvious of the use you will be able to put this technique to and its appropriateness to your situation.

Employee Selection Process

Who makes the selection decision, the roles of operating management/human resource management specialists, general selection criteria, and the reliability and validity of job interviews are explored.

Job Analysis

Job analysis can be defined as the determination of the essential characteristics of a job in order to produce a job specification. In this section use of job analysis in the employee selection process is explained.

Job Interviews—Purpose and Validity

The two-fold purpose of job interview is explained, as well as a critical look at their validity is explored.

Establishing Job Constructs for the Job Interview

The job constructs (dimensions) and the sub-dimensions, against which applicants are to be evaluated for suitability and compatibility are shown under:

- Communication skills.
- Self-motivation.
- Setting of work standards—self/others.

- Interpersonal/ability to sell self and ideas.
- Leadership potential and skills.
- Decision-making abilities.
- Judgement abilities.
- Knowledge bases/technical skills.
- Management abilities.

Profile Analysis

Profile analysis is a tool to maximize the probability of matching people to job positions. In this 'how to' section, the construction of position profiles and imposing data collected from applicants, is explained. Profile analysis has other uses in human resource management and these are also expounded.

Job Interview Outline Guide

The mechanics of conducting a professional job interview explained. There are some informal do's and don'ts for the job interview, in this article they are listed.

User Guide

This places all of the above together in an organized and planned methodology so that you will be able to individualize interview questions to the unique experiences of each prospective candidate, for each of the key constructs for the job being interviewed for. The Acrobat PDF version contains well over 600 job interview questions categorized by job construct.

CASE STUDY: AUSTRALIAN HOTEL INDUSTRY

The Australian hotel industry is at the crossroads. As part of the tourism strategy of the present Federal Government, it is charged with catapulting Australia out of its economic malaise. The industry is, however, constrained in its development by market fluctuations, an oversupply of accommodation and outdated human resource management practices. Several recent research studies have underlined the significant costs of labour in overall industry costs, and the pressing need to reduce these costs and improve profitability and competitiveness by effective and innovative human resource management strategies.

Hotels in Australia, as compared to their international counterparts, are less productive, less profitable and less labour intensive. The challenge is to develop innovative human resource management practices which will enhance productivity and profitability without increasing staff levels. Significant contributions to industry viability will be achieved through comprehensive and integrated human resource management systems which ensure that the right staff are recruited, trained, monitored and appropriately rewarded in line with institutional and industry requirements.

Introduction

The primacy of the service sector, and in particular tourism, to economic recovery in Australia has became almost a truism in the last decade. Successive federal and state government ministers, from John Brown to Alan Griffiths, have emphasised the potential economic contributions and demands of this industry sector to productivity, growth and regional competitiveness. Alan Griffiths, the current federal Tourism Minister, recently described the tourism industry as the "economic star of the 1990s", (ABC Lateline, 1992) predicting inbound tourist growth to reach more than half of all travellers in Australia by the magical year 2000.

Despite current hiccups in infrastructure growth, especially oversupplies of hotel accommodation in capital cities and leisure resorts resulting from the hotel-building boom of the late 1980s, the same minister projected a need to continue building hotels at a frantic pace in order to cater for anticipated levels of tourism from Southeast Asian countries. (ABC Lateline, 1992). Whether or not the industry is primed to pull Australia out of its economic malaise or merely to survive in continuing difficult economic times, the importance of tourism, and in particular the contributions of its accommodation segment, is unlikely to diminish in the next decade.

Industry analysts, citing the negative impact of events such as the 1980s Pilots' Dispute and the current recession and the Barcelona Olympic Games, (ABC Lateline, 1992) seriously question these predictions, especially in view of industry indicators such as hotel receivership levels[1] and staffing reductions.

There are varying statistics[2] on the employment and financial contributions of the hotel industry to the Australian economy. Anne Rein, Chief Executive of Tourism Training Australia, is perhaps closest to reality—current employees, 320,000 people in some 25,000 mainly small establishments, contributing 5.4 per cent of GDP, accounting for 6 per cent of the overall Australian workforce and amounting to $ 6.7 billion in export earnings (Rein, 1992). In order to assure the ongoing effectiveness and global competitiveness of the hotel industry in Australia, significant issues concerning the style of service provided by hotels, their human resource management practices and overall management processes, demand to be confronted and resolved.

This chapter, aiming to contribute to the debate on quality assurance in the Australian hotel industry, focusses on the crucial components of effective human resource management programmes in resolving and value-adding service, productivity and profitability in this industry. Considerable problems currently exist. However, substantial opportunities are also available to hotel managers, supervisors and human resource specialists to ensure effectiveness, cost-effectiveness and global competitiveness within this crucial industry sector.

Industry Characteristics

Nils Timo (Timo, 1992) observes that the "Australian hotel industry is characterised by...gendered labour markets, a relatively young transient workforce, a culture of casualisation, seasonability, and the development of internal labour markets." Not an ideal scenario for a burgeoning and crucial economic sector! The recent Australian Workplace Industrial Relations Survey (AWIRS) (Callus, 1991) confirms some, but not all, of these assumptions.

Gendered Labour Markets

On the issue of "gendered" labour markets, AWIRS found that some 56 per cent of employees in the "recreation, personal services and others" category are female, comparable to the proportions indicated by the Australian Bureau of Statistics studies (Timo,

1992). However, this proportion may be misleading, as the category subsumes all such industries, and fails to isolate the hotel sector.

The Bureau of Tourism Research's figure of 60 per cent may be more realistic (BTR, 1990). A smaller, more recent, survey indicates that the representation of females in the hotel industry may be even greater than both studies suggest—69.4 per cent (Nankervis, 1991). This survey also indicates that such proportions vary with hotel classifications. Five-star hotels appear to employ equal proportions of male and female employees, whilst three- and four-star hotels seem imbalanced towards female employees. Both traditionally female occupations (e.g. housekeeping, guest relations) and the part-time, or casual, nature of "service" occupations presumably influence these statistics.

A Culture of Casualisation

Whilst the "gendered labour market" of the hotel industry may, or may not, be a crucial issue, it is important that the "culture of casualisation" is addressed by the Australian hotel industry in order to ensure future success. The conjunction of "casualisation" and the high proportions of female employees may represent discriminatory and exploitative practices which are inimical to such progress. The AWIRS study suggests that within the overall category of "recreation, personal services and other" around 54 per cent of employees, the highest of all industries surveyed, are employed on a part-time basis, with some 68 per cent of hotels employing more than half of their staff on these conditions (Callus, 1991). Another study, (Nankervis, 1991) taking a different perspective, suggests a relationship between gender and work status—whilst 57 per cent of staff are employed on a full-time basis, 71 per cent of these are male, often in managerial positions.

Recent revisions to the award which covers hotel employees, renamed in 1989 the Hotels, Resorts and Hospitality Industry Award implies the regularisation of casual employment "...employees who have worked a roster of at least fifteen hours per week for a period of not less than six months" (Bodi, A., *et al.*, 1991)—but still fails to provide job security. No doubt justification for continued, irregular, employment of large numbers of "casuals" in the hospitality industry relates to the industry need for numerical flexibility, especially in resort locations, and overall industry seasonal fluctuations. It may not, however, provide either the optimal staffing scenario, nor an adequate justification for the high prevalence of female workers in this category.

Young, Transient Workforce

The recent AWIRS study, defining youth workers as those 20 years or younger, found that some 55 per cent of surveyed organisations in the "recreation, personal and other, category employed no young workers (Callus, 1991). This figure is no doubt skewed due to the inclusion of non-hotel sector organisations. Few reliable statistics exist on the levels of youth employment in the hotel industry. However, another survey (Nankervis, 1991) suggests that there is a strong preference (75.4%) for the employment of employees with prior industry experience, which may support the AWIRS findings. This preference is highest, as might be expected, in four-star (90%), five-star resort (75%) and five-star capital city sectors (72.7%).

Transience may be indicated by comparatively high labour turnover rates, which are confirmed by both Bureau of Tourism Research (BTR, 1990) and AWIRS studies (Callus, 1991)—45 per cent annually[3], especially in kitchen, housekeeping, front-of-house and bar occupations. Labour stability appears correspondingly low, with few employees overall staying more than five years (Callus, 1991). The preponderance of low-skilled occupations, "normal" seasonal fluctuations, and the apparent overall scarcity of value-added human resource activities (training, career paths, rewards systems), may contribute to these statistics, which severely challenge government and industry predictions about the contributions of this industry sector to national economic recovery.

Salary Levels/Union Involvement

Hotel employees have traditionally been perceived as among the lowest paid of all Australian workers, partly due to their transience, low skills levels (and historic lack of skills accreditation), and lack of union support. These perceptions are confirmed by several studies—the AWIRS findings (Callus, 1991) and a more recent survey (Nankervis, 1991)—which indicate that less than 30 per cent five-star city hotels, 45 per cent resorts, 40 per cent four-star and 22 per cent three-star hotels pay more than the award rates. In contrast, many hotels pay their managerial staff, often male, substantial salary supplements, especially in five-star sectors.

Presumably, some hotels will increase employee wages as the result of new enterprise agreements and award restructuring activities, based upon the abolition of penalty rates and productivity initiatives. Already, a major Australian hotel chain has successfully negotiated an enterprise agreement with its employees, involving the substitution of penalty rates for higher hourly rates and increased job flexibilities (Smith, 1992). More are likely to follow. As a highly labour-intensive industry, the hospitality sector will fail to thrive if the only solution to its problems focuses on salary disincentives and corresponding job flexibilities.

Union participation is also unusually low in the Australian hotel industry—AWIRS estimates the level of unionised workplaces in the "recreation, personal and other services" category as 67 per cent, the lowest, alongside "wholesale and retail trade" and "finance, property and business services"; a comparable survey suggests that 73.9 per cent respondents in the hotel industry have less than half of their employees covered by relevant unions (Nankervis, 1991).

Such low levels undoubtedly reflect casualisation, gender imbalances, transient workforces and the historically weak positions of relevant industry unions. They also provide substantial opportunities for astute hotel managers and their human resource specialists to negotiate creative enterprise agreements, covering job flexibilities, performance-based rewards systems and career management programmes.

Labour Costs and Overall Industry Costs

As a highly labour intensive industry, the hotel sector is naturally becoming concerned to identify the actual relationships between labour costs and institutional profitability and competitiveness. The opportunities for increasing labour flexibility, and thus potentially reducing these costs as a proportion of overall operating costs, as well as the increasing use of minor technologies to substitute for labour (e.g. greater use of computerised front office systems, self-service automated telephone and mini-bar operations), are predicated on industrial relations and operations changes. The AWIRS study suggests that half of their respondents in the "recreation, personal and other services" category estimate that between 21-40 per cent of their overall operating costs directly relate to labour costs (CaEus, 1991).

A more focussed study (Tourism Task Force, 1992) found that "...the Australian hotel industry has one of the highest labour cost components when expressed as a percentage of revenue and an amount per available room." Using international comparisons, the study also found (see Table 2.1) that Australian hotels have both "...the highest percentage payroll cost and the second lowest employee per room (next to Europe) statistic..."(TTF, 1992). Accordingly, the Tourism Task Force concludes that the Australian hotel industry "...ranks last in terms of hotel Gross Operating Profit (GOP) as a percentage of revenue and GOP per available room" (see Table 2.2).

Labour costs include direct wages, overtime, penalty rates, holiday and long service leave, training, meals, payroll tax and workers' compensation premiums. Significant components of labour costs are actual wages, penalty rates, holiday pay and payroll taxes.

Australian hotels thus appear to employ less staff overall than their European, United Kingdom and Asian competitors, but provide them with greater salary and benefits systems. Ironically, however, the salary levels of employees in this industry are amongst the lowest of all Australian employees. Not surprisingly then, any modification of labour costs must concentrate on the "peripherals" (penalty rates, holiday pay and leave loadings), the arena for negotiation in recent award restructuring initiatives.

However, concentration on labour cost modification alone as an impetus for industry growth and international competitiveness is insufficient, especially as the principal "product" of at least the four-and five-star hotel segment is quality service, which necessarily requires ongoing high levels of staffing. Of perhaps more value is a comprehensive industry strategy reviewing all aspects of human resource management practices, and devising unique and long-term solutions to ensure continuing productivity, profitability, and thence competitiveness.

Table 2.1: International Labour Cost Comparison

	Australia	*Far East/Asia*	*North America*	*Europe*	*United Kingdom*
Payroll Per Available Room (US$):					
Rooms	$4,028	$1,962	$2,836	$3,551	$3,430
F&B	5,325	3,158	4,078	5,989	5,851
A&G	1,813	1,280	1,236	1,847	1,779
Market	523	450	643	384	445
Maint	614	350	675	629	568
Payroll as a % of Sales:					
Rooms	23.4	13.0	18.0	19.3	17.6
F&B	44.0	31.0	43.5	34.7	30.7
Tele	21.4	11.9	30.2	13.4	11.7
Total Payroll as a % of Total Revenue	37.2	25.8	34.7	31.2	28.3

Note: (1) All amounts are medians.

(2) All dollar amount stated in US$.

Source: Horwath International.

Table 2.2: Comparative International Profitability Data

	Australia	*Far East/Asia*	*North America*	*Europe*	*United Kingdom*
GOP per Available Room (US$)	$4,883	$7,921	$5,880	$10,586	$13,518
Room Dept. Profit (% of Sales)	65.2	77.5	72.5	71.88	75.1
Food & Beverage Profit (% of Sales)	11.4	26.9	15.7	26.1	31.1
GOP percent (% of Total Revenue)	20.4	34.8	24.7	29.2	33.9
Occupancy %	58.3	70.2	64.5	65.5	65.0
Average Room Rate (US$)	$82.80	$65.60	$72.00	$80.00	$79.42

Note: All amounts are medians.

Source: Horwath International.

As an illustration of this approach, a comparative study of middle-range hotels in Germany and the United Kingdom discovered that German hotel workers are generally better-trained and vocationally accredited, have greater skills flexibility and exercise far broader discretionary authority than their British counterparts (Prais, 1989). Additionally German hotels appear to utilise more systematic work processes, have lower turnover rates and staffing levels, their managers focus on longer-term human resource planning and marketing strategies, and are enthusiastic about the implementation of minor technological systems (e.g. user-friendly building design; comprehensive computer systems; industrial, rather than domestic, vacuum cleaners, etc). Not surprisingly then, this study found that the labour productivity of German hotels was between one and half to two times higher than in British hotels. Despite generally higher wages in German hotels, room prices were 20 per cent lower than their United Kingdom counterparts.

So neither labour costs alone, nor staffing ratios alone, are sufficient to account for the comparative competitiveness of the hotel industry. A similar study in Singapore hotels (Debrah, 1991) confirms the global dilemma faced by the industry, that: "we cannot afford to continue to manage hotels in Singapore the same way we are managing today."

The State of Human Resource Management in the Australian Hotel Industry

As indicated, the hotel industry in Australia appears to be considerably less productive and less profitable than many of its overseas counterparts. Some of the problems can be traced to the turbulence of the Australian domestic economy, industrial relations factors, tourist choices and internal supply/demand fluctuations.

However, significant difficulties exist within industry operations and management styles which contribute to the current state of malaise. The dearth of historic industry research, perceptions of industry leaders and individual hotel management have been relevant in the failure of the industry to date to face its fundamental and crucial problems. The earlier cited studies (Horwath; Prais, Jarvis and Wagner; AWIRS) all conclude that industry productivity and international competitiveness directly relate to the efficacy of the industry's management of their workforce.

Simple solutions would suggest the ruthless reduction of the workforce, immediate and significant skills and conditions flexibilities, massive technological change and close scrutiny of financial management. Timo suggests that some of these approaches are already being implemented: "Because the level of demand for such services is highly volatile, unpredictable and perishable, management strategy has increasingly focused upon the extension of labour antiflexible specialisation through a complex process of deskilling and reskilling" (Timo, 1992). He warns, however, that these processes, combined with the use of increasing numbers of transient or short-term visa employees "...engender higher turnover...and retard skill formation for some occupations..." (Timo, 1992). In order then for the Australian hotel industry to regain its competitive position, hotel managers and industry leaders need to focus on the most effective ways of improving productivity levels, including the reduction of overall labour costs, value-added skills development and the avoidance of expensive wastage and turnover levels, realistically within the Australian socio-economic and industrial relations context. Such strategies require attention to a broad range of human resource management practices within a long-range plan for development.

The hotel industry is perhaps the least advanced of all industries in its use and integration of modern human resource management activities. A recent study (Nankervis, 1991) found that, whilst most hotels surveyed, did in fact have a designated position as Personnel/Human Resource Manager, Training Manager, or some esoteric combination, few utilise innovative recruitment methods (e.g. relationships with hotel training colleges, secondary schools, older and/or disabled employees); management development, career or succession planning; performance management systems, flexible salary programmes or applied wastage/labour turnover studies.

Service Standards

Perhaps even more importantly, whilst most hotels possess general mission/vision statements, hardly any operationalise their definitions of "service" into behavioural standards for housekeeping, front-of-house, and food and beverage occupations. Most appear to focus on general qualities such as the "friendliness", "refinement", "spontaneity" or "consistency" of staff.

Whilst it is not suggested that hotels should adopt standardised, rigid McDonalds-style patter, the absence of specific behavioural standards impacts on recruitment/selection accuracy, training and skills development programmes, appraisal and rewards systems. It also largely precludes consistency and hence the fulfilment of guest expectations, especially in four-and five-star establishments. The development of national competency standards and benchmarks for service occupations by Tourism Training Australia and the National Training Board is a step in the right direction, as a basic skills expectation, nationally accredited. It does not, however, preclude individual hotels from adding value to their own staff, by defining additional specific behaviours relevant to their unique ambience. Failure to do so imposes constraints on quality service and hinders subsequent employee development, appraisal and appropriate remuneration, and thence enhanced productivity levels.

In the current industrial relations and labour market climate significant opportunities exist for proactive hotel, and human resource managers to recruit more selectively; create considerable skills flexibility coupled with subsequent training and career development opportunities; and free up the historic inflexibility of hotel employees' salary systems.

Recruiting Opportunities and Options

For effective exploitation of the increased numbers and varied experience of the Australian labour market in the 1990s, more innovative recruitment strategies require consideration. As earlier indicated, the predominance of casual or part-time and female workers especially in service occupations (e.g. front office, housekeeping, food and beverage), may reflect traditional, rather than necessarily effective, sources of hotel staff. Recent increases in the supply of trained and accredited hotel employees through TAFE colleges, private hotel schools and training establishments, certainly provide a wider and more secure source of staff. However, it may be additionally useful for hotel recruiters to consider broader options such as developing ongoing relationships with hotel schools, local secondary schools and even sources of disabled, or older, mature and generically experienced workers. In a different labour market, some Singaporean (Debrah, 1991) and German (Prais, 1989) hotels consciously seek out more mature workers for highly specialised, and sensitive, positions such as concierges, front-of-house receptionists and guest liaison. Some writers (Tanke, 1990, Heskett, 1990, Zeithaml, 1990) suggest that North American trends in hotel employment are increasingly focused on "older" employees, especially 25-34 year old, and disabled workers, due to their low turnover and higher productivity rates (Tanke, 1990). In a scarce labour market, Singapore hotels are even resorting to "bring a friend" incentives and cash rewards for referral. On the other hand, "boutique" or resort hotels may prefer to recruit younger staff for easier assimilation with hotel philosophy and guest markets.

The point here, however, is that recruitment and selection practices should reflect actual expected occupational standards and overall management philosophies. (indicates the current use of recruitment practices in Australian hotels. More use of appropriate applicant testing schemes, site tours and probationary periods may yield considerable benefits to potential employers). Innovative sources and recruitment practices will ensure value-added recruits who are already oriented to the demands and opportunities of a career within the hotel industry.

Industry Promotion and Institutional Development

Associated with innovative, and focused recruitment programmes, the hotel industry would be well-advised to adopt more strategic industry and individual hotel campaigns to apprise prospective employees of the future opportunities offered by the industry. Many regional and resort hotels already operate community-based programmes emphasising their local involvement and investments (Blackwell, 1989). The tourism industry and its leaders have also significantly reversed the traditionally unattractive image of occupations in the hotel industry by media campaigns, work-experience programmes and career advice.

The Australian industry shares perhaps some of the perceptions noted by a Singaporean researcher: "...serving people has traditionally been perceived as degrading work in Chinese culture...low social status. There is also a moral element. Many conservative parents do not want their children to work in hotels. Similarly many men do not want their wives to work in hotels. These people see hotel jobs as one step from working in a night club" (Debrah, 1991). However, the semi-skilled nature of many such jobs and the relative absence of true career paths within this industry may still act as a disadvantage for potentially valuable recruits. This continuing perception of hotel occupations, overcome by necessity in recessionary times, can be addressed by both ongoing and broad industry promotional campaigns, and the development of human resource management programmes post-recruitment aimed at career paths, job rotation, multi-skilling and flexible remuneration systems.

On the subject of the development of employee careers as a means of attracting and retaining quality, productive staff less likely to leave, Anne Rein of Tourism Training Australia suggests "...a nationally-recognised pattern of career advancement, linked to qualifications recognised by (and portable between) employers and education and training establishments," (Rein, 1992). Support for the industry in its value-adding process for staff is considerable from such organisations. Individual hotel human resource managers will, however, have to be sufficiently prescient to recognise the value of such programmes, and incorporate them in their award restructuring negotiations. Recent revisions of the industry award, retitled the Hotel, Resorts and Hospitality Industry Award (1989), permit the employment of 'regular casuals', traineeships, reduced working hours, redundancy and modified termination procedures. Several hotels have already taken advantage of the flexibilities offered by award restructuring and enterprise agreements—the Melbourne International" (Bodi, A. *et al.*, 1992). HR manager "...believes the new job classification structure can provide the first step to achieving a better working environment based on the existence of clear career opportunities." Wisely this process has been closely monitored to ensure it is used positively and developmentally rather than merely for unwarranted employee promotions.

Similarly, the Sheraton hotel chain, commencing in its Melbourne operations, has recently traded restrictive penalty rates for higher hourly rates and increased job flexibility tied to career paths. The Southern Pacific Hotels group is trialling similar approaches (Smidi, 1992). Thus, in these somewhat isolated instances, human resource managers are beginning to recognise the productivity impact of increased flexibility, including career pathing, and exchanging extrinsic (penalty rates) for intrinsic rewards (job enrichment, multi-skilling).

RESEARCH AND PRACTICE IN HUMAN RESOURCE MANAGEMENT IN HOTELS

Apart from clearly-defined performance expectations of hotel employees, accurate job descriptions, and career opportunities, human resource managers in hotels, as their counterparts in other industries, need to become increasingly aware of other elements of an integrated human resource management strategy designed to meet corporate objectives and increasingly raise productivity, and thence profitability levels. These practices include job rotation, training and development, performance management, effective employee communication, rewards system, turnover and wastage analyses. The cardinal principle behind all these activities, however, is that they are effectively integrated within the mission/strategy of particular hotels and their clientele, responsive to their specialised labour markets (e.g. capital city, region) and economic conditions. It is insufficient, and unproductive, to regard any of these human resource management activities as a solution in itself for long-term profitability.

Job Rotation, Performance Management and Rewards Systems

Often based upon European or North American models, and sometimes encouraged by the approaches of hotel training schools, hotel occupations have traditionally been segmented into particular departments. Whatever progression has occurred, has largely focused on promotion within rather than across hotel departments. Thus, housekeeping staff may be recruited at base level, and eventually rise through the various available supervisory levels in that department. Front-of-house, and food and beverage staff, similarly, largely remain within their original departments. Even within departments, staff may only progress through specific occupational routes (e.g. porter, porter supervisor, concierge) rather than generic departmental paths (e.g. porter, receptionist, front office manager). Whilst it is argued that this instils occupational depth and provides substantial experience, it may also fail to utilise employees' broader skills, result in competitive segregation and act destructively toward productive teamwork perspectives.

A more productive approach to employee motivation and commitment, involving a perception that it is "...everyone else's responsibility (apart from front line workers)...to, 'serve' those who directly serve the customer" (Heskett, 1990), will be enhanced by job rotation schemes, which provide both multi-skilling (for subsequent promotion and vacancy-filling options) and team-building opportunities. Job rotation schemes are currently in minimal use (less than 39.1) according to a recent survey (Nankervis, 1991). Perceptive human resource managers will use award restructuring negotiations to develop job rotation schemes in concert with other forms of multi-skilling, training and development programmes.

Performance management programmes appear to be increasing in use in the hotel industry, especially in its upper segments. This is somewhat surprising, given the relative lack of both career and adequate remuneration plans, and may even be self-defeating if such programmes are not subsequently developed.

As already indicated, hotel salaries are generally far lower than average, even though they contribute significantly to overall operating costs. Award restructuring negotiations, as in the case of the Sheraton hotel chain, provide opportunities for modifications to penalty rates, and ultimately, holiday leave loadings, in return for increases in salary levels for most hotel occupations. Job stability, in terms of secure employment, career development, training programmes and less casualisation, may well-compensate for continuing low levels of salary, especially if combined with increasing opportunities for self-development including multi-skilling. Over time, the add-on costs for full-time, as opposed to casual staff rates, may also prove both more productive and less costly.

The issues of differential rewards within occupational classifications on a performance-based system, and additional non-cash rewards (e.g. dinners, holidays, discounts, etc) may also contribute to ongoing performance and productivity, especially in occupations with little promotional opportunity.

Training and Development, Employee Communication

Recent developments in the establishment of a plethora of tourism training institutions and colleges, coupled with portable national competency standards for a variety of hotel occupations, will no doubt ensure a skilled pool of potential employees. Linking such training to individual occupational criteria, and supplementing it with thorough orientation programmes, on-the-job training modules and appropriate supervision, will no doubt fill this previous gap in human resource management for the hotel industry. These developments parallel the findings of the previously-mentioned United Kingdom-Germany study (Prais, 1989), which found that Germany's productive edge was at least partly due to its nationally-accredited vocational training system.

Studies of some of the best United States and Australian hotels (Gray, 1992) also suggest that the cement which binds skilled and motivated employees to their organisation, who are thus more enthusiastic, more committed and potentially more productive than their competitors' employees, is clear and ongoing communication between hotel managers and their employees. The "messages" sent through the host of human resource activities, strategies, policies and procedures need to be congruent and consistent, and might include promotion of mission statements, the nature of the physical working environment, plasticised credo cards, "management by walking around", staff-supervisor meetings, active (and positive) use of guest feedback, and grievance mechanisms.

Turnover Wastage Analyses, Human Resource Planning

It has already been indicated that labour turnover levels in the Australian hotel industry are disproportionately high in comparison with other industries. This is largely attributed to perceptions of the nature of hotel occupations by both potential employees and their managers, and the "culture of casualisation" referred to by Nils Timo. It may also be partly caused by the lack of careers, low job satisfaction and inadequate salaries. Whilst 60.9 per cent of hotels surveyed (Nankervis, 1991) report using methods for analysing the reasons for, and solutions to, high turnover/wastage rates, only 30.4 per cent respondents appear to use formal exit interviews.

Few human resource managers in hotels appear to undertake comprehensive human resource planning, although pre-opening strategies no doubt include some degree of labour market analysis. It is however important that human resource specialists maintain strategic approaches to labour demand and supply projections, including examination of turnover/wastage levels, in order to ensure effective, and cost-effective, utilisation of their employees to accountably contribute to the productivity of their establishments.

Conclusions

This paper has explored the nature of the Australian hotel industry, and in particular its human resource management practices. Using a variety of national, and international research studies, the paper argues the case for a comprehensive and integrated human resource management strategy encompassing innovative recruitment, selection, training, development and performance management techniques, which will effectively contribute to industry productivity and profitability.

The industry, appears to be characterised by a culture of "casualisation", like its international competitors, significant gender imbalances, a largely transient workforce which is relatively underpaid and under-represented by industry unions. As a highly labour-intensive industry, it is also disproportionately expensive, less productive or profitable than its counterparts.

Human resource management practices remain fragmented and short-term oriented and without direct significance to overall hotel productivity.

CASE STUDY: THE SOCIETY FOR HUMAN RESOURCE MANAGEMENT

The Society for Human Resource Management (SHRM) is the world's largest professional association devoted to human resource management. Our mission is to serve the needs of HR professionals by providing the most current and comprehensive resources, and to advance the profession by promoting HR's essential, strategic role. Founded in 1948, SHRM represents more than 225,000 individual members in over 125 countries, and has a network of more than 575 affiliated chapters in the United States, as well as offices in China and India.

SHRM is an individual membership organization, and our members include HR professionals with the following titles:

- President, CEO, Chairman, Partner, Principal.
- Chief HR Officer.
- Vice-President of HR, Personnel.
- Assistant/Associate Vice President of HR.
- Director of HR, Personnel.
- Assistant/Associate Director of HR.
- Manager of HR, Personnel.
- HR Generalist.
- Supervisor.
- Specialist.
- Consultant.
- Administrator.
- Representative.
- Legal Counsel.

Nearly forty per cent have titles of director or above. Approximately fifty per cent of members work in organizations with more than 500 employees, and approximately thirty-five per cent are in manufacturing or service industries.

SHRM has more than 560 affiliate chapters both in the United States and abroad, and provide additional programming and networking opportunities in your local area. SHRM chapters are autonomous organizations, so it is not automatic that you will be a member of your local chapter when you join SHRM at the national level, and vice versa.

MASTER OF ARTS IN HUMAN RESOURCE MANAGEMENT: CASE STUDY OF HAWAII PACIFIC UNIVERSITY

Today, many businesses and organizations are facing the growing challenge of managing one of their most important assets—people. This is reflected in the dynamic and rapidly growing area of human resource management and the demand for skilled and knowledgeable human resource managers.

Students in the Hawaii Pacific University Master of Arts in Human Resource Management (MA/HRM) degree programme learn in a dynamic and interactive classroom environment from experienced faculty who use case studies, multimedia technology, experiential exercises, small group activities, and field projects. The faculty is veteran business professionals who enrich the classroom experience by integrating real-world experiences with theory. The HPU MA/HRM degree programme is designed for students who wish to specialize in the field of human resource management and its applications to other areas of organizational activity. The MA/HRM emphasizes the study and practices of human relations and management of people.

Decisions about managing people make a difference. As a manager, you will face intense pressures to achieve success through the people you lead. Your decision will affect not only your own success, but also your employees' behaviours and sense of fair treatment as well.

Faced with the pressures of global competition, social change, and accelerating technological advances, managers are urged to take action. Solutions are not always simple, nor are they unchanging. What works in one set of circumstances may not apply in another setting or with other employees. Thus, the search for "the answer" lies in an analysis of the conditions and people involved.

The MA/HRM degree programme at Hawaii Pacific University will help you understand what to consider in such an analysis so that you can make effective decisions. The potential returns from decisions about employees can match or surpass the returns from decisions on other organization resources.

SYLLABUS ON HOSPITALITY MANAGEMENT: CASE STUDY OF SCOTTSDALE COMMUNITY COLLEGE

Description of Course

HRM 110 presents an overview of the hospitality industry including the hotel, restaurant and travel segments. Prerequisites: None.

Primary Objectives (Competencies) of the Course

1. Identify major components of the hospitality and Tourism industry and explore the roles of each.

2. Identify and describe career opportunities in the hospitality and tourism industry and explore an individual career plan.
3. Identify and describe the components of the tourism industry and its operations.
4. Identify and describe the components of the food service industry and review its operations.
5. Identify and describe the components of the lodging industry and review its operations.
6. Identify and describe the characteristics of various hospitality and tourism market segments.
7. Identify and describe methods to attract and manage customers in different hospitality and tourism settings.
8. Identify and describe the major components of contemporary hospitality management.
9. Demonstrate effective communication and presentation skills.

Textbook Required for the Course

Introduction to *Hospitality Management*; John R. Walker; Published by Pearson, Prentice Hall, 2004.

Policy for Late Assignments and Make-up Tests

Weekly assignments must be submitted on their due dates. Assignments will not be accepted after the due date (NO Exceptions). Being absent from class is no excuse for a missed assignment. You must submit assignments electronically through Blackboard. Make-up tests will be at the discretion of the instructor, and grade assignment for missed work is also at the discretion of the instructor.

Class Changes

It may be necessary to change some part of this syllabus or course because of the level of student achievement or new information presented by the industry.

Challenges

If you have difficulty with the course material or method of instruction, please talk to me about it. It is my desire to help you be successful with your educational goals.

Evaluation Techniques

The final grade will be determined by a composite evaluation of your performance in the following areas:

1.	Attendance and Class participation	100	Pts
2.	Assignments	230	Pts
3.	Career Plan	300	Pts
4.	Tests and Quizes (5)	250	Pts
5.	Final Exam	200	Pts
6.	Extra Credit points		Pts
	(Approximately) Total	1,085	pts

A = 90% to 100% C = 70% to 79%

B = 80% to 89% D = 60% to 69%

Attendance/Participation and Assignments

Students are required to attend all classes. There are a variety of activities occurring each week and you must be present to learn effectively. If you plan to become a leader in the hospitality industry it is important that you learn some of the essential values of the industry. Three of the most important industry values are those of self-motivation, dependability and participation.

Twenty-five (25) points will be deducted for each missed class after the first two (the first two are free passes; use them wisely). Six missed classes total (for any reason) = Drop.

The text is an important tool in gathering information and gaining a perspective about technology management in this dynamic industry. It is also used as a base for presentation and discussion in class. Completing the written assignments is an excellent way to retain information. The course schedule will list for you the days in which you will need to come to class having read the chapter and completed assignments. All assignments are due at the beginning of class. Points will be awarded on the basis of quality of the paper. Grammar, spelling and comprehension are critical elements in the business environment and this class will maintain those standards (see Blackboard: *Communication Skills Standards*). It is also important to be able to take quality class notes.

Career Plan

The Career Plan is an essential segment of the course competencies and will be an integral part of your future career plans. It is imperative that every section of this plan is completed in order for you to comprehend the impact this will have on your future. You will not earn a passing grade in this class unless all five career plan modules are completed. This will provide a wonderful starting point for your motivation in the HRM programme.

Opportunities for Excellence-Tests

The testing portion of the course will consist of four (4) tests during the semester. The tests will consist of three methods of examining your knowledge; true/false, multiple choice and short essay or practical assessment. A study guide will be offered for each of the examinations. As the tests are about 35 per cent of the final grade, it becomes more important to complete the other areas of the course requirements. For those of you that plan to come to class just on test days, plan again.

Extra Credit

You will have several opportunities to earn extra credit throughout the semester. Completing a formatted restaurant review, you will discuss your review with the class before turning it in for credit. Each review (a maximum of three) is worth 10 points. The restaurant must be a full serve facility located in the greater Phoenix area. NO QSR's! Only one review per week...NO reviews after the fifteenth week. Other extra credit assignments will be available for those that don't frequent restaurants. I will accept NO work of any kind after week #15.

Grading

You will receive a grade of F if you fail to complete the course or without benefit of an official withdrawal.

NOTES

1. (ABC Lateline, 1992) More than 50 major capital city/resort hotels are currently in receivership, representing more than 10,000 tourist beds.
2. Compare UK/German hotel labour statistics—United Kingdom: 250,000 equivalent full-time employees, female, 41 per cent part-time. Germany—190,000 full-time equivalents, 19 per cent part-time (*Source*: Prais, S.J. *et al.*, p. 52).
3. Callus, R. *et al.*, 1992: p. S7—81 per cent organisations in the "recreation, personal and other services" category report none of their employees remaining after five years. Only 6 per cent retained half of their employees during this period.

3

Training and Development in Human Resource Management: Case Studies from Hotel, Restaurant and Hospitality Agencies

TRAINING AND HUMAN RESOURCE MANAGEMENT

The HR functioning is changing with time and with this change, the relationship between the training function and other management activity is also changing. The training and development activities are now equally important with that of other HR functions. Gone are the days, when training was considered to be futile, waste of time, resources and money. Now-a-days, training is an investment because the departments such as, marketing and sales, HR, production, finance, etc., depends on training for its survival. If training is not considered as a priority or not seen as a vital part in the organization, then it is difficult to accept that such a company has effectively carried out HRM. Training actually provides the opportunity to raise the profile development activities in the organization. To increase the commitment level of employees and growth in quality movement (concepts of HRM), senior management team is now increasing the role of training. Such concepts of HRM require careful planning as well as greater emphasis on employee development and long term education. Training is now the important tool of Human Resource Management to control the attrition rate because it helps in motivating employees, achieving their professional and personal goals, increasing the level of job satisfaction, etc. As a result training is given on a variety of skill development and covers a multitude of courses.

Role of HRD Professionals in Training

This is the era of cut-throat competition and with this changing scenario of business; the role of HR professionals in training has been widened. HR role now is:

1. Active involvement in employee education.
2. Rewards for improvement in performance.
3. Rewards to be associated with self-esteem and self-worth.
4. Providing pre-employment market oriented skill development education and post-employment support for advanced education and training.
5. Flexible access i.e. anytime, anywhere training.

Training/Facilitation Competencies

Competencies	*Behaviours*
Presentation Effectiveness	• Is organized and prepared for training sessions • Possesses a reasonable knowledge of subject matter • Connects classroom content to participant's job responsibilities • Demonstrates a participant-centered approach • Provides an interactive learning experience and encourages learner involvement • Presents in an interesting and understandable manner • Displays a passion for training and a sincere interest in helping the participants improve their skills • Uses a variety of resources to add value to the class (audio/visual, case studies, activities, handouts)
Participant Management	• Maintains focus on key training objectives • Aware of different adult learning styles and adapts class to the individual participant's needs • Able to engage and motivate individuals • Uses group facilitation techniques to maintain a balanced environment (control dominating students, involve reticent learners) • Conveys ideas with poise, confidence, and enthusiasm • Proficient use of presentation tools in order to avoid disruption in the learning experience

(Contd.)

Competencies	*Behaviours*
Evaluation/Assessment	• Conducts a training needs assessment prior to the class to ensure that the class content addresses the training objectives • Learns about the participant's individual strengths and challenges in order to adapt the class to their unique needs and interests • Seeks confirmation that students are understanding the content throughout the class and makes adjustments to ensure a positive learning experience • Conducts evaluations at the end of each class to monitor student response and uses the information to improve future classes • Conducts formal evaluations on the job to determine if the training is having a positive effect on changing behaviour in the workplace

Instructional Design Competencies

Competencies	*Behaviours*
Technical Knowledge	• Develops a working knowledge of all aspects of the operation and draws on the professional expertise of subject-matter experts for course content development • Possesses a thorough understanding of the business objectives, metrics and strategic plans of the organization • Understands adult learning principles and how to apply them to curriculum • Demonstrates an understanding of needs analysis and performance improvement processes • Possesses key skills necessary from programme development—computer literacy, technical-writing skills, editing/proofing skills • Able to demonstrate the ROI value of a programme in clear financial and business terms to key decision makers within the organization
Programme Design	• Prioritizes projects based on company's objectives and most important business needs • Obtains input from various stakeholders prior to the development of new programmes • Utilizes project management techniques to ensure that development is on schedule and all resources are managed for maximum effectiveness

(Contd.)

Competencies	*Behaviours*
Process Improvement	• Establishes clear training objectives prior to the development of a new programme • Pilot tests programme to ensure that training needs and objectives are being met and design achieves desired results • Manages all current training programmes to ensure their accuracy and credibility • Constantly seeking input from a variety of stakeholders on changing business needs and develops training interventions that meet their needs • Aligns training curriculum with company's strategic goals and objectives • Monitors training to ensure consistent delivery of current programmes • Formally conducts evaluation of programmes to ensure their effectiveness. • Updates programmes based on current standard operating procedures • Responds in a timely manner with solutions to operational requests

Management Competencies

Competencies	*Behaviours*
Operational Knowledge	• Possesses a clear understanding of the organization's structure. • Constantly reviews organizational design to identify adjustments that may lead to greater effectiveness • Strong awareness of strategic objectives of the organization • Identifies and select training interventions that address company's goals and objectives • Ensures that training programmes are designed with a focus on company's values/guiding principles • Distinguishes between training solutions and operational roadblocks
Project Management	• Identifies corporate development needs based on strategic objectives and goals • Prioritize training development based on a criteria of projects most likely to positively affect the business • Review projects based on a return on investment model, approving those that deliver positive value

(*Contd.*)

Competencies	Behaviours
	• Coordinate efforts of developers to ensure that projects address training needs and are developed on time and within budget • Coordinate workflow of designers/trainers to maximize team's focus on key business objectives • Frequently review training curriculum to ensure that the right programmes are being delivered to address company's changing needs
Coaching and Development	• Demonstrates an awareness of staff member's strengths and challenges • Consistently improves skill set of instructional design team and trainers by offering constructive feedback • Places a high value on the ongoing development of staff • Delegates challenging projects and tasks to appropriate team members • Leads team through strategic planning process to identify specific goals and objectives for their areas • Provides opportunity for team members to develop by encouraging attendance and conferences, supporting additional formal education or cross-training experiences

Leadership Competencies

Competencies	Behaviours
Communication/Influence	• Demonstrates the ability to motivate others through influence rather than formal authority • Utilizes active listening skills and effective negotiation techniques when working with others to understand needs and develop solution options • Develops strong working relationships with senior management and operations • Incorporates company mission, vision and values into communication with others • Viewed as the corporate expert on all aspects of training, ranging from executive coaching and development to crew level orientation • Serves as a champion throughout the organization for the needs of the Training Department and its members

(Contd.)

Competencies	Behaviours
Business Acumen	• Viewed as a leader within the organization for all matters pertaining to staff and leadership development • Thoroughly understands the company's strategic objectives, financial metrics, goals and objectives • Able to help the company achieve its goals through the timely development of its personnel • Recognizes the importance of succession planning and is viewed as an expert in this key area • Skilled at developing business plans and proposals for training initiatives that demonstrate business results • Utilizes sound business rationale and fiscal responsibility for all Training Department projects
Strategic Planning	• Has earned a "seat at the table" to assist in developing corporate plans • Provides a strategic viewpoint on projects and tasks to inform others of the impact of various options • Consistently delivers on promises and proactively demonstrates Training's value to the organization • Keeps senior management and operations updated on projects and key training initiatives • Capable of synthesizing large amounts of data and bringing clarity to the results of training's efforts • Sought after for his/her expertise on the impact of training and development on company's success

TRAINING AND DEVELOPMENT IN HOSPITALITY SECTOR

Hospitality sector is growing at a very fast rate in India. The sector is growing at a rate of approximately 8 per cent. This sector can be classified into hotel industry, travel and tourism, restaurants, pubs, clubs and bars, contract catering and aviation. Other than that, opportunities also exist in universities, sporting venues, exhibition centres and smaller events management companies. The major challenge of this sector is shortage of skilled employees along with the challenge of attrition rate. Skilled chefs and managers are in great demand. Managers require huge range of competencies such as, people management, viable skills, business insights, analytic skills, succession planning, and resource development in order to get success in this sector. In addition to that, employees are not enough trained on Business Etiquettes, Courtesy and Business Communication. Hospitality is all about handling people. So an employee must have right attitude, tolerance, and listening skills in order to move up the hierarchy. There is still a long way to go to inculcate good public relation, inter-personal skills. With the increase in competition due to the coming up of major players like Four Seasons, Shangri-La, Aman Resorts, etc., the need to train employees has increased more than ever before. The major players are now strategizing to increase the turnover of the customers by training their employees on Communication, Dining and Business etiquettes, etc. Some of the essentials required by this sector are:

- Good infrastructure.
- Trained trainers.
- Quality of content.
- Certification of training course.
- Effective Training evaluation.

Training programmes are available for the following areas:

- Food Production.
- Food and Beverage Service.
- Front Office.
- Housekeeping.

HUMAN RESOURCE MANAGEMENT IN THE HOTEL INDUSTRY: STRATEGY, INNOVATION AND PERFORMANCE

Over the last decade, human resource management has come to be viewed as the dominant paradigm within which analyses of the world of work have been located. This illustration examines the nature and assesses the impact of HRM within a highly under-researched division of the service sector, namely the UK hotel industry. Common perceptions of management practices in the hotel industry typically include work intensification, high labour turnover, lack of training and poor career prospects, and casualised terms and conditions of employment. Using data from a survey of over 200 hotels, this illustration challenges such stereotypes by demonstrating that this part of the service sector is just as likely to have experimented with new approaches to HRM as the manufacturing industry. It suggests that primary influences on managerial decision-making in the hotel industry are no different from the primary influences affecting decision-making elsewhere, countering the argument that mainstream management theories are inapplicable within the hotel industry. Furthermore, where hotels emphasise the importance of service quality enhancement and where they introduce HRM as an integrated, mutually supporting package of practices, a strong relationship between HRM and organisational performance is proposed. Human Resource Management in the Hotel Industry is essential reading for students and researchers with a specific interest in the hotel and catering industry, but will also be of interest to researchers with a wider interest in HRM issues.

PREDICTING UNION CERTIFICATION ELECTIONS IN THE HOSPITALITY INDUSTRY: A CASE STUDY

A study of union certification elections conducted between January 1999 and December 2001 isolated two factors that significantly affected the elections' outcome. Those factors were the size of the prospective bargaining unit and the presence of more than one union on the ballot. The study considered 190 union ballots, 54 per cent of which resulted in the union's certification. Either of two large unions, Hotel Employees and Restaurant Employees (HERE) and the International Brotherhood of Teamsters (IBT), was involved in 46 per cent of the elections. One peculiar finding was that the presence of HERE in an election seemed to depress the turnout. The average size of the bargaining unit in the elections being studied was 56. On balance, unions did better when the bargaining unit was smaller than that number and they tended to lose elections when the unit was larger than the average. A union also prevailed significantly more often in elections in which more than one union participated. One can infer that the heightened emotions in a multiple-union campaign are to the union's benefit. One factor that did not seem to influence the outcome of elections was the presence of right-to-work laws, but the relative dearth of elections held in the 22 right-to-work states was noticeable in the data.

A study of the variables that are associated with the success of union organizing efforts for hotel workers found that certain factors are associated with greater union success. The study examined 190 certification elections between January 1999 and December 2001, nearly half of which involved either Hotel Employees and Restaurant Employees or the Teamsters. The average bargaining-unit size was fifty-six. Unions won just over half of the elections, and nearly half of those were decided by fewer than ten votes. Only two of six factors under consideration significantly affected election outcomes. Those were the size of the bargaining unit (a large unit diminishes the likelihood of union success) and the presence of more than one union on the ballot (on the theory that the intensity of employees' involvement increases in such elections). Oddly, although few elections were held in right-to-work states, that factor did not significantly affect outcomes.

A recent survey conducted by the Centre for Hospitality Research at Cornell University reported that the most important issue cited by U.S. hospitality executives was the management of human resources.

(1) Since the hospitality industry is labour intensive, employees can affect both an operation's cost and its service. The importance of labour is complicated by the fact that a shortage of qualified labour is expected to continue for the next few years and will become more acute as the economy picks up. Therefore, it is not surprising that researchers have started paying attention to the HRM policies and practices in the hospitality sector.
(2) Progressive HRM practices result in satisfied employees, reduced turnover, greater employee morale, and improved customer service.
(3) Since employees are key in ensuring high customer satisfaction and long-term organizational viability in the service industry, a number of operators in the hospitality sector have developed strong HRM practices (e.g., flexible work schedules, solid benefit packages) as a form of competitive advantage. But many managers in this sector also accept low wages, high turnover, and long working hours as standard operating practice.
(4) Labour costs can account for nearly 44 per cent of operating costs in the hospitality sector.
(5) Various strategies by firms to reduce costs and increase efficiency, coupled with the recent economic slowdown, have made many hotels good prospects for union recruitment efforts. Unions that have lost members in the shrinking manufacturing sector have turned their attention

to the service sector, which provides nearly four out of five jobs in the United States.

(6) Over ten million people work in the hospitality portion of the service sector. A large proportion of them are immigrants (legal and illegal) and Hispanics, a rich source of new union members.

(7) In addition, a study of U.S. hotels by American Federation of Labour-Congress of Industrial Organizations's (AFL-CIO) Working for America Institute in 2002 reports that from 1992 through 2000, hotel workers had more occupational injuries than did private sector workers as a whole.

(8) Such a situation provides an opening for unions, as workplace safety is a major recruitment issue. The purpose of the study described in this article is to examine factors that influence the results of union certification elections. According to the Working for America Institute, unionized hotel workers earn nearly 17.6 per cent more per hour than do nonunion hotel workers.

(9) However, this figure does not control for factors like occupation, location, and local economic conditions that may explain part of the union-non-union wage differential. In addition, the institute reports that hotel workers earn 16.1 per cent more per hour if they are located in areas where unions represent a large percentage of hotel employees, such as Boston, Chicago, Honolulu, Las Vegas, Los Angeles, New York, San Francisco, and Washington, D.C. Again, this statistic ignores the possible effects of factors like demographic, economic, and location characteristics, as well as the extent of union representation. In these areas, union wages set standards for the local labour market. Thus, non-union employers in these areas have to pay union or above—union wages to avoid unionization.

(10) Research studies on unionization in the United States fall into two groups—namely, studies on the voting intent of non-unionized employees in a hypothetical union election and studies on actual election outcomes in certification elections conducted by the National Labour Relations Board (NLRB). The first group of studies primarily

investigates voting behaviour and factors that can influence an individual to vote in a certain way. A major limitation of studies in this group is that self-reported prounion voting intent may not translate into votes for unionization in an actual election. The second group of studies focuses on variables that affect the collective decision of a majority of the individuals in an actual NLRB-conducted election to vote either for or against a union. The study described in this article falls into this latter category.

A search on ABI-INFORM revealed no previous empirical study that has examined the factors underlying the outcome of union elections in the hospitality sector. Since we believe that most managers want to avoid unionization, it may be useful to many hospitality business owners to know the factors that may cause unionization.

THE COUNCIL OF HOTEL AND RESTAURANT TRAINERS (CHART): A CASE STUDY

CHART is one of the oldest and largest non-profit organizations dedicated to training in the hospitality industry. Members number over 500 and represent multi-unit restaurant and hotel companies. A typical CHART member holds over 10 years of training and human resources experience and impacts over 5,000 employees in 80 units. By helping trainers do their jobs better, CHART positively impacts millions of employees, customers and companies and the industry as a whole.

Like many professional associations, the Council of Hotel and Restaurant Trainers (CHART) was founded by an informal group of peers who were passionate about their profession. In this case, the year was 1970 and this forward-thinking group already understood the connection between great people practices and organizational achievement. More importantly, they understood the critical *training and human resource role* in this equation. The founders held common beliefs that continuing learning, sharing information, developing personally and building relationships were vital if one wished to achieve a high standard of professionalism and contribute to their company's growth and profitability.

Today, CHART is the oldest and largest non-profit organization dedicated to training in the hospitality industry. Made up of over 500 human resources and training professionals, CHART represents practitioners responsible for the creation and implementation of training programmes for over 350 restaurant and hotel companies. The founding beliefs endure today as CHART's guiding principles of *Learning, Sharing, Growing, Caring.*

Vision: CHART is the premier training association in the hospitality industry.

Mission: CHART develops hospitality training professionals to advance industry training practices and improve operational results by providing access to education, tools and resources.

Guiding Principles

The essence of CHART is evident in CHART's guiding principles of *Learning, Sharing, Growing, Caring.* If you wish to improve the performance of your business by improving your training and human resources practices, we invite you to access the resources of CHART.

Access Learning: CHART members can choose from two energizing conferences per year to continue their education. These forums are unique in that members share their best programmes, practices and ideas, giving attendees practical take aways that can be brought home and immediately used. Three days of interactive workshops cover in-depth topics, such as cost/benefit analysis, technology-based training, diversity, managerial and leadership development and customer service. Regional meetings continue the learning throughout the year.

Access Sharing: Sharing ideas and solutions is what gives CHART its true strength and unique character as an organization. Members say CHART is like an extension of their own training and human resources department. The Ask My Peers listserv, where members email their questions to all members and receive replies from trainers that have helpful information, is one example. Recent discussion topics include, "How do you recognize employees?" and "What are good teambuilding exercises?" and "What are your turnover statistics?"

Access Growing: CHART can be one of the most important and influential forces in a trainer's professional growth and success.

Members report that their personal influence and impact on their company has increased dramatically due to the interactions and ideas CHART provides.

Access Caring: Networking does not even come close to describing the lifelong bonds that members share. That is truly CHART's unique difference; members have walked in each other's shoes and sincerely want to help each other solve challenges.

Goals and Strategies

CHART's objective is to be a recognized, necessary workforce resource to the hospitality industry by providing hospitality trainers inimitable access to the industry's best and brightest training professionals, innovations and solutions. CHART helps trainers do their jobs better by pursuing the following goals:

- Providing a forum for members to grow and become more effective trainers, programme designers and managers.
- Building awareness that effective training and development is an investment that contributes to productivity gains.
- Understanding human resource priorities affecting the development of our employees.
- Providing high quality, low cost educational opportunities. and
- Providing opportunities for professional networking among members to build lasting relationships that will provide long-term personal resources.

The key strategies under CHART 's 2005-2007 Strategic Plan are:

1. Know and Grow Membership.
2. Refine and Grow Product and Service Mix.
3. Grow Partnerships and Industry Alliances.
4. Strengthen Organizational Structure.

Volunteer Opportunities

CHART helps create great leaders! CHART is a volunteer organization, and members consistently view the volunteer work they do with CHART as a significant growth tool in their careers. Members report that their personal influence and visibility within their own organizations and within the industry has increased due to the interactions and ideas CHART provides. If you get involved, CHART can be one of the most important and influential forces in your professional growth and success.

INTERNATIONAL COUNCIL ON HOTEL, RESTAURANT AND INSTITUTIONAL EDUCATION (I-CHRIE): A CASE STUDY

Founded in 1946, the International Council on Hotel, Restaurant, and Institutional Education is the global advocate of hospitality and tourism education for schools, colleges, and universities offering programmes in hotel and restaurant management, foodservice management and culinary arts. In recent years, International CHRIE's focus has expanded and its mission statement has evolved, making it a marketplace for facilitating exchanges of information, ideas, research, products and services related to education, training and resource development for the hospitality and tourism industry (food, lodging, recreation and travel services). Serving as the hospitality and tourism education network, we strive to unite educators, industry executives and associations.

FAQs w.r.t. I-CHRIE

Q. 1. *How do I submit Professional Opportunities for the CHRIE Communiqué?*

Ans. Information on how to submit advertisements appearing in the Professional Opportunities section of the CHRIE Communiqué can be found on I-CHRIE's website at *http://www.chrie.org/i4a/pages/Index.cfm?pageID=3402*

Q. 2. *How do I submit a Professional Opportunities advertisement for online posting on the I-CHRIE website?*

Ans. Information on how to submit online Professional Opportunities advertisements can be found on the I-CHRIE website at *http://www.chrie.org/i4a/pages/Index.cfm?pageID=3412*

Q. 3. *Do we have a listing of schools that offer hospitality programmes?*

Ans. A list of member institutions is made available to I-CHRIE members and can be found in the "Members Only" section of the

I-CHRIE website. International CHRIE also publishes a *Guide to College Programmes*. To order, visit, *http://www.chrie.org/i4a/pages/Index.cfm?pageID=3394* or call the call International CHRIE at (804) 346-4800 and we can help you place your publication order.

Q. 4. *How can I get information on joining International CHRIE?*

Ans. Membership information can be found on the I-CHRIE website at *http://www.chrie.org/i4a/pages/Index.cfm?pageID=3290*. This page gives pricing and benefit information. If you would like to fill out and submit a membership application online, click on the "Join Now" hyperlink found on this page which links to an electronic membership application.

Q. 5. *How do I log on the I-CHRIE member's area page?*

Ans. To log in into the CHRIE MEMBERS ONLY area, use your last name as your login and your CHRIE member ID number as your password. If you have forgotten your password, there is a hyperlink which appears below the Login/Password box that will email your password to you. In most cases, it only takes a few minutes to receive your password. If you are still experiencing difficulty with your login and/or your password is not operational, it may be for one of the following reasons:

1. Your membership HAS RECENTLY expired. Your access rights to the I-CHRIE MEMBERS ONLY section have been removed.
2. Your membership expired, but you have recently renewed. Once your I-CHRIE membership has expired, it normally takes 7-10 days for your member record to be reinstated on the website.
3. You just applied for I-CHRIE membership. It normally takes 7-10 days to process your new membership and to allow your web access rights to be instituted on the I-CHRIE website.

Please note that if you have logged on to the Members Area and updated your last name field in the directory, you must enter your last name EXACTLY as it now appears in order for your log in name to be accepted. For example, you changed your LAST NAME (i.e., Smith) to Smith, Ph.D. You must enter your last name exactly as it matches the changes you have made to your record or your log in will fail.

Q. 6. *How do I change my password to access the "members only" section of the I-CHRIE website?*

Ans. Your "default" password is your I-CHRIE membership identification number. To change your ICHRIE website password, all you need to do is:

1. Go to the I-CHRIE Website at *http://www.chrie.org/i4a/pages/Index.cfm?pageID=1* and select the "Members" tab on the upper right-hand corner of the I-CHRIE home page.
2. Enter your name and password (one last time using your member ID as your password).
3. Scroll down the right-hand side of the page until you find the hyperlink for the "Member Directory" and click on the hyperlink. Then, enter search information to find your I-CHRIE member listing.
4. Click on "Edit my profile" and Proceed to create a custom password. If you forget your new password, it can be emailed to you by selecting the link found below the member log-in screen. After just a few minutes, you will receive an email notification of your password.

Q. 7. *What is the difference between an individual an institutional membership?*

And. With an institutional membership, you receive a full-page programme description in the *Guide to College Programmes,* discounts on advertising rates for ads placed in I-CHRIE publications, and reduced pricing for conference exhibition space. Your school will also have their career day schedule listed on the I-CHRIE career day calendar that is posted twice a year on our website. As an institutional member, your school will also be eligible to receive free copies of the bi-annual I-CHRIE posters which promote the industry to hospitality and tourism students.

Another advantage of being an institutional I-CHRIE member is the right to apply for and/or maintain chapter status as an approved *Eta Sigma Delta* Honour Society chapter which recognizes the top students in hospitality and tourism management programmes at 4-year and 2-year schools.

Q. 8. *How do I submit articles to the HOSTEUR™, JHTE or JHTR?*

Ans. The current guidelines for submissions to I-CHRIE publications vary according to the approved criteria for each publication. Specific submission information can be found by visiting the I-CHRIE website at *http://www.chrie.org/i4a/pages/Index.cfm?pageID=3396*. Before submitting your article, please carefully read the stated guidelines. Because of production costs and deadline schedules, strict adherence to these guidelines will be enforced.

Q. 9. *How do I join a listserv?*

Ans. Log on to the website as a member and on the members only tab of the website, the drop down box should show an option for ListServ (if you are not logged on as a member, this option will not appear on your screen). Please note, you must be a member of International CHRIE in good standing to join a listserv.

Q. 10. *How do I access a link that appears on the site as a red "X"?*

Ans. The problem is your web browser is not JAVA-enabled. You will need to go to *http://www.sun.com/* and download Java for Windows at the following link: *http://java.sun.com/j2se/downloads*. In some countries, JAVA may not be a commonly-known operating system.

Q. 11. *Is there a banking fee when paying by wire transfer?*

Ans. Currently, our bank charges are $US30 per wire transfer, so when paying by wire transfer, you must add the $US30 wire transfer fee to your total dues in order for your dues or service payment to be processed.

SOCIETY FOR FOODSERVICE MANAGEMENT (SFM): A CASE STUDY

The Society for Foodservice Management is the pre-eminent national association serving the needs and interests of executives in the onsite foodservice industry. Our principal role is to enhance the ability of our members to achieve career and business objectives in an ethical, responsible and professional climate. With members from coast to coast and overseas, SFM members are the best and brightest in onsite foodservice. The society represents major corporate liaison personnel and independent operators as well as national and regional foodservice contract management companies. Consultants and companies providing products and services to the onsite market are also SFM members. Additionally, the association includes faculty and students at HRI programmes.

History

The Society for Foodservice Management (SFM) was founded in 1979 *via* a merger of the National Industrial Cafeteria Managers Association (NICMA) and the Association of Food Service Management (AFSM). Richard Ysmael of Motorola, and Phillip Cooke of Foodservice Associates (now FSA Group) were key players in SFM's formation, with Ysmael an influential NICMA member and Cooke the manager of NICMA's affairs.

Vision Statement

SFM: Knowledge, experience and opportunities essential for success.

Mission Statement

The Society for Foodservice Management provides professional development through research and information, continuing education and member interaction in a collaborative environment.

Resources

Original Research: Recent reports include, "The Strategic Value of Onsite Foodservice: An Industry Perspective" and the "SFM 2005 Industry Standards and Benchmark Comparison." Read descriptions of these reports and view a sample page of each.

Industry Articles and Reports: Read articles and reports submitted to or developed by SFM for their interest to our members.

FastFacts is SFM's member newsletter and is a great resource for keeping SFM members connected with and informed about Society events. Distributed monthly *via* email, FastFacts provides information on regional and national events, member news, research projects and much more. Recent issues are linked below for your review.

Article—SFM President Jim Wulfurst explains Duke University's successful foodservice provider evolution programme. Submitted by Foodservice Director.

Article—Industry writer Donna Boss researches employee retention and how keeping good employees must be a top priority in all types of foodservice organizations.

WOMEN'S FOODSERVICE FORUM (WFF): A CASE STUDY

For 18 years, the Women's Foodservice Forum (WFF) has led the industry's efforts to develop gender-diverse leadership talent for all segments of the foodservice industry—operators, manufacturers/suppliers and distributors.

Since its inception, WFF has made important differences in the personal and professional lives of individual members and the foodservice industry at large. Through the Annual Leadership Development Conference, Regional Connect events, Executive Women's Summit, Signature mentoring programmes and facilitated teleforums, WFF provides members with the tools needed to make a positive difference in their careers. Like all organizations and professionals intent on staying on the leading edge, WFF continues to set goals and overcome challenges to remain relevant and compelling. On behalf of our 3,000+ WFF members, we remain committed to leading the transformation of our industry through gender-diverse leadership.

Networking

WFF delivers exceptional networking opportunities through our local, regional and national events. Members can search our database to maintain connections all year long.

Year Round Events

From our signature Annual Conference to the Executive Women's Summit and Regional Connects, members can build skills through our exceptional events.

Professional Development

Unique programming to build leadership competencies for emerging leaders and senior executives in the industry.

HOSPITALITY HR.COM: A CASE STUDY

No matter how you refer to them, their goals are still the same—matching the right candidates with the right companies and job opportunities.

HospitalityHR.com was conceived as a one stop source for candidates in search of recruiters that specialize in the Restaurant and Hospitality industries.

The recruiters you'll find here represent the best career opportunities with the finest restaurant groups in the country—*local to national, big and small, fast food to Four Star*.

If you're a successful Restaurant Manager, Chef, or Hospitality Executive in search of new job and career opportunities, then you've come to the right place.

The recruiters in our directory work with the best known restaurant, hotel and hospitality management groups in the US, and represent the finest Restaurant Management and Chef jobs available today.

With their years of experience and established relationships, these recruiters can help broaden your job search horizons with a range of opportunities you might never find on your own—including many jobs you won't find on any job board.

State and National Restaurant Associations

Restaurant Associations

- National Restaurant Association.
- Alabama Restaurant Association.
- Alaska Cabaret, Hotel, Restaurant and Retailers Association.
- Arizona Restaurant and Hospitality Association.
- Arkansas Hospitality Association.
- California Restaurant Association.
- Colorado Restaurant Association.
- Connecticut Restaurant Association.
- Delaware Restaurant Association.
- Restaurant Association of Metropolitan Washington (DC).
- Florida Restaurant Association.
- Georgia Hospitality and Travel Association.
- Hawaii Restaurant Association.

- Idaho Lodging and Restaurant Association (currently does not have a website).
- Illinois Restaurant Association.
- Restaurant and Hospitality Association of Indiana.
- Iowa Hospitality Association.
- Kansas Restaurant and Hospitality Association.
- Kentucky Restaurant Association.
- Louisiana Restaurant Association.
- Maine Restaurant Association.
- Restaurant Association of Maryland, Inc.
- Massachusetts Restaurant Association.
- Michigan Restaurant Association.
- Minnesota Restaurant, Hotel and Resort Association.
- Mississippi Restaurant Association.
- Missouri Restaurant Association.
- Montana Restaurant Association.
- Nebraska Restaurant Association.
- Nevada Restaurant Association.
- New Hampshire Lodging and Restaurant Association.
- New Jersey Restaurant Association.
- New Mexico Restaurant Association.
- New York Restaurant Association.
- North Carolina Restaurant Association.
- North Dakota Hospitality Association.
- Ohio Restaurant Association.
- Oklahoma Restaurant Association.
- Oregon Restaurant Association.
- Pennsylvania Restaurant Association.
- Rhode Island Hospitality and Tourism Association.
- Hospitality Association of South Carolina.
- South Dakota Retailers Association Restaurant Division.
- Tennessee Restaurant Association.
- Texas Restaurant Association.
- Utah Restaurant Association.
- Vermont Lodging and Restaurant Association.
- Virginia Hospitality and Travel Association.
- Washington Restaurant Association.
- West Virginia Hospitality and Travel Association.
- Wisconsin Restaurant Association.
- Wyoming Lodging and Restaurant Association

WOMEN'S FOODSERVICE FORUM: A CASE STUDY

The WFF was formed in 1989 by a group of 14 women with a radical notion for the times. The WFF's formation was actually rooted in a roundtable discussion that was held during the 1988 National Restaurant Association Show in Chicago. Peter Berlinski, then editor of Restaurant Business magazine, called to express interest ingathering data on the state of women in the foodservice industry. He brought together a group of women to talk about issues of developing leadership talent and ensuring career advancement among executive women in the foodservice industry, which remained highly male-dominated—particularly within the leadership ranks.

That early roundtable became known as the Women's Council, forerunner to the Women's Foodservice Forum, which was founded formally a year later.

The round table discussion resulted in major foodservice-trade coverage, including a cover story, "Bridging the Gender Gap" which appeared in the September 1, 1988 edition of Restaurant Business.

Now, WFF is a vibrant, highly charged organization committed to helping women at all levels in their careers, entry-level to emerging leader to executive, envision and achieve their highest potential.

To accomplish this, the WFF invested significant time talking with corporate leaders to identify the critical business skills that set leaders apart. It is providing the opportunity to develop these skills in our members that form the foundation of the WFF, it mission, vision and ultimate goals.

By doing so, the WFF hopes to elevate women leaders in order to elevate the entire foodservice industry. This spirit and dedication has set it apart from any other organization serving the foodservice industry.

Mission and Resources

Women's Foodservice Forum is the premier leadership development community for collective insights and connections that empower women in the foodservice industry to envision and achieve their highest potential.

We engage the foodservice industry to develop leadership talent and ensure career advancement for executive women.

WFF is leading the transformation of the foodservice industry by enhancing the industry's business performance through gender-diverse leadership.

Programming Design

WFF Skill-Building Programmes

WFF Leadership Competency Assessment (LCA)

An online benchmarking tool to measure your current skills against the WFF 10 Core Leadership Competencies.

Mentor Programmes

High impact and engaging mentor programmes pair mentors and protégés in a facilitated programme. Our Leadership Round table series brings together informal groups of women and an industry leader.

WFF Teleforums and Book Club Discussions

Quarterly events led by industry leaders and moderators addressing topics and business books relevant to the WFF 10 Core Leadership Competencies.

Volunteer Committee Service

Over 400 volunteers hone existing skills, develop new ones and interact with peers as a volunteer or leader of a WFF Committee.

Programmes and Services

Develop your personal roadmap to success and WFF programmes will help you get there. At the heart of the Women's Foodservice Forum mission are the 10 Core Leadership Competencies, defined and developed in tandem with foodservice CEOs as the critical leadership skills to master. WFF has developed an online *Leadership*

Competency Assessment (LCA) to help members assess their strengths and weaknesses in these competencies. To assist with growing and refining women's skills WFF offers programmes that range from mentoring to facilitating executive women as they assume senior leadership roles within their companies and pursue opportunities to serve on private and public boards.

WOMEN CHEFS AND RESTAURANT (WCR): A CASE STUDY

Mission

The mission of Women Chefs and Restaurateurs is to promote and enhance the education, advancement and connection of women in the culinary industry.

History

Formed in 1993 by eight of the nation's top women chefs and restaurateurs, WCR has grown to a membership of over 2,000 members, offering a variety of networking, professional and support services.

Founding Members

- Lidia Bastianich, co-owner of Felidia and Becco, New York.
- Elka Gilmore, chef, San Francisco.
- Joyce Goldstein, author/restaurant and food consultant, San Francisco.
- Johanne Killeen, co-owner of Alforno, Providence, RI.
- Barbara Lazaroff, owner of Spago Beverly Hills and Imaginings Interior Design, CA.
- Mary Sue Milliken, co-owner of Ciudad and Border Grill, Santa Monica, CA.
- Anne Rosenzweig, owner of Inside, New York City.
- Barbara Tropp, author/chef/consultant, San Francisco (deceased).

Founding Corporate Members

- Allied Domecq Spirits and Wine.

- American Express Travel Related Services, Inc.
- Beringer Vineyards.
- Champagne Veuve Clicquot.
- Citicorp Diners Club.
- The Culinary Institute of America.
- *Food Arts* Magazine.
- The French Culinary Institute.
- MasterCard International.
- Robert Mondavi Winery.
- San Pellegrino U.S.A., Inc.
- Starbucks Coffee Company.
- Visa USA, Inc.

Corporate Support

WCR enjoys the corporate support of many corporate sponsors, such as our founding corporate members listed above, and our current corporate members:

- All-Clad MetalCrafters, Inc.
- American Express.
- American Roland Food Corp.
- ARAMARK.
- Art Institute of New York City.
- Bon Appétit at the Getty Center.
- Bon Appétit Management Company.
- Cabot Creamery Cooperative.
- California School of Culinary Arts.
- CanolaInfo.
- The Culinary Institute of America.
- Food Arts Magazine.
- The French Culinary Institute.
- FullBloom Baking Co, Inc.
- Guittard Chocolate Company.
- Indian Harvest Specialtifoods, Inc.
- The Institute of Culinary Education.
- Johnson & Wales University.
- JW Marriott Orlando, Grande Lakes.
- Kimpton Restaurant Group.
- KitchenAid.

- Marriott International.
- Nation's Restaurant News.
- Nestlé Waters North America.
- Royal Cup Coffee.
- Sid Wainer & Son Specialty Produce.
- Sur La Table.
- Visa USA.

Membership

Seven membership categories are offered:

- Student.
- Beginning Restaurant Professional.
- Culinary Professional.
- Executive Member.
- Friend of WCR.
- Small Business Member.
- Corporate Membership.

Goals

Exchange

To facilitate communication and exchange of ideas between members and to promote professional contacts.

Education

To provide educational opportunities for professional and personal development for women in all sectors of the restaurant industry.

Enhancement

To create and expand professional and business opportunities for women working in or wishing to enter the restaurant industry.

Equality

To provide support and foster an environment which ensures

women equal access to the position, power and rewards offered by the restaurant industry.

Empowerment

To examine the issues of women in the workplace and to advocate the improvement of work environments in the restaurant industry.

Entitlement

To provide opportunities, encouragement and support for women of all backgrounds who wish to enter or advance in the restaurant industry.

Environment

To promote efforts to safeguard and improve the global food and water supply.

Excellence

To foster standards of excellence and integrity within the restaurant industry.

Awards Programme

WCR launches a call for nominations for the "Women Who Inspire Awards" in the spring of each year. Hundreds of women are nominated for these prestigious awards. The winners are announced at a gala dinner held during the annual conference in the fall. Sponsorships are available for this programme. Learn more about the WCR Awards programme on the Website.

Scholarship and Internship Programme

WCR sponsors a unique Scholarship and Internship Programme that includes international travel, culinary school opportunities, wine studies and internships in member restaurants. Applications are taken January through March. The scholarship committee reviews the applications in March and April and the scholarships are awarded in June. Sponsorships are available for this programme. The prior year Scholarship and Internship Programme is posted on the WCR Website.

National Conference

In the fall of each year, WCR hosts a National Conference that consists of master cooking classes, keynote presenters, panel discussions, culinary tours, champagne receptions, awards dinner, networking lunches and a mini trade show. Sponsorships are available for this programme.

Mentorship Programme

WCR launched a new Mentorship Programme in 2002. WCR has always been about "women-helping-women" in the culinary field. The mentorship programme formalized the informal mentoring that has always existed.

Local Exchange

The WCR Local Exchange programme offers culinary educational programmes in local markets. These meetings take place across the country and are both educational and networking opportunities for our members and prospective members. Sponsorships are available for this programme.

Media Contact

Women Chefs and Restaurateurs
304 W. Liberty St., Suite 201
Louisville, KY 40202-3068
toll free: 877-927-7787
fax: 502-589-3602
wcr@hqtrs.com

INTERNATIONAL HOTEL AND RESTAURANT ASSOCIATION (IH & RA): A CASE STUDY

Founded in 1946, the IH and RA is the only business organisation representing the hospitality industry worldwide. Its members are national hotel and restaurant associations throughout the world, and international and national hotel and restaurant chains representing some 50 brands. Officially recognised by the United Nations, IH&RA monitors and lobbies all international agencies on behalf of this industry, estimated to comprise 300,000 hotels and 8 million restaurants, employ 60 million people and contribute 950 billion USD annually to the global economy.

What is the International Hotel and Restaurant Association?

The IH & RA is the only international trade association exclusively devoted to promoting and defending the interests of the hotel and restaurant industry worldwide. It is a non-profit membership organisation dedicated to helping members achieve their business objectives and prepare for the future.

Members

- International and National Hotel and/or Restaurant Chains.
- Independent Hoteliers and Restaurateurs.
- National Hotel and/or Restaurant Associations.
- Providers and Supporters of the Industry.

IH&RA headquarters are in France, 48 Boulevard de Sébastopol, 75003 Paris.

- Industry Watchdog: Protecting your business interests.
- High profile events: Building your business network.
- Timely News Reports: Keeping you informed.
- The IH&RA is run on a not-for-profit basis with a team led by a Chief Executive.
- It is governed by a General Assembly and a Board of Directors.

The IH&RA Foundation for the Future (FFF) is a registered Swiss charity established in 1989. Its purpose is to contribute to the development of education, specifically in the hospitality industry, to contribute to research on this industry and to promote projects in developing countries.

The FFF was set up with an initial donation from the American Express Foundation of CHF 300,000. It currently runs an annual summer scholarship programme for deserving young professionals in the hotel and restaurant industry. This is financed by donations for individual scholarships (worth US$ 4000 each) from individual hotels and Affiliate Members (totalling some US$ 35,000 per year) and by funds raised through the annual IH&RA congress. These include the Silent Auction and voluntary contribution from registration fees, amounting in all to around US$ 15 000. Participating hotel schools also provide discounts on tuition. Every year 10 to 15 summer scholarships are awarded. Thanks to this mode of financing, the scholarship programme is virtually self-sufficient and has shown a small increase of income over expenditure year on year.

Programmes

The Foundation for the Future runs the following Programmes.

Visiting Professor Programme

The FFF developed the visiting professor programme taking the academic to the students and thereby avoiding travel, accommodation and visa problems for the students as well as allowing them to continue their usual employment.

Summer Scholarship Programme

For a number of years the FFF ran an annual summer scholarship programme for deserving young professionals in the hotel and restaurant industry. This was financed by donations (value $US 4000 each) for individual scholarships from individual hotels and Affiliate Members (providing approximately US$ 35,000) and by funds raised through the annual IH&RA congress (mainly the Silent Auction, breakfast Mini Chat sessions, along with a voluntary contribution from registration fees, amounting in all to around US$ 15,000). Participating hotel schools also provided discounts on tuition. Every year 10 to 15 scholarships were awarded and in this way, some 200 young people, particularly from developing countries, were able to improve their skills through training in reputable hotel school Summer programmes. The scholarship programme was self-financing and showed a small increase of income over expenditure year on year.

Youth Career Initiative

The Youth Career Initiative (YCI) uses resources within the hotel industry to prepare young people in poor countries for careers in hospitality and other service sectors. The aim is to ensure participants' long-term social and economic security by providing them with professional training and experience that enhances their earning potential, their self-esteem and their ability to make informed decisions about their lives.

THE HOTEL ASSOCIATION OF CANADA (HAC): A CASE STUDY

The Hotel Association of Canada supports, protects and promotes our members so they can excel in today's challenging business world. For over 90 years, we have helped them to compete by building and maintaining a high profile with governments, developing innovative marketing programmes, hosting events to celebrate excellence, and providing current industry information and resources. All of our activities share a singular goal: to help our members be more competitive and successful.

The Hotel Association of Canada is your voice—we advocate on your behalf to build a favourable business climate and influence policies for your success. We offer cost-effective, innovative marketing programmes, and celebrate excellence through our annual conference. Our data and statistics keep you informed on the industry trends.

Our members are an important part of the HAC network; a network that is over 7,000 strong and encompasses Hotel Companies, hotels, resorts, provincial and international lodging associations, industry suppliers and educators.

Strategic Partnerships

Hotel Association of Canada (HAC) Strategic Partners are leading organizations and companies involved in a wide range of industry sectors and activities. Although these areas of activities may differ, they are all committed to their work with the lodging industry.

Benefits

Participating in select HAC activities provides the Strategic Partners with the unique occasion of forging a broad network of national and international contacts. In the process, partners gain an opportunity to share their expertise, work closely with their lodging customers, acquire valuable insight into the latest industry developments and work with HAC and its members in providing solutions to the industry's challenges and priorities.

HAC Strategic Partners

Air Canada

Air Canada is Canada's largest domestic and international full-service airline and the largest provider of scheduled passenger services in the domestic market, the transborder market and each of the Canada-Europe, Canada-Pacific, Canada-Caribbean/Central America and Canada-South America markets. Passenger transportation is the principle business. Headquartered in Montreal, Air Canada is a wholly owned subsidiary of ACE Aviation Holdings Inc. (ACE).

Avaya Communication

Leading hospitality firms must leverage every possible advantage in the ongoing battle to attract and retain customers, including the use of technology. Avaya Intelligent Communication Solutions provide powerful technology for just such an advantage, whether in the area of customer experience, process efficiency, or productivity.

In today's environment, providing guests with the desired experience in a high-quality, consistent manner can be a formidable challenge. However, customer loyalty depends on the ability to do so:

- Intelligent Communications Technology.
- The Guest Experience.
- Efficiency and Productivity.
- Resources.

The Association of Corporate Travel Executives (ACTE)

The association of corporate travel executives is a not-for-profit association providing executive-level global education to business travel leaders in 50 countries. ACTE was the first organization in the business travel industry to recognize Corporate Social Responsibility (CSR) as a key issue, including holding the industry's first 'carbon low' global education conference in 2006.

Based on the Green Key Eco-Rating Programme ACTE and HAC have developed a Checklist for Corporate Travel Managers to use in assessing environmental practices at lodging facilities which is available complimentary to ACTE members at *http://www.acte.org/*.

Chase Paymentech

The single source for Visa, MasterCard, American Express and Interac Direct Payment processing. Today, thousands of Canadian companies like yours rely on us to provide products and services essential to their continued growth and profitability. Our business focuses on Merchant Solutions—delivering much more than just convenient, secure payment options.

Our leading-edge technical capabilities and vast industry experience enables us to deliver an exceptional and innovative suite of electronic payment opportunities to you. No matter where your customers are, we offer the best possible business-building options from point-of-sale terminals to gift card programmes and best-in-class Internet payment solutions that will keep you connected.

Department of Foreign Affairs and International Trade—Programme for Export and Market Development (PEMD)

Foreign Affairs and International Trade Canada supports Canadians abroad; helps Canadian companies succeed in global markets; promotes Canada's culture and values; and works to build a more peaceful and secure world.

PEMD's goal is to increase the prosperity and competitiveness of Canadian businesses in the international marketplace. Since its inception in 1971, PEMD has assisted over 28,000 Canadian businesses in marketing their products and services abroad. Specifically, the PEMD objective is to increase export sales of Canadian goods and services by sharing the costs of activities that companies could not or would not undertake alone, thereby reducing the risks in entering a foreign market.

The programme is divided into two broad categories—one targeted to companies and the other to national trade or industry associations.

Diners Club International

Diners Club offers Cardmembers and corporate clients its expertise in managing their business travel and entertainment expenses worldwide. Many of Canada's top 500 corporations as well as government departments currently use a Diners Club expense management solution.

Diners Club is the smart payment choice for mid-to-large corporations, individual business people and professionals. It is the only card/payment solution provider that combines a superior product package, unsurpassed service and award winning rewards with universal acceptance.

Hcareers is the leading job board for the hospitality and restaurant/foodservice industries. A unit of onTarget jobs of Fort Worth, Texas, Hcareers operates three websites, each serving the United States, Canada and the United Kingdom. Hcareers is known for being the leader in providing industry-specific online recruitment solutions, with the most relevant jobs and job seekers in their niche market. Hcareers started in 1998 and has rapidly become the number one choice for both job seekers and employers in the hospitality and foodservice industry.

HLT Advisory Inc.

HLT Advisory Inc. provides specialized consulting and support services to the Canadian and international hospitality, leisure and tourism industries including gaming, lodging, travel/tourism, recreation, sport, entertainment and public assembly venues.

Hospitality Talent Network (HTN)

The Hospitality Talent Network is a network of job boards dedicated to the foodservice, hospitality, travel and tourism industries. A job or resume posted on one job board is automatically posted on all job boards in the network. Employers use the job board to post-foodservice, hospitality, travel and tourism jobs and shortlist employees using Hospitality Talent Network's advanced profiling and matching technology. Job seekers create profiles, attach resumes, apply for jobs, and monitor employer interest free!

Natural Resources Canada/Office of Energy Efficiency

The Office of Energy Efficiency (OEE), Canada's centre of excellence for energy conservation, energy efficiency and alternative fuels information, is playing a dynamic leadership role in helping Canadians save millions of dollars in energy costs while addressing the challenges of climate change.

Established in April 1998 as part of Natural Resources Canada, the OEE's mandate is to renew, strengthen and expand Canada's commitment to energy conservation and energy efficiency. The OEE originated out of Canada's commitment to reduce greenhouse gas emissions by 6 per cent below 1990 levels by the period between 2008 and 2012, as agreed to in the Kyoto Protocol.

PKF Consulting

PKF Consulting, with offices in Toronto and Vancouver, was established in Canada in 1970 and provides a comprehensive range of services to the hospitality and tourism industries across the country. Our clients include the largest and the smallest of hotels and hotel companies, owners, operators and lenders as well as a broad cross section of both private sector and public sector clients. The two Canadian consulting offices and our ten U.S. consulting offices focus totaling on serving the needs of the hospitality and tourism industry in North America and are supported by similar consulting practices in the United Kingdom, Europe, Asia and Caribbean.

VIA Rail Canada

VIA Rail Canada is an independent Crown corporation established in 1978. VIA operates trains in all regions of Canada over a network spanning the country from the Atlantic to the Pacific, and from the Great Lakes to Hudson Bay.

VingCard Elsafe

VingCard Elsafe has products installed in more than 33,000 properties worldwide, securing in excess of 5.5 million hotel rooms, continuing to offer advanced technology solutions to provide security and peace of mind for both hospitality providers and their guests. VingCard Elsafe's extensive international network covers more than 150 countries worldwide. VingCard Elsafe is part of the company ASSA ABLOY, the world's leading provider of locking solutions.

Programmes/Services

Travel and tourism is one of the world's fastest growing business segments and the lodging industry plays an important role in this growth. As hoteliers our responsibility is two-fold: to successfully manage our real estate assets and to fulfill the needs of our guests. With this in mind, the Hotel Association of Canada is committed to helping our members by providing services and programmes that encourage and strengthen the lodging industry across Canada.

Canada Select

"Canada Select" is an industry led, consumer sensitive rating programme, developed for the purpose of providing the travelling public with a national consistent standard of quality within categories of accommodation.

Canada select inspects and rates all participating properties to ensure they meet consumer expectations. Ratings are based on extent and quality of facilities, services and amenities. The higher the star rating, the more extensive are the facilities, guest services and amenities.

"Canada Select" was developed after extensive consumer research into what was expected and considered important at various star levels and categories of accommodations. Presently nine provinces and one territory are delivering the "Canada Select" programme. New found land and Labrador, New Brunswick, Prince Edward Island, Nova Scotia, Ontario, Alberta, Saskatchewan, British Columbia, Manitoba and the Yukon.

As can be appreciated, comparing a hotel to a bed and breakfast would be like comparing apples and oranges. Current consumer research indicates that roofed accommodations should have six distinct categories.

Each accommodation category is comprised of properties having similar characteristics; however, actual facilities, amenities and services may vary.

The six categories are:

- Hotel/Motel.
- Hunting/Fishing Lodges.
- Inns.
- Resorts.
- Bed and Breakfast/Tourist Homes.
- Cottages.

Once a property has been categorized it is evaluated for physical quality of the property, content of facilities, services and amenities provided. All properties, regardless of their star level, must also meet stringent cleanliness and state of repair guidelines.

Each category and star level has distinct criteria which must be achieved.

A star rating from (1 to 5; in ½ star increments), is awarded based on the results of the evaluation. Each star level reflects specific consumer expectations.

A one star rating reflects that a property is clean and comfortable and has met or exceeded nationally accepted criteria in the areas of facilities, services, amenities and quality of the accommodation. Additional stars are awarded depending on the extent of facilities, services, amenities and quality of accommodations.

Where the quality of facilities is superior, a property may be awarded a half-star above its criteria rating, i.e., a two star property may warrant a 2½ star rating, depending on the overall quality assessment.

The following are the star rating descriptions:

- At this level, guests should expect clean and well-maintained accommodations providing the necessary facilities for an enjoyable stay. Criteria includes standards such as room size, window screens and coverings, clothes storage, linens, door lock, smoke detector, and parking facilities.
- This level equates to what is popularly considered "mid-range" accommodation. It exceeds the 1 star level in quality of mattress, bed linen, floors/window/wall coverings, and in provision of bedside and seating area lighting, additional room furniture and parking space.
- These properties will offer larger units with additional room furniture, coordinated furnishings, better quality mattresses and linens, and will be equipped with clock/alarm, extra amenities in washrooms, etc. Private baths for all BB rooms is a requirement for a 3 star and higher rating. Three star properties offer above average facilities and services.
- This rating indicates exceptional quality in all areas of facilities and services offering superior quality throughout the property in areas of guestrooms, bath and common areas. The property typically provides laundry/valet service as well as many additional amenities.
- A 5 star property is luxurious at a world standard, offering outstanding facilities, guest service and amenities.

Remember, although in many provinces the Canada select programme is voluntary, some provinces have mandatory licensing requirements which are administered in conjunction or separate from the rating programme. In these provinces, properties MUST be licensed prior to obtaining a rating. In order to be in a position to be rated, a property must obtain the "1" star level in areas of facility requirements (clean, comfortable accommodations). Properties which do not obtain this level cannot be rated.

Benefits of "Canada Select" to the Owner/Operator

- Provides an effective marketing tool. Extensive Advertising and Promotional Campaigns inform consumers of the "Canada Select" programme. Star ratings are published, with the operator's consent, in provincial tourism literature, providing participating properties international and domestic exposure as preferred properties.

A new marketing strategy has been developed to further enhance consumer awareness of Canada Select properties. All Canada Select properties may use the Canada Select logo in its marketing and is provided Canada Select signage as part of the rating fee.

- Improves industry standards. Evaluation and rating of properties ensures and enhances minimum standards and stimulates improvements.
- Assists in the development of policy. An inventory of accommodations, coupled with research on market mix, assists industry and government in the development of policies and strategies to help industry grow.

Consumer Benefits

- "No surprise is the best surprise."
- Provides accurate information consistent from coast to coast, "Canada Select's" national rating standard provides reliable information to the travelling public on what to expect from a roofed accommodation.

Access Canada Standards and Training Programme

Recognizing that 15 per cent of the world's population is comprised of seniors and persons with disabilities, the Hotel Association of Canada (HAC) developed access canada.

Access Canada is the rating of lodging properties based on the level of accessibility offered to guests with disabilities. The ratings, from Level 1 to 4, are based on extent and quality of accessible facilities, services and amenities, including sensitivity training for staff. The higher the rating, the more extensive are the facilities, services and amenities.

The programme, offered in both official languages, consists of two components: sensitivity training for staff; and standards of facility accessibility.

The sensitivity training is designed for all members of hotel staff and includes recognition of various types of disabilities and how to serve guests with disabilities.

The standards clearly define four levels of facility accessibility for hotel certification. When hotels confirm to the HAC that they have met the standards of one of the four access levels they receive certification from the HAC.

Completion of both components is required in order to be recognized by the Hotel Association of Canada as an Access Canada property.

The Access Canada Standards and Training Programme is currently undergoing revisions in order to reflect recent changes in legislation, building code updates, as well as evolving market demands. Administration of the programme is on hold until Spring 2007 when it is anticipated that updates and revisions will be complete. Properties that currently hold an Access Canada rating are still recognized for their participation in the programme.

Green Key Eco-Rating Programme

The Hotel Association of Canada's (HAC) Green Key Eco-Rating Programme is a graduated rating system designed to recognize hotels, motels, and resorts that are committed to improving their fiscal and environmental performance.

Based on the results of a comprehensive environmental audit, hoteliers are awarded a 1-5 Green Key rating and given guidance on how to "unlock" opportunities to reduce operating costs and environmental impacts through reduced utility consumption, employee training, and supply chain management. Members also benefit from powerful sales, marketing, public relations, and team building opportunities, not to mention positive feedback from guests.

The HAC Green Key Eco-Rating Programme is a voluntary programme, although hoteliers are encouraged to participate, not only for the health of the planet but also for the 'health' of their business. Energy retrofits do lead to significant monetary savings over the long run. The programme is open to any lodging property in Canada regardless of whether they are members of the HAC.

The Green Key Audit

The HAC Green Key Eco-Rating Programme is unique in that it is administered entirely on line. Once a hotelier has registered for the programme, they are granted instant access to the member section of the Green Key website which includes the online audit.

The audit consists of 5 sections: Corporate Environmental Management, Housekeeping, Food and Beverage Operations, Conference and Meeting Facilities and Engineering. Each section is comprised of a number of "multiple choice"—style questions related to the following areas of sustainable hotel operations:

- Energy conservation.
- Water conservation.
- Solid waste management.
- Hazardous waste management.
- Indoor air quality.
- Community outreach.
- Building infrastructure.
- Land use.
- Environmental management.

Each question has been designated a specific value based on the environmental and social impacts of a particular action and its associated impact on guests, employees, management, and the local community.

The audit also takes limited-service hotels into consideration—in situations where a lodging property does not offer either Food and Beverage Services and/or Conference and Meeting Facilities, the hotelier is given the option to indicate that this is not applicable to their operation. The audit is designed to take this into account when tallying their final score and their final score is not affected.

Within minutes of completing the audit, the Green Key system calculates the property's rating and sends a congratulatory email. A property-specific report highlighting accomplishments and recommendations, as well as a Green Key plaque, is then forwarded to the property by the Hotel Association of Canada.

Rating Descriptions

1 Green Key: A hotel that has taken steps to reduce environmental impacts by analyzing its operations and identifying opportunities for improvement. An action plan focusing on resource conservation and waste minimization has been established, and is supported by a firm commitment to continual improvement.
2 Green Keys: A hotel that has taken considerable strides to identify environmental impacts and implement policies and programmes to minimize its ecological footprint. A firm commitment to continual improvement has resulted in programmes and actions that have shown effective results.
3 Green Keys: A hotel that has taken significant steps to protect the environment. Strong environmental programmes, best management practices, training programmes, and engineering solutions have been implemented which have benefited the environment and the local community.
4 Green Keys: A hotel that has shown national industry leadership and commitment to protecting the environment through wide ranging policies and practices. Hotel has mature programmes in place that involve management, employees, guests, and the public, and which have shown substantial and measurable results.
5 Green Keys: A hotel that exemplifies the highest standards of environmental and social responsibility throughout all areas of operations. The hotel employs cutting edge technologies, policies, and programmes that set the international standard for sustainable hotel operations.

Travel

It is a domain name exclusively for businesses, organizations and individuals in the travel industry. Travel has an exclusive space for the travel and tourism industry on the Internet.

How is it different from .com, .ca and other domain extensions?

Almost anyone can purchase a .com, .ca name even if the name is not relevant to the products/services they offer. This can create confusion among consumers and frustration for legitimate businesses/organizations.

To hold a travel name the registrant must be a verified business, organization or individual in the travel industry. Upon registration an authorized "Authenticating Agent" reviews the application to ensure the information is valid.

Why does the world need Travel?

The travel industry is one of the largest worldwide and its continued rapid growth on the Internet makes it difficult for consumers to locate accurate travel info online.

Travel is unique because it is more than just a search engine. It is an industry directory containing detailed information on all products and services being offered by travel participants. This info is provided by, and updated by, the travel businesses themselves so it will be comprehensive and accurate, making any search far more efficient.

Benefits

- Access is free—Consumers do not pay for access to the directory.
- Consumers will have greater confidence in the validity of the information they find knowing that those in the .travel directory have met certain published standards and criteria.

The travel industry will benefit as follows:

- You are instantly seen by consumers as a recognized travel business.
- It enables travel businesses to safely and confidently do business with other travel businesses.

Some Value-added Services

- Alphabetical (and by country) directory of travel providers and suppliers featuring their key products and services, contact and other relevant information.
- A "WHOIS" directory, providing information about who owns a particular domain name i.e. Who is hotel associationofcanada travel.
- Easy access, e.g. typing *http://www.directory.travel/* into your browser takes you to the directory.

Because only bona fide travel companies may purchase a travel domain name, the process for obtaining a travel domain name is unique.

Obtaining a travel name

Step 1: Pre-authentication

To pre-authenticate your eligibility for a .travel domain name(s), you must complete an information form and forward the Hotel Association of Canada (HAC) some supporting documents. Visit the "authentication data" link below, click the "get started" link and follow the instructions. HAC will review your data and confirm your eligibility based on the information you supply. Once you have been authenticated you are sent an email confirming your eligibility.

Step 2: Name Validation

HAC will then review the "Additional Names", or Names List, you have selected to ensure that they meet the following criteria *(we strongly recommend you to provide us with supporting documentation to ensure prompt validation)*:

- Incorporation (legal) Name/Partnership Name/Individual Name.
- Doing Business As; Trade Name; or Usual Business Name; or Usual Business Name as currently used in an active URL.
- Trade Mark.
- Service Mark.
- Club or Association Name.
- Vessel Name.
- Competition/Event Name.
- Division Name.
- Subsidiary Name.
- Acronym (the first letter of the primary words of the name, not including words such as: the (unless the first word of the name), and, as, of, &, or. Contractions or short forms of words, such as "Chas" for "Charles" or "Bros" for "Brothers" are not permitted as acronyms.

Step 3: Purchasing Your travel Names

Once you are authenticated and your names have been validated you are then ready to proceed with the purchasing of your travel domain names. The official travel registrar for the Hotel Association of Canada is EnCirca. Your travel name registration fee includes not only the cost of your Pre-Authentication, but also your Directory listing. Please note that the policy for registering any travel domain name is first-come, first-served, therefore, we urge you to get authenticated and register your chosen domain name(s) as quickly as possible.

The Hotel Association of Canada offers members a competitive 5 per cent discount. This means that to purchase a travel name for a 1 year period you'll only pay about $95 USD.

NATIONAL RESTAURANT ASSOCIATION (NRA): A CASE STUDY

Founded in 1919, the National Restaurant Association is the leading business association for the restaurant industry. Together with the National Restaurant Association Educational Foundation, the Association's mission is to represent, educate and promote a rapidly growing industry that is comprised of 945,000 restaurant and foodservice outlets employing 13.1 million people.

Our Members

The National Restaurant Association represents more than 380,000 member restaurant establishments. Our membership base consists of many different facets of the industry.

- Our *restaurant members* represent table service and quick service restaurant operators, chains, franchisees and independents.
- Our *allied members* are suppliers, distributors and consultants.
- The *student and faculty memberships* represent those in the education field.
- The *international membership* allows those companies outside the U.S. to enjoy the benefits of the Association.

- And the *not-for-profit members* gain access to information to better their organizations.

IH and RA

The National Restaurant Association is a member of the International Hotel and Restaurant Association (IH&RA), a network of national associations, international chains, hotel operators, restaurateurs and supplier companies in more than 150 countries, representing over 750,000 establishments. Its mission is to protect, promote and inform the hospitality industry, which comprises over 300,000 hotels and 8 million restaurants worldwide, employs 60 million people and contributes $950 billion annually to the global economy.

History

For more than 80 years, the National Restaurant Association has represented, educated and promoted the restaurant industry. Here's a taste of the Association's history.

1917: When egg brokers try to demand a price of 65 cents a dozen, the year-old Kansas City Restaurant Association, one of the restaurant industry's earliest professional associations, organizes an egg boycott. Egg prices plummet to 32 cents. The seeds of a national movement are sown.

1919: Kansas City restaurateurs launch a national organization, holding the first meeting of what is today's National Restaurant Association on March 13 in Kansas City. The fledgling organization represents an industry of 43,000 restaurants.

1920: Prohibition begins in 1920, kicking off a 13-year ban on alcohol sales. Restaurants that are used to serving free sandwiches with five-cent beers need to develop new marketing tactics—and they do. Despite Prohibition, the industry thrives, riding a wave of national prosperity. Howard Johnson's opens its first franchises, White Castle's five-cent burgers grow popular, and Willard Marriott opens his first Hot Shoppes.

1927: The growing National Restaurant Association moves its headquarters from Kansas City to Chicago.

1930s: Prohibition ends, but the Depression is in full swing. Congress's National Recovery Act requires each industry to prepare a "Code of Fair Competition" in 1933. The National Restaurant Association quickly complies.

1930s: In an appeal to customers in bleak times, the National Restaurant Association tries out two advertising slogan: "Enjoy Life—Eat Out More Often" and "Take Her Out to Dinner at Least Once a Week."

1940s: World War II gas rations and travel restrictions result in the cancellation of national restaurant conventions from 1942 to 1945. In their place, the National Restaurant Association institutes a programme of wartime conferences dealing with such concerns as food, equipment and labour shortages.

1940s: Post-World War II restaurant sales hit a new high. The number of meals served triples from a pre-war level of 20 million meals a day to a post-war level of more than 60 million meals a day. The National Restaurant Association launches an Educational Department to help busy restaurateurs do their jobs better. The Association also produces its first film: "America's Heritage of Hospitality," to promote the industry and recruit new employees.

1950s: The National Restaurant Association endorses the use of credit cards, and supports a new type of dinner—the "take home" meal—that families could enjoy at home in front of their new black and white television sets. McDonald's launches its "Speedee System," and fast food is born. To whet customers' appetites for eating out, the National Restaurant Association commissions two songs: "Pass the Meat, Pass the Potatoes" (1951) and "Let's Go Out to a Restaurant" (1953).

1960s: The association celebrates its 50th anniversary in 1969 at the National Restaurant Association Convention and Exposition. The theme: "Golden Opportunities." The industry evolves, in an age of national experimentation, more restaurateurs forgo traditional French cooking techniques. New ethnic flavors and locally-grown produce make their way on to menus.

1970s: The energy crisis, inflation, beef shortages and more government mean growing pains for the restaurant industry. In 1979, the National Restaurant Association relocates its headquarters from Chicago to Washington, DC, to better communicate the industry's messages to lawmakers.

1981: National Restaurant Association launches *Restaurants USA* magazine and the *Washington Weekly* newsletter to keep members abreast of industry news.

1987: In response to the industry's growing professionalism, the Association creates what is now known as the National Restaurant Association Educational Foundation to produce educational programmes and materials on everything from food safety to responsible beverage-alcohol service.

1980s: The National Restaurant Association becomes more politically active. Tip-reporting rules, tip taxes, business meal deductibility, employment law, minimum wage and other public-policy issues take centre stage for the restaurant industry.

1999: *Fortune* magazine names the National Restaurant Association the 10th most powerful lobbying organization in the country, up from #15 in 1998 and #24 in 1997.

1999: The U.S. Department of Commerce declares 1999 the "Year of the Restaurant" in recognition of the industry's significant contribution to the U.S. economy.

1999: The National Restaurant Association Educational Foundation certifies its one millionth restaurant-industry professional in its ServSafe food-safety training programme.

2000: The National Restaurant Association's 81st Annual Restaurant, Hotel-Motel Show in May is the largest NRA Show ever. Show attendees walk through miles of aisles of products and services—including the wares of 250+ technology exhibitors—covering 1.3 million square feet of exhibit floors.

So here we are today...With 13.1 million employees, the restaurant industry is now the nation's largest private-sector employer.

In 2000, Americans are spending more than 45 per cent of their food dollar at eating-and-drinking places, up from 25 per cent in 1955. By 2010, Americans are expected to spend more than half of their food dollar at an anticipated one million eating-and-drinking places.

As the industry flourishes, the National Restaurant Association continues to help restaurateurs meet new challenges. Right now, that's labour shortages and increased competition. Stay tuned...

PARK GROUP (INDIA): A CASE STUDY

Park group optimizes hrm across all units in india. the park group of hotels has optimized human resource management and standardizing and integrating processes across the organization.

TCS implemented SAP ERP—Human Capital Management (HCM) across Park units at Delhi, Bangalore, Kolkata, Chennai and Vizag. The deployments make the hotel chain the first company in the Indian hospitality sector to go-live on SAP.

SAP was selected to provide a flexible and reliable HCM solution for managing and improving the range of transactional, tactical, and strategic processes associated with human resources. Through the implementation the organization aims at enabling HR systems and processes to add value to the overall business strategy and prepare for the challenges of a fast-growing and expanding organization.

The challenges faced by The Park Hotels before deploying SAP solutions included an archaic system with lack of real time benefits and in need of consistency and integration across the organization. Following the SAP implementation, The Park has derived business benefits like standardized and uniform HR system and processes, improved planning and decision-making through real-time reporting mechanisms, increased efficiency through process automation and enhanced employee engagement levels through automation and interactive self-service convenience.

"As an organization, we are witnessing remarkable growth every year and the importance of having a best-in-class system to complement this growth and prepare for the challenges cannot be overstated. Our people are our key strength and pivotal to our success. Hence, amalgamating our HR knowledge and functions with our business process and strategy through SAP has helped us to maximize our human resources potential. SAP solutions have enabled us in managing change and getting people and processes together on a common platform" said Mr. Vijay Dewan, Managing Director, The Park Hotels.

"The hospitality industry in India is increasingly leveraging information technology to improve operational efficiencies and sharpen its competitive edge. We are delighted to support The Park with our industry-leading human capital management solutions and provide the tools necessary to manage their most important asset—their people," said Mr. Ranjan Das, President and CEO, SAP Indian Subcontinent. "We look forward to work closely with The Park on their business transformation journey."

About The Park Hotels

The Park Hotels is a unique collection of contemporary luxury boutique hotels in India. The Park is present in Bangalore, Chennai, Kolkata, Navi Mumbai, New Delhi and Visakhapatnam and have recently acquired land in Hyderabad for a 280 room hotel scheduled to be ready by end 2008. Pioneers of the boutique hotel concept in India, the hotels are a part of the Apeejay Surrendra Group. The Park in Bangalore, Chennai, New Delhi and Kolkata are a part of the Design Hotels ™. Design Hotels Inc. represents and markets its international collection of design-oriented city hotels and exceptional leisure resorts. Member hotels need to distinguish themselves through innovative interior design and architecture, uncomplicated service, a sense for creative details and a distinct identity.

The preferred address for many corporate and leisure travellers, The Park is the natural choice for anyone looking for a luxurious downtown location with easy access to key commercial and leisure districts and their award winning, dining and entertainment options provide excitement.

The first hotel in The Park collection opened on November 1, 1967 with 150 rooms on the fashionable Park Street in Kolkata. The ever-evolving street lends its name and character to the company. The following year a beautiful beachside hotel The Park, Visakhapatnam became the group's second hotel and the first deluxe hotel of Andhra Pradesh. The Park, New Delhi was launched in November 1987, in the heart of the Capital on Parliament Street with 224 rooms. The Park, Bangalore, an urban retreat, with 109 rooms opened its doors in 2000 in the Silicon City of India. The Park, Chennai, an urban haven of 215 rooms, on Anna Salai—the heart of the business district of Tamil Nadu's vibrant capital, opened in May 2002. In February, 2007 we opened in Navi Mumbai.

The Park has remained contemporary throughout the 40 years of operation, bringing in fresh concepts and learning from the world over.

About SAP

SAP is the world's leading provider of business software*. Today, more than 43,400 customers in more than 120 countries run SAP® applications—from distinct solutions addressing the needs of small businesses and midsize companies to suite offerings for global organizations. Powered by the SAP NetWeaver® technology platform to drive innovation and enable business change, SAP software helps enterprises of all sizes around the world improve customer relationships, enhance partner collaboration and create efficiencies across their supply chains and business operations. SAP solution portfolios support the unique business processes of more than 25 industries, including high tech, retail, financial services, healthcare and the public sector. With subsidiaries in more than 50 countries, the company is listed on several exchanges, including the Frankfurt stock exchange and NYSE under the symbol "SAP." (Additional information at <http://www.sap.com/>).

(*) SAP defines business software as comprising enterprise resource planning and related applications such as supply chain management, customer relationship management, product life-cycle management and supplier relationship management.

4

Human Resource Training in Tourism and Travel Industry: Selected Case Studies

Competitive and flexible firms in the tourism sector are important to generate sustained growth of this important sector of the Armenian economy. Modernizing human resource management of tourism firms is one way to enhance the quality of companies and services provided to tourists.

HUMAN RESOURCE TRAINING NEEDS: ASSESSMENT FOR ARMENIAN TOURISM COMPANIES

The survey was conducted through a custom designed questionnaire and interviews with tour operators and travel agencies, hotels, restaurants and associations. Detailed interviews were conducted with 21 entities, and complemented with analysis of the current situation in the Armenian tourism sector from other research and survey findings. The survey revealed that the structure of the human resources management functions performed by the companies is less than ideal. The functions of job analysis and development of job descriptions, implementation of human resources policy, procedures and systems, are performance appraisal are not accomplished by the overwhelming majority of considered companies. The reported annual average turnover rate of personnel was relatively high at more than 10 per cent but reaching 20-30 per cent at some companies. The relatively high workforce turnover at some hotels and restaurants can be overcome through the application of the effective types of employee recruitment and selection, as well as strengthening of the employee motivation. The major human resource management problems hindering the effective activities of tourism companies are the lack of qualified specialists, difficulties with recruitment, limited knowledge of labour legislation and labour ethics, absence of specialized regular tourism schools, and weak cluster relationships between the tourism sector companies and educational establishments. Revising the curricula of educational establishments in accordance with the best international standards is critical for tourism development in the country. Many firms agreed that overcoming of the identified difficulties in complying with labour regulations requires provision of the advisory services or organization of training courses on this issue. The analysis of consultancy needs of companies showed that the company needs are concentrated on human resources management, labour legislation, human resources policy, effective recruitment and selection, performance appraisal and reward systems.

The survey of the human resources in the tourism sector was conducted based on a questionnaire and was completed through personal interviews. The interviews with the representatives of selected tour operators and travel agencies, hotels, restaurants and associations were conducted between January 22-31, 2007 and lasted between 40 minutes to 1.5 hours. Twenty-one respondents were covered including 9 tour operators and travel agencies, 10 hotels and 2 restaurants. The list of surveyed associations included the Union of Incoming Tour Operators of Armenia (UITO), the Armenian Hotel Association (AHA) and the Armenian Restaurant Association (ARA). The staff of surveyed companies made up 700 employees. The respondents were concentrated in the capital city. The sample selection was based on the existing and renewed database of tourism companies, and consultations with CAPS staff. Only locally owned establishments were included in the sample.

Results of the survey were analyzed using the SPSS statistical software and MS Excel. The largest employers in the sample were in the hotels and restaurants. The share of employees at the hotels and restaurants made up more than 90 per cent of the total number of the employed at the observed companies. The average company size in hotels and tour operators was 58 and 7 employees respectively. The survey revealed that more than a half of the employed at the companies are females (60%). The human resources functions at the companies are performed by the Executive Director in 48 per cent of those companies surveyed or

Human Resources manager in the other 52 per cent. At the small companies the HR functions are performed mainly by the Executive Director while at the large companies a Human Resources Manager performs these functions. The analysis of human resources management functions performed by the respondents revealed that such functions as job analysis and development of human resources policy, procedures and systems (at only 1% correspondingly), performance appraisal (at 7%) have the lowest share in the total number of HRM functions implemented by the companies.

THE ASSOCIATION OF TOURISM TEACHERS AND TRAINERS (ATTT): A CASE STUDY

The ATTT is committed to enhance the body of knowledge in tourism and to provide tools for tourism educators, trainers and professionals. ATTT also aims to extend links and partnership between education and training interests and employers in all sectors in the industry. A wide range of initiatives, such as the Tourism Education Exchange, the Tourism Literature Access Scheme, and the Who is Who in Tourism Education, as well as Professional Development seminars and other activities are undertaken in order to facilitate these objectives. Increasingly it is recognised that human resources and intellect become some of the most important assets of the tourism industry. Hence, the competitiveness of tourism destinations and organisations of the future will depend on their ability to educate and train their managers and employees continuously throughout their career. Innovation, flexibility and interactivity will be critical for satisfying tourism demand and education and training are of paramount importance in order to develop these attributes. The above arguments illustrate the need for dissemination of knowledge, not only for the new generations of tourism managers, who are currently students in colleges and universities around the country, but also for teachers, lecturers, managers and professionals in the tourism industry.

Educators in their everyday life are asked to recommend suitable resources for students and also to get inquiries from the industry asking for references in several research areas. In order to achieve the dissemination of knowledge, the ATTT committee decided to publish a guide in the best tourism and hospitality books. The bibliography includes a number of book reviews as well as detailed bibliographical reference to over 300 books in tourism and hospitality providing a unique source for the industry and academia.

BC'S TOURISM INDUSTRY: A CASE STUDY

Although many of us have been "tourists" at some point in our lives, defining what tourism actually is can be difficult. Tourism is the activities of persons travelling to and staying in places outside their usual environment for not more than one consecutive year for leisure, business or other purposes. Tourism is a dynamic and competitive industry that requires the ability to constantly adapt to customers' changing needs and desires, as the customer's satisfaction, safety and enjoyment are particularly the focus of tourism businesses.

Types

Tourism encompasses:

(*a*) *Outbound Tourism*: Outbound tourism is what you may be most familiar with. It involves the business of people going from British Columbia to other provinces, territories or countries. For example, going to Hawaii in February is considered outbound tourism.

(*b*) *Inbound Tourism*: BC competes in a global market to attract tourists from the United States, Japan, Germany and many other countries. We also implement marketing campaigns aimed at attracting travellers from other parts of Canada. The tourists coming to BC from other places are called inbound tourists.

(*c*) *Sectors*: The tourism industry is divided into five different sectors:

(*i*) Accommodation.
(*ii*) Food and Beverage Services.
(*iii*) Recreation and Entertainment.
(*iv*) Transportation.
(*v*) Travel Services.

The diversity of these five sectors shows that the career options in the tourism industry are unlimited. Depending on your interests and skills, you can work indoors or out, nine to five or midnight to noon. You can work in an office, an airport or out of your home. You can have one career in the winter and another in the summer. In short, you can make your career fit the lifestyle you want.

go2 was created by the BC tourism industry in 2003, on the recommendation of an 18 month task force involving more than 100 industry representatives and stakeholders around the province, to deal with the labour shortage and other HR issues. Through its programmes and services go2, an independent, non-profit industry association, assists BC's tourism industry to recruit, retain and train employees to support industry growth. Following are some of the ways go2 is helping industry to address the labour shortage challenge:

Tourism Career Awareness

go2, with the support of industry, launched an advertising and PR campaign called MOVE ON UP™ with a career in tourism. The campaign is intended to be multi-year and is targeted to youth, their influencers and under-represented labour groups. The campaign includes the following tactics:

- Print and radio advertising.
- Public relations activities to promote careers in tourism.
- Career awareness presentations in high schools and to under-represented groups.
- Exhibiting at career fairs.
- Partnerships with associations such as the BC Chefs' Association and Canada West Ski Areas Association to profile careers in specific sectors of tourism.
- Moveonup.ca website and e-newsletter.

Research and HR Planning

go2 is coordinating regional labour market research around BC. The Sea-to-Sky region (Whistler) was the first to start, followed by the Kootenay Rockies. Other regions are planned to follow upon receipt of funding. The go2 is assisting these regions with development of strategic human resource plans based on the research to help them address labour shortages.

Compensation Survey

In 2005, go2, working with other Western provinces, released the Western Canadian Tourism Industry Compensation Study. The study shows a current review of wage, salary and benefits in Western Canada. It was updated in 2007 to include 1,153 organizations from across Canada.

Educating Employers on HR Best Practices

go2 educates employers on HR issues such as recruitment, retention, training and legal issues through the go2hr.ca portal website, e-newsletter, articles in trade publications and speaking regularly at industry events and conferences. go2 also sponsors awards to highlight BC tourism employers with exemplary HR and leadership practices.

Industry Training Initiatives

go2 was recently selected by the Industry Training Authority to take on a new training mandate for tourism in BC. The mandate will be to provide an effective industry-driven training function by defining training needs, setting industry training and occupational standards, measuring training results and directly interfacing with training providers. Apprenticeship programmes for Cook, Baker and Meatcutter will fall under the jurisdiction of go2's industry training division.

Advocating for Policy Changes

go2 is working with other industry associations and all levels of government to address the foreign worker and immigration policies as part of the strategy to deal with labour shortages. In the short term, go2 is advocating to improve existing programmes to make it easier for employers to access them. Longer term, our goal is to encourage government to revamp the immigration and foreign worker programmes to align them with current labour market conditions.

Temporary Foreign Worker Guide

go2 has published a guide to assist employers with accessing the Temporary Foreign Worker programme. Registered tourism employers can contact us for a free copy.

Labour Shortage Strategy

There is no 'silver bullet' to address the labour shortage issue. go2 is proposing that BC's tourism industry needs to have a multi-faceted strategy to be successful.
The following Goals and Objectives have been identified:

- Become better employers.
- Retain existing workers.
- Increase investment in training.
- Raise awareness of careers in tourism.
- Increase productivity in business operations.
- Increase recruitment efforts to include targeting under represented groups.
- Recruit workers from other parts of the province and across Canada.
- Recruit workers from other countries.

Training and Education

The more training you have, the more you have to offer potential employers, thus increasing your chances of landing the job that you want! So check out your tourism education and training options below.

BC Tourism Learning System

The BC Tourism Learning System (TLS) includes the laddered tourism and hospitality education programmes shown here. These programmes follow an 'industry approved' core curriculum—

making sure you get practical training and education that is valued by employers!

BC Centres of Leadership and Innovation

The BC Centre for Tourism Leadership and Innovation and the BC Centre for Hospitality Leadership and Innovation are working on your behalf to help support and promote programmes in the BC Tourism Learning System (TLS). They encourage innovative education and training at colleges and universities across BC. The centres have partnered with go2 to showcase your education options and help you Move On Up to your dream career even faster!

Education Options

Secondary School Programmes

A head start for your career in tourism!

- Tourism 11 and 12 classes.
- The Canadian Academy of Travel and Tourism (CATT).
- Tourism Career Awareness Programme (TCAP).
- Secondary school apprenticeship programmes.

Industry Credentials

Apprenticeships

Earn while you learn!

- Apprenticeship is paid work-based training combined with post-secondary education.
- Tourism apprenticeships are available for cooks, bakers and other specialized trades.

Certificate/Diploma Programmes

Learning the essentials!

- These tourism and hospitality programmes are offered at public and some private colleges and universities.

- Certificates are one year in length or less and prepare you for front-line positions in the industry.
- Diplomas are usually two years in length and prepare you for front-line or supervisory-trainee positions.

Skills Certificates

A great starting point!

- FOODSAFE™—A provincial programme which focuses on safe food handling.
- Serving It Right™—BC's mandatory self-study programme for the responsible service of alcohol.
- SuperHost®—Internationally recognized workshops for training in customer service.
- FirstHost—A customer service workshop, promoting excellence in aboriginal hospitality skills.

Degree Programmes

Building on the essentials!

- Typically four years in length, degree programmes challenge you to learn the management level skills required to enjoy life long career opportunities in senior positions.

National Certification

emerit...great for those already working in tourism!

- A national certification process that challenges an individual to demonstrate they have mastered the required skills and met the standards of their profession in a practical job setting.

Post-Graduate Programmes

Taking it to another level!

- Masters and doctoral programmes are available for those

that want to pursue advanced level of studies and research relating to the tourism industry.

Apprenticeship Training: go2 Industry Training Division

In the fall of 2006 go2 was approved to become the new Industry Training Organization for BC's tourism industry. As such, go2's Industry Training Division was created.

Why was go2's Industry Training Division Formed?

Industry Training Organizations (ITOs) are responsible for all designated trades training in BC. They are created by a provincial government agency called the Industry Training Authority (ITA).

The goal of the ITA is to increase the number of participants in apprenticeship trades training. In doing so, they also seek to increase the number of individuals that complete apprenticeship training and continue on to receive provincial and sometimes inter-provincial designations and credentials.

In order to accomplish these goals, the ITA creates ITOs for each industry. Currently there are 6 ITOs in BC, one of which is the tourism ITO that will be managed by go2's Industry Training Division.

Industry is the key word in the title of Industry Training Organization. It represents the fact that industry members will play a leading role in defining the standards and requirements for apprenticeship training. It is go2's role to engage industry members and evolve the apprenticeship programmes to meet industry needs.

What is Apprenticeship?

Apprenticeship is a distinct form of training, where the majority of the learner's time is spent training on the job. In order to become an apprentice, one must first register provincially and then formally engage an employer to sponsor their learning. During their work periods, they must also participate in short periods of technical training or school-based learning at designated times of the year.

Some advantages of apprenticeship training are:

- It allows the learner to instantly apply theory.
- The learner can earn a wage while receiving an education.
- For some, it is a preferred learning model to the alternative of attending school full-time.

As go2's Industry Training Division evolves it will take on increasing responsibility for the management of the apprenticeship training for the trades under its umbrella. To start, go2 has been assigned 3 designated trades:

- Cook.
- Baker.
- Meatcutter.

Going forward go2's Industry Training Division's role will be to examine the tourism sector as a whole and look for opportunities to expand the number of designated occupations through which a person apprentices. Check back frequently for updates.

Tourism in BC is a growing, dynamic industry. Following is a snapshot of what the tourism industry means for our province:

- British Columbia hosts more than 22.5 million overnight visitors a year.
- Tourism generated $9.98 billion in revenues in 2006.
- Tourism returns approximately $1 billion to the provincial treasury in the form of taxes and fees every year.
- Tourism is a labour intensive industry, employing 267,000 British Columbians (117,500 directly), and has been one of the fastest growing industries over the past decade.

There are nearly 18,000 tourism-related companies in British Columbia, with between 300 to 500 new tourism businesses started each year. Getting more background information on the industry will help you to better position your business moving forward or help you to identify the wealth of career opportunities. The articles in this section will tell you more about the industry and changing trends, such as the emergence of culinary tourism and the growth of adventure tourism, as well as provide an overview of the industry, its sectors, and the news about the 2010 Olympic Games.

TOURISM INDUSTRY ASSOCIATION OF CANADA (TAAC): A CASE STUDY

TIAC represents the broad interests of Canada's tourism industry nationally, getting action on the issues important to its members through effective advocacy and lobbying. It is the lead organization on national tourism issues, and also works to support provincial, territorial, regional or municipal tourism industry organizations when requested. TIAC's advocacy activities involve identifying, promoting and supporting policies, programmes and courses of action that will benefit the industry's growth and development. In fulfilling this core function, TIAC advocates tourism interests to a range of sectors that might impact tourism, including various organizations, businesses, the media and the general public. Those efforts are complemented by lobbying activities that focus on legislators and regulators—specifically, government. TIAC has successfully influenced government thinking and action on behalf of Canadian tourism businesses since 1930, promoting positive measures that enhance the industry's prospects for growth and profitability, as well as the removal of barriers to the achievement of these goals. Actions in support of TIAC's ongoing advocacy and lobbying efforts include working with Parliamentarians from all parties in Ottawa. This helps TIAC and the tourism industry maintain a strong and meaningful federal presence, promotes awareness of government policies and issues affecting Canadian tourism, and identifies TIAC as the national resource on tourism issues. Meanwhile, TIAC's annual Tourism Lobby Day on Parliament Hill gives members an opportunity to meet with MPs, Senators and senior government officials to discuss their views about policies and programmes that affect their business, their region and the tourism industry as a whole.

Representing Tourism Businesses

Every business owner in the tourism and travel industry must manage the internal challenges that confront all businesses, including staffing, training, advertising and sales. The larger the business, the more these concerns are delegated to managers with expertise in a particular field. But there are also external influences—such as taxation, regulation and competition—that impact every tourism operation, large or small. And they need to be managed, too. TIAC is tourism's expert manager with the responsibility of representing the industry's interests on such external matters.

Key Wins

TIAC has been tackling difficult and often complex issues affecting Canadian tourism. This section of the website contains information on TIAC's advocacy and lobbying activities in current issue areas such as public health, safety and security, customs administration and border management, employment insurance, infrastructure, human resources, marketing, sustainable tourism and transportation.

Most recently, TIAC contributed to, among others:

- A new airport rent policy (May, 2005) that is expected to result in close to $8 billion in rent relief for Canada's airport authorities over the course of their existing leases.
- Progressive reductions in Employment Insurance premiums.
- The reduction of the Air Travellers Security Charge (ATSC) from $24 to $14 in the 2003 federal budget, to $12 in the 2004 budget, and to $10 in the 2005 budget.
- The introduction of a rebate ability for consumers who overpaid their ATSC.
- The introduction of a "deemed rehabilitated" option for visitors with previous driving-under-the-influence (DUI) convictions more than ten years old. The assessment of economic impact in decisions to allow foreign tour directors to meet their tours in Canada.
- The introduction of an insurance programme to increase the confidence of foreign buyers of Canadian tourism products.
- Substantial funding increases for the maintenance and enhancement of Canada's national parks and historic sites.
- Heightened awareness of liability insurance challenges.

It is also important to recognize the many ways in which Canadian tourism businesses continue to benefit from TIAC's past successes on the advocacy and lobbying front. Over the past 75 years, TIAC has contributed to many programmes and initiatives that continue to benefit Canada's tourism industry, including:

- A GST rebate for business travellers and international tourists.
- More traffic and streamlined travel to Canada through Open Skies, more liberalized air charter services, and improved customs procedures at Canada's borders.
- The creation of the Canadian Tourism Commission and incremental funding increases, from $15 million to $50 million and now $83 million.
- Recognition of tourism's unique financing needs.
- The building of the Trans-Canada Highway.
- The establishment of standards-based certification programmes.
- A uniform start and end to Daylight Savings Time for traveller convenience.
- A tax exemption on tourism promotional literature.
- Government recognition that tourism is an industry!

Clearly, the Canadian tourism environment is better today because the Tourism Industry Association of Canada was a driving force in the resolution of a wide range of important issues.

TIAC continues to help the industry successfully manage change and confront new challenges, representing its interests forcefully and effectively at the national level.

Rules and Regulations Regarding TIAC National Tourism Awards

The TIAC National Awards for Tourism Excellence presented by *The Globe and Mail* are a celebration of Canada's best in tourism products, services and people. They attract national attention within the tourism community, and among the travel trade and news media. The awards are presented annually at a gala evening during Canada's Tourism Leadership Summit. The next Summit is taking place November 4-6, 2007, at the Fairmont Empress in Victoria, British Columbia.

Award Categories and Criteria—Select Award by Name

- Tourism Toronto Business of the Year Award—Multiple-Unit.
- CTHRC/emerit Award for Excellence in Human Resources.
- Delta Hotels Limited Employee of the Year Award.
- Air Canada Business of the Year Award—Single-Unit.
- Metro Toronto Convention Centre Event of the Year Award
- Starwood Hotels and Resorts Worldwide Inc. Corporate Partner of the Year.
- Parks Canada Sustainable Tourism Award.
- The BDC New Business of the Year Award.
- The Globe and Mail Travel Media Award.
- Deloitte Programme Innovator of the Year Award.
- Canadian Travel Press Lifetime Achievement Award.
- VIA Rail Canada Volunteer of the Year Award.
- Fairmont Hotels and Resorts Marketing Campaign of the Year Award.

Eligibility Criteria

- Applications will be accepted from all organizations or businesses that support the Canadian tourism industry and contribute to the development of Canada as a must-see destination.
- The tourism-related product or service must have been offered within the 18 months concluding June 30 of the current year.
- Organizations or businesses are encouraged to put forward their own nominations for this award.

Nomination Deadline

Nominations for the 2007, TIAC National Awards for Tourism Excellence presented by *The Globe and Mail* will be accepted until 12:00 p.m. EDT on Monday, August 13, 2007.

Nomination Process

Simply complete the online nomination form, which will prompt you to provide information relating to each of the judging criteria for the selected award(s) and provide electronic links to any supporting material where applicable.

Judging Process

To be eligible, all nominations must be received by 12:00 p.m. EDT, August 13, 2007. Nominations for 11 of the 13 awards will be reviewed and scored online by a tourism industry judges panel; the exceptions are the CTHRC/emerit Award for Excellence in Human Resources, and the Travel Press Lifetime Achievement Award (see below). Completed judging forms will be sent to an independent auditor who will tabulate the scores for each entry and report the results to the Tourism Industry Association of Canada; all decisions rendered by the auditor will be final. Three finalists will be announced on September 14, 2007, for each award except the Travel Press Lifetime Achievement Award.

The judging process for the CTHRC/emerit Award for Excellence in Human Resources will be managed by the Canadian Tourism Human Resource Council staff. A national judging committee will judge all nominations. Three finalists will be selected by the national judging committee consisting of persons who are not associated with the nomination process or any of the nominees.

The recipient of the Travel Press Lifetime Achievement Award will be determined by the Chair of the Board of Directors of the Tourism Industry Association of Canada.

Finalist Recognition

The three finalists in each category will be advised by September 14, 2007. The finalists will be honoured by their peers at Canada's Tourism Leadership Summit. Each finalist will receive two complimentary tickets to the National Awards for Tourism Excellence Gala Event and two tickets to the Finalists' Reception prior to the gala dinner.

Winner Recognition

- A custom-designed, mouth-blown and hand-cut crystal art award crafted by NovaScotian Crystal will be presented at the gala awards event during Canada's Tourism Leadership Summit.
- Use of award logo on marketing materials.
- News release with good media pickup.
- Posting on the Tourism Industry Association of Canada's website.
- Receipt of National Awards for Tourism Excellence Finalist Certificate.

Award Categories and Judging Criteria

Tourism Toronto Business of the Year Award—Multiple-Unit

1. *Excellence in Field of Endeavour (10 Points)*

- Describe any recognition, acclaim and awards previously received by the Nominee.
- Highlight any previous successes enjoyed by the Nominee.

2. *Contribution to Tourism (10 Points)*

- Describe how the nominee's work has contributed to the promotion or support of the tourism industry.
- Show the nominee's record of involvement or volunteerism with the tourism community.

3. *Sustainability of Tourism (10 Points)*

- Describe how the nominee's efforts will contribute to the sustainability of the tourism industry. (Definition of "sustainable tourism" used by the Tourism Industry Association of Canada: Sustainable tourism actively fosters appreciation and stewardship of the natural, cultural and historic resources and special places by residents, the touirsm industry, governments and visitors. It is tourism that can be sustained over the long-term because it results in a net benefit for the social, economic, natural and cultural environments of the area in which it takes place.)

4. Description of Accomplishments (25 Points)

- Describe the specific action or initiative and/or the long-term body of work and effort for which this nomination is being presented.

5. Objectives and Evaluation (10 Points)

- Describe the nominee's use of research, objectives and evaluation relative to the work being recognized in this nomination.

6. Visitor Expectations (15 Points)

- Demonstrate the nominee's ability to successfully satisfy visitor expectations.
- Present how the nominee managed visitor expectations.

7. Human Resource Management (15 Points)

- Describe any successes the nominee has had in employee retention, training, motivation and development.

8. Professionalism and Image (5 Points)

- Describe how the nominee has contributed to the enhanced professionalism and image of the tourism industry.

CTHRC/Emerit Award for Excellence in Human Resources

1. Business HR Practices (Total Points = 30)

(*a*) State or describe turnover rate (%) by position or for all employees for last completed fiscal year. *5 points*

(*b*) State percentage of payroll spent by business on training. *5 points*

(*c*) Describe other incentives provided for employee professional development. *5 points*
(*d*) Describe benefits package offered to employees. *5 points*
(*e*) Provide the number of promotions from within as a percentage of positions filled during the last completed fiscal year. *5 points*
(*f*) Provide the number of employees enrolling in and achieving professional certification, designation, or credentials from an outside organization. *5 points*

2. *Awards or Recognition (Total Points = 20)*

(*a*) Identify awards or recognition received for excellence in human resources development by the business since its establishment. *15 points*
(*b*) Identify awards or recognition received for excellence in human resources development by the business in the last year (June 1, 2006 to May 31, 2007). *5 points*

3. *Contribution to Workforce Development (Total Points = 20)*

(*a*) Identify the number of student work placements (high school or post-secondary) provided in the last year (June 1, 2006 to May 31, 2007) with a brief description. *5 points*
(*b*) Identify other activities supporting tourism education such as participating in community, secondary or post-secondary institution career fairs; providing funding to support tourism education; participating on the advisory committees for high school or post-secondary tourism-related programmes, *e.g.* Canadian Academy of Travel and Tourism, hospitality or tourism programmes at colleges and universities. *5 points*
(*c*) Identify activities related to hiring and supporting in the workplace people from disadvantaged groups, *e.g.* new immigrants, Aboriginals, people with disabilities. *10 points*

4. *Human Resource Planning (Total Points = 10)*

(*a*) Describe business's activities related to research, analysis and evaluation in the areas of recruitment, training, and evaluation of employees and how the findings and recommendations have been used by the business. *10 points*

5. *Customer, Visitor Impact/Response (Total Points = 20)*

   (*a*) Describe customer satisfaction results, particularly if they can be related to business' HR activities. *10 points*
   (*b*) Describe employee satisfaction results. *10 points*

Delta Hotels Limited Employee of the Year Award

1. *Excellence in Field of Endeavour (20 Points)*

   - Describe any recognition, acclaim and awards previously received by the Nominee.
   - Highlight any previous successes enjoyed by the Nominee.

2. *Contribution to Tourism (20 Points)*

   - Describe how the nominee's work has contributed to the promotion or support of the tourism industry.
   - Show the nominee's record of involvement or volunteerism with the tourism community.

3. *Sustainability of Tourism (5 Points)*

   - Describe how the nominee's efforts will contribute to the sustainability of the tourism industry. (Definition of "sustainable tourism" used by the Tourism Industry Association of Canada: Sustainable tourism actively fosters appreciation and stewardship of the natural, cultural and historic resources and special places by residents, the tourism industry, governments and visitors. It is tourism that can be sustained over the long-term because it results in a net benefit for the social, economic, natural and cultural environments of the area in which it takes place.)

4. Description of Accomplishments (30 Points)

- Describe the actions and initiatives undertaken by the Nominee over a period of at least three years for which the nomination is being presented.

5. Visitor Expectations (10 Points)

- Demonstrate the nominee's ability to successfully satisfy visitor expectations.
- Present how the nominee managed visitor expectations.

6. Human Resource Management (5 Points)

- Describe any successes the nominee has had in employee retention, training, motivation and development, either personally or through contributions to the efforts of others.

7. Professionalism and Image (10 Points)

- Describe how the nominee has contributed to the enhanced professionalism and image of the tourism industry.

Air Canada Business of the Year Award—Single-Unit

1. Excellence in Field of Endeavour (10 Points)

- Describe any recognition, acclaim and awards previously received by the nominee.
- Highlight any previous successes enjoyed by the nominee.

2. Contribution to Tourism (10 Points)

- Describe how the Nominee's work has contributed to the promotion or support of the tourism industry.
- Show the Nominee's record of involvement or volunteerism with the tourism community.

3. Sustainability of Tourism (10 Points)

- Describe how the nominee's efforts will contribute to the sustainability of the tourism industry. (Definition of "sustainable tourism" used by the Tourism Industry Association of Canada: Sustainable tourism actively fosters appreciation and stewardship of the natural, cultural and historic resources and special places by residents, the tourism industry, governments and visitors. It is tourism that can be sustained over the long-term because it results in a net benefit for the social, economic, natural and cultural environments of the area in which it takes place.)

4. Description of Accomplishments (25 Points)

- Describe the specific action or initiative and/or the long-term body of work and effort for which the nomination is being presented.

5. Objectives and Evaluation (10 Points)

- Describe the nominee's use of research, objectives and evaluation relative to the work being recognized in this nomination.

6. Visitor Expectations (15 Points)

- Demonstrate the nominee's ability to successfully satisfy visitor expectations.
- Present how the nominee managed visitor expectations.

7. Human Resource Management (15 Points)

- Describe any successes the nominee has had in employee retention, training, motivation and development.

8. Professionalism and Image (5 Points)

- Describe how the nominee has contributed to the enhanced professionalism and image of the tourism industry.

Metro Toronto Convention Centre Event of the Year Award

1. *Excellence in Field of Endeavour (20 Points)*

- Describe any recognition, acclaim and awards previously received by the Nominee.
- Highlight any previous successes enjoyed by the Nominee.

2. *Contribution to Tourism (20 Points)*

- Describe how the nominee's work has contributed to the promotion or support of the tourism industry.
- Show the nominee's record of involvement or volunteerism with the tourism community.

3. *Sustainability of Tourism (5 Points)*

- Describe how the nominee's efforts will contribute to the sustainability of the tourism industry. (Definition of "sustainable tourism" used by the Tourism Industry Association of Canada: Sustainable tourism actively fosters appreciation and stewardship of the natural, cultural and historic resources and special places by residents, the tourism industry, governments and visitors. It is tourism that can be sustained over the long term because it results in a net benefit for the social, economic, natural and cultural environments of the area in which it takes place).

4. *Description of Accomplishments (30 Points)*

- Describe the event for which the nomination is being presented.

5. *Visitor Expectations (10 Points)*

- Demonstrate the nominee's ability to successfully satisfy visitor expectations.
- Present how the nominee managed visitor expectations.

6. Human Resource Management (5 Points)

- Describe any successes the nominee has had in employee retention, training, motivation and development.

7. Professionalism and Image (10 Points)

- Describe how the nominee has contributed to the enhanced professionalism and image of the tourism industry.

Starwood Hotels and Resorts Worldwide Inc Corporate Partner of the Year Award

1. Excellence in Field of Endeavour (20 Points)

- Describe any recognition, acclaim and awards previously received by the Nominee.
- Highlight any previous successes enjoyed by the nominee.

2. Contribution to Tourism (25 Points)

- Describe how the nominee's work has contributed to the promotion or support of the tourism industry.
- Show the nominee's record of involvement or volunteerism with the tourism community.

3. Sustainability of Tourism (5 Points)

- Describe how the nominee's efforts will contribute to the sustainability of the tourism industry. (Definition of "sustainable tourism" used by the Tourism Industry Association of Canada: Sustainable tourism actively fosters appreciation and stewardship of the natural, cultural and historic resources and special places by residents, the tourism industry, governments and visitors. It is tourism that can be sustained over the long-term because it results in a net benefit for the social, economic, natural and cultural environments of the area in which it takes place.)

4. Description of Accomplishments (30 Points)

- Describe the specific action or initiative and/or the long-term body of work and effort for which the nomination is being presented.

5. Visitor Expectations (10 Points)

- Demonstrate the nominee's ability to successfully satisfy visitor expectations.
- Present how the nominee managed visitor expectations.

6. Professionalism and Image (10 Points)

- Describe how the nominee has contributed to the enhanced professionalism and image of the tourism industry.

Parks Canada Sustainable Tourism Award

1. Commitment to Excellence (25 Points)

- Describe any recognition, acclaim or awards previously received by the nominee for sustainable tourism development or promotion.
- Describe how the nominee has demonstrated a commitment to encouraging appreciation of and respect for, Canada's natural, cultural and aesthetic heritage.

2. Achievement of Sustainable Tourism Development (50 Points)

- Describe how the nominee has strived to achieve tourism development in a manner which harmonizes economic objectives with the protection and enhancement of Canada's natural and cultural heritage.
- Describe how the tourism products and services offered by the nominee are consistent with community values and the surrounding environment.

3. Promotion of Sustainable Tourism (25 Points)

- Describe how the nominee has cooperated with colleagues and the tourism industry in promoting sustainable development.
- Describe how the nominee has fostered greater public awareness of the economic, social, cultural and environmental significance of tourism.

The BDC New Business of the Year Award

1. Excellence in Field of Endeavour (10 Points)

- Describe any recognition, acclaim and awards previously received by the Nominee.
- Highlight any previous successes enjoyed by the nominee.

2. Sustainability of Tourism (10 Points)

- Describe how the nominee's efforts will contribute to the sustainability of the tourism industry. (Definition of "sustainable tourism" used by the Tourism Industry Association of Canada: Sustainable tourism actively fosters appreciation and stewardship of the natural, cultural and historic resources and special places by residents, the tourism industry, governments and visitors. It is tourism that can be sustained over the long-term because it results in a net benefit for the social, economic, natural and cultural environments of the area in which it takes place.)

3. Objectives and Evaluation (25 Points)

- Describe the nominee's use of research, objectives and evaluation relative to the work being recognized in the nomination.

4. Visitor Expectations (30 Points)

- Demonstrate the nominee's ability to successfully satisfy visitor expectations.

- Present how the nominee managed visitor expectations.

5. Human Resource Management (15 Points)

- Describe any successes the nominee has had in employee retention, training, motivation and development, either personally or through contributions to the efforts of others.

6. Professionalism and Image (10 Points)

- Describe how the nominee has contributed to the enhanced professionalism and image of the tourism industry.

The Globe and Mail Travel Media Award

1. Excellence in Field of Endeavour (15 Points)

- Describe any recognition, acclaim and awards previously received by the Nominee.
- Highlight any previous successes enjoyed by the Nominee.

2. Contribution to Tourism (50 Points)

- Describe how the nominee's work has contributed to the promotion or support of the tourism industry.
- Show the nominee's record of involvement or volunteerism with the tourism community.

3. Sustainability of Tourism (5 Points)

- Describe how the nominee's efforts will contribute to the sustainability of the tourism industry. (Definition of "sustainable tourism" used by the Tourism Industry Association of Canada: Sustainable tourism actively fosters appreciation and stewardship of the natural, cultural and historic resources and special places by residents, the tourism industry, governments and visitors. It is tourism that can be sustained over the long-term because it results in a net benefit for the social, economic, natural and cultural environments of the area in which it takes place.)

4. Description of Accomplishments (20 Points)

- Describe the specific action(s) or initiative(s) and/or the long-term body of work and effort for which the nomination is being presented. Submission must include at least one work which was published or broadcast between July 2006 and June 2007.

5. Objectives and Evaluation (10 Points)

- Describe the nominee's use of research, objectives and evaluation relative to the work being recognized in the nomination.

Deloitte Innovator of the Year Award

1. Excellence in Field of Endeavour (10 Points)

- Describe any recognition, acclaim and awards previously received by the nominee.
- Highlight any previous successes enjoyed by the nominee.

2. Contribution to Tourism (20 Points)

- Describe how the nominee's work has contributed to the promotion or support of the tourism industry.
- Show the nominee's record of involvement or volunteerism with the tourism community.

3. Sustainability of Tourism (5 Points)

- Describe how the nominee's efforts will contribute to the sustainability of the tourism industry. (Definition of "sustainable tourism" used by the Tourism Industry Association of Canada: Sustainable tourism actively fosters appreciation and stewardship of the natural, cultural and historic resources and special places by residents, the tourism industry, governments and visitors. It is tourism that can be sustained over the long-term because it results in a net benefit for the social, economic, natural and cultural environments of the area in which it takes place).

4. Description of Accomplishments (30 Points)

- Describe the innovation for which the nomination is being presented.

5. Objectives and Evaluation (15 Points)

- Describe the nominee's use of research, objectives and evaluation relative to the work being recognized in the nomination.

6. Visitor Expectations (10 Points)

- Demonstrate the nominee's ability to successfully satisfy visitor expectations.
- Present how the nominee managed visitor expectations.

7. Professionalism and Image (10 Points)

- Describe how the nominee has contributed to the enhanced professionalism and image of the tourism industry.

Canadian Travel Press Lifetime Achievement Award

1. Excellence in Field of Endeavour (20 Points)

- Describe any recognition, acclaim and awards previously received by the nominee.
- Highlight any previous successes enjoyed by the Nominee.

2. Contribution to Tourism (40 Points)

- Describe how the nominee's work has contributed to the promotion or support of the tourism industry.
- Show the nominee's record of involvement or volunteerism with the tourism community.

3. Sustainability of Tourism (5 Points)

- Describe how the nominee's efforts will contribute to the sustainability of the tourism industry. (Definition of "sustainable tourism" used by the Tourism Industry Association of Canada: Sustainable tourism actively fosters appreciation and stewardship of the natural, cultural and historic resources and special places by residents, the tourism industry, governments and visitors. It is tourism that can be sustained over the long-term because it results in a net benefit for the social, economic, natural and cultural environments of the area in which it takes place.)

4. Description of Accomplishments (30 Points)

- Describe the long-term body of work and effort for which the nomination is being presented.

5. Professionalism and Image (5 Points)

- Describe how the nominee has contributed to the enhanced professionalism and image of the tourism industry.

VIA Rail Canada Volunteer of the Year Award

1. Excellence in Field of Endeavour (20 Points)

- Describe any recognition, acclaim and awards previously received by the Nominee.
- Highlight any previous successes enjoyed by the nominee.

2. Contribution to Tourism (40 Points)

- Describe how the nominee's work has contributed to the promotion or support of the tourism industry.
- Show the nominee's record of involvement or volunteerism with the tourism community.

3. Sustainability of Tourism (5 Points)

- Describe how the nominee's efforts will contribute to the sustainability of the tourism industry. (Definition of "sustainable tourism" used by the Tourism Industry Association of Canada: Sustainable tourism actively fosters appreciation and stewardship of the natural, cultural and historic resources and special places by residents, the tourism industry, governments and visitors. It is tourism that can be sustained over the long-term because it results in a net benefit for the social, economic, natural and cultural environments of the area in which it takes place.)

4. Description of Accomplishments (30 Points)

- Describe the specific action(s) or initiative(s) and/or the long-term body of work and effort for which the nomination is being presented.

5. Professionalism and Image (5 Points)

- Describe how the nominee has contributed to the enhanced professionalism and image of the tourism industry.

Fairmont Hotels and Resorts Marketing Campaign of the Year Award

1. Contribution to Tourism (30 Points)

- Describe how the nominee's work has contributed to the promotion or support of the tourism industry.
- Show the nominee's record of involvement or volunteerism with the tourism community.

2. Sustainability of Tourism (5 Points)

- Describe how the nominee's efforts will contribute to the sustainability of the tourism industry. (Definition of "sustainable tourism" used by the Tourism Industry

Association of Canada: Sustainable tourism actively fosters appreciation and stewardship of the natural, cultural and historic resources and special places by residents, the tourism industry, governments and visitors. It is tourism that can be sustained over the long-term because it results in a net benefit for the social, economic, natural and cultural environments of the area in which it takes place.)

3. *Description of Accomplishments (25 Points)*

- Describe the marketing campaign for which the nomination is being presented.

4. *Objectives and Evaluation (25 Points)*

- Describe the nominee's use of research, objectives and evaluation relative to the marketing campaign being recognized in the nomination.

5. *Visitor Expectations (10 Points)*

- Demonstrate the nominee's ability to successfully satisfy visitor expectations.
- Present how the nominee managed visitor expectations.

6. *Professionalism and Image (5 Points)*

- Describe how the nominee has contributed to the enhanced professionalism and image of the tourism industry.

THE CANADIAN TOURISM HUMAN RESOURCE COUNCIL (CTHRC): A CASE STUDY

The CTHRC works on behalf of the 164,000 businesses that make up Canada's vibrant tourism sector. Established in 1993, the CTHRC promotes professionalism throughout the sector and addresses key labour market issues. Collectively, Council members and the CTHRC bring together Canadian tourism businesses, labour unions, associations, educators and governments to co-ordinate human resource development activities and contribute to a sustainable, globally competitive tourism sector. The CTHRC provides resources that include more than 50 national occupational standards as well as online and paper-based training tools. Through these and our Professional Recognition and Professional Certification programmes, the CTHRC is working with the sector to build a Canadian tourism work force that is truly world class.

Tourism is the world's largest and fastest-growing sector. It includes accommodation, food and beverage services, transportation, recreation and entertainment, and travel services. In 2006, tourism spending in Canada reached $66.9 billion and tourism's share of economy wide Gross Domestic Product (GDP) was 2.1 per cent. The total tourism sector employs 1.66 million people, or 10.1 per cent of the Canadian labour force.

Established in 1993, the Canadian Tourism Human Resource Council (CTHRC) addresses labour market issues and promotes professionalism in the Canadian tourism sector. Collectively, council members work on behalf of 164,000 businesses that make up the sector. The CTHRC brings together tourism businesses, labour unions, associations, educators and governments to coordinate human resource development activities in support of a globally competitive and sustainable Canadian tourism sector. Through its *emerit* tourism training brand, the Council provides resources that include

- More than 50 National Occupational Standards.
- Online and paper-based training tools.
- National Professional Recognition.
- Professional Certification for 26 occupations.

Through its programmes and initiatives, the Council works to build the most professional Canadian tourism work force possible. We promote the varied employment opportunities in the sector, provide resources to help individuals obtain necessary training and workplace experience and provide national recognition for the skills, knowledge and experience individuals acquire.

The Council undertakes various initiatives to capture, document and disseminate Labour Market Information (LMI) to the tourism sector. Through publications like the *Total Tourism Employment Study* and various research documents the CTHRC provides practical, detailed and timely information about the state of the Canadian tourism sector.

Through the Discover Tourism website the Council provides new Canadians, persons with disabilities, mature workers, Aboriginals and career seekers of all ages with an introduction to the tourism sector. Visit discovertourism.ca to learn about tourism myths and facts, training, career paths and so much more.

The *Ready-to-Work* programme is a national, sector-based internship programme that assists individuals by preparing them for the world of work. The programme offers a mix of classroom and on-the-job training that provides people with the skills, knowledge, attitudes and experience required for long-term stable employment in tourism.

National Professional Recognition

Branded under the new *emerit* tourism training name, professional recognition is available at various stages in the career of a tourism employee. Recognition is a way for employers to show their commitment to their employees and a way for employees to make themselves more employable. The pinnacle of recognition is National Professional Certification, an industry-recognized credential granted to candidates who successfully demonstrate competence as defined in National Occupational Standards. Currently, there are 26 certifiable tourism occupations.

Occupation-Specific Training

This training, also under the *emerit* brand, is available online and in paper-based format. Self-study workbooks and their accompanying trainer's guides take learners beyond the walls of the classroom by offering flexible, practical and comprehensive learning tools. Many occupation-specific learning tools are now available online and offer learners even greater flexibility in their training options.

Education

As the Canadian tourism sector grapples with a pending labour shortage and increased competition from other industries for the best and brightest minds, the need to attract, train and retain people is increasingly important. For this reason, ongoing dialogue and the alliance we have built with the education establishment across Canada is vital. Through education partnership and consultation the CTHRC is able to promote tourism as a viable career or job choice and influence curriculum development to ensure its relevance to the industry as a whole.

We continue to partner with the Canadian chapter of the *International Council on Hotel, Restaurant and Institutional Education* (Canada CHRIE) and the Association of Canadian Community Colleges (ACCC) on a number of initiatives. We also work closely with the Canadian Academy of Travel and Tourism (CATT) to introduce future leaders to our sector.

In addition to working with the formal education community, the Council produces career planning and awareness materials that inform career seekers about the Canadian tourism sector and the wealth of job and career opportunities the sector offers.

FAQ about CTHRC

Q. *What is the role of the Council?*

Ans. As Canada's Sector Council for the tourism sector, the CTHRC brings together industry, labour, government and education to discuss and find solutions to ongoing and pending human resource needs.

Q. *What are the main human resources challenges facing the Canadian tourism sector?*

Ans. The pool of youth to draw from is shrinking. This is a key concern for our sector because tourism has traditionally been dominated by a younger workforce. In Canada overall, 37.4 per cent workers are 34 years of age or younger whereas in tourism, 42.8 per cent fall into this category.

Turnover within the sector is an ongoing challenge. Average turnover rates in the Canadian workforce range from 20.4-22.5 per cent in the last two census periods *versus* 31.9-38.2 per cent for the tourism sector during the same periods. As an industry, we need to look at ways to decrease this turnover rate that include investing in employees through training initiatives, flexible work arrangements and the job incentives or "perks".

At the same time as the supply side of our industry (its workforce) is decreasing, the demand side is increasing. Research conducted by the Council estimates that well over 280,000 new jobs will be created in the Canadian tourism sector by the year 2015. Filling these positions will require a focus on attracting and supporting under-represented groups such as qualified immigrants, Aboriginals and recent retirees.

Q. *What training materials are available to assist with my HR needs?*

Ans. The CTHRC supplies an impressive range of occupation-specific and business "how to" products through our tourism training brand, *emerit. Emerit* products are designed to assist the industry in attracting, training and retaining its workforce. You'll find an extensive selection of online and paper-based training resources available in both French and English at http://www.emerit.ca/.

Q. *What does the CTHRC do for the Canadian tourism sector?*

Ans. Through its *emerit* training brand, the CTHRC provides training products and professional recognition programmes that help to reduce employee turnover, ensure a skilled labour force and improve quality of service by ensuring employee knowledge and performance is consistent with the appropriate *emerit* National Occupational Standards. These standards exist for over 50 tourism occupations in both official languages. They are set by the industry, for the industry and to date nearly 10,000 individuals from across Canada have been Professionally Certified in their tourism occupations.

Q. *What does the CTHRC do to prepare new entrants into the tourism workforce?*

Ans. Since 1995, the CTHRC's highly successful national preparation-for-work programme, Ready-to-Work, has introduced and trained over 10,000 individuals for a career in the tourism sector.

The Canadian Academy of Travel and Tourism, another CTHRC initiative, offers tourism courses, projects and activities as part of the high school curriculum in selected schools across Canada. Currently, 19 schools in seven provinces are involved. While the Council and industry are helping youth and other new entrants to make a fresh start, they are also helping to alleviate the problem of under-skilled workers and creating a more positive image for the Canadian tourism sector. Through participation at

Career Fairs and Expos as well as presentations across the country, the Council provides career awareness and planning information to attract people to the sector and inform them of the vast array of career options and opportunities available.

Education

As the Canadian tourism sector grapples with a pending labour shortage and increased competition from other industries for the best and brightest minds, the need to attract, train and retain people is increasingly important. For this reason, ongoing dialogue and the alliance we have built with the education establishment across Canada is vital. Through education partnership and consultation the CTHRC is able to promote tourism as a viable career or job choice and influence curriculum development to ensure its relevance to the industry as a whole.

We continue to partner with the Canadian chapter of the *International Council on Hotel, Restaurant and Institutional Education* (Canada CHRIE) and the Association of Canadian Community Colleges (ACCC) on a number of initiatives. We also work closely with the Canadian Academy of Travel & Tourism (CATT) to introduce future leaders to our sector.

In addition to working with the formal education community, the Council produces career planning and awareness materials that inform career seekers about the Canadian tourism sector and the wealth of job and career opportunities the sector offers.

MODEL COURSE ON ORGANISATIONAL BEHAVIOUR AND HRM IN THE TRAVEL AND TOURISM INDUSTRIES BY LONDON METROPOLITAN UNIVERSITY

BU2F04 Organisational Behaviour and HRM in the Travel and Tourism Industries

Module Summary

Code: BU2F04C

Title: Organisational Behaviour and HRM in the Travel and Tourism Industries.

Brief Description: The aim of this unit is to allow students to have a clear understanding of the meaning and nature of organisational behaviour and HRM, and its implications for management in the travel and tourism industries.

Semester: Autumn

Prerequisite: None

Assessment: In course assessment (40%), and an unseen examination (60%)

Summary Description of Assessment Items

Assessment Type	*Description of Item*	*% Weighting*	*Qual Mark*	*Qual Set*	*Tariff*	*Week Due*
CWK	Using a variety of approaches such as a case study or a number of individual questions with an essay type answer.	40	–	–	–	12
EXU	Unseen examination	60	–	–	–	–

Module Aims

The principal Graduate Attributes developed by this module are A1, A2 and A3.

1. The aims of this unit is to allow students to have a clear understanding of the meaning and nature of organisational behaviour and HRM, and its implications for management in the travel and tourism industries.
2. The unit seeks to develop an understanding of the behaviour of people, through the analysis of individual processes at work.
3. The unit also aims to develop knowledge of groups and group processes and in turn relate these to leadership and conflict resolution.
4. To give students an appreciation of interpersonal processes such as motivation and their impact on people within the organisation.
5. To develop an understanding of individual differences such as personality and learning and their impact upon the recruitment, selection and retention of individuals.
6. To develop in students an awareness and understanding of contracts of employment including the psychological

contract and its implications for flexibility and employee relations.

7. To allow students to gain knowledge of techniques for effective communication in a range of work related situations.
8. To allow students to appreciate the range of HRM involvement from human resource planning to appraisal.

Syllabus

- Management approaches: scientific-human relations.
- Organisational Structures and culture.
- Motivation theories and management practice.
- Groups and group dynamics.
- Flexibility within the work place.
- Personnel management/HRM/International HRM.
- Recruitment, selection and retention.
- Contracts of employment.
- Role of HRM department.
- Effective communications.

Learning and Teaching

Delivery will mostly be in the form of one-hour lectures to cover key areas of the syllabus. The one-hour tutorials will use a range of student centred approaches such as case studies, role-play exercises, videos and presentations.

Learning Outcomes

Upon completion of the unit the student should be able to:

1. Understand the contributions of theorists, such as Taylor, Fayol and behavioural science to management and their use in appreciating how human behaviour is influenced in organisations. [A2]
2. Define what is meant by motivation and explain how it can be used to influence the contribution and performance of individuals and groups working in the travel and tourism industry. [A2]

3. Understand the nature of service industries and appreciate the challenges of managing and motivating a diverse workforce operating in a range of environments such as the back office, front office, and in the field. [A1, A2]
4. Understand and recognise the importance of leadership and good communications, including how to recognise barriers to good communication. [A1, A2]
5. Identify differences in personality and learning approach including how to overcome barriers to learning and the contribution learning makes to organisational effectiveness. [A1, A2]
6. Recognise the importance of contracts of employment in the travel and tourism industry, and especially the psychological contract. [A1, A2, A3]
7. Apply the procedures and skills associated with the major areas of HRM for example recruitment, selection, retention, appraisal and grievance/disciplinary handling to the travel and tourism industry. [A1, A3]
8. Appreciate how personality, personal-, and social costs and benefits, and the seasonal nature of the sector affect recruitment and retention in the travel and tourism industry. [A1, A2]

Assessment Strategy

In course assessment: 40 per cent course work based, using a variety of approaches such as a case study or a number of individual questions with an essay type answer.

The end of semester exam will comprise an unseen examination. This element will account for the remaining 60 per cent of the overall unit assessment.

NEW ZEALAND TOURISM RESEARCH INSTITUTE (NZTRI)

The New Zealand Tourism Research Institute, based at the Auckland University of Technology, brings together experts in the tourism and hospitality arena. Our goal is to develop timely and innovative research solutions for the tourism industry and those who depend on it. Our focus is on helping to develop a profitable and sustainable industry which provides tangible benefits for business, residents and visitors. The strategic role of HRM in SME performance: The case of accommodations sector in New Zealand.

The past two decades have witnessed a significant growth of tourism in New Zealand and many other countries. As a vital component of the tourism industry, the accommodation sector is attracting increased research interest. The accommodation sector in New Zealand is largely made up of Small and Medium Enterprises (SME) employing less than 20 staff. It is estimated that there are some 2,000 small and medium accommodation businesses in this country.

KERALA TOURISM LAUNCHES 'LET'S LEARN': CASE STUDY OF AN INDIAN HR INITIATIVE

The tourism season is just a few months away and the Tourism Department has launched its novel initiative for skill up gradation in the sector. Through Let's Learn, the department has started a first-of-its-kind HR initiative in the industry.

The programme incorporates learning modules, both for hospitality and tour operations, aimed at brushing up communication and inter-personal skills and improving services and operations of everyone involved in the sector.

Primarily an orientation programme, Let's Learn has modules designed by institutions such as Kerala Institute of Tourism and Travel Studies (KITTS) and Institute of Hotel Management and Catering Technology (IHMCT).

"The state has emerged as a leader in the tourism sector. We need to maintain it and Let's Learn would help us to be up there. In fact, the government is giving a platform for all players in the field to upgrade their standards. Therefore, the onus is on the employers to help their staff make use of it," V. Venu, Tourism Secretary, said.

The programme falls under Synergy, the latest public-private sector partnership in tourism.

The modules in hospitality section include sessions for front office, food and beverage services and guest handling. Those for tour operations cover travel counselling, tour executives and senior/middle level executives.

The duration and content of the programmes vary according to the nature of service of the participants. Advertisements to this effect have already been placed and communication has already been sent to all the players in the hotel, tourism and travel industry.

The modules will be repeated depending on the number of participants. The department plans to hold sessions in Thiruvananthapuram, Kochi and Kozhikode for the convenience of the participants.

"Let's Learn has originally been designed as an annual programme for the months of July and August. We are waiting to knowhow the industry is going to react to it," Venu said.

"Since experts will be handling the sessions, the participants will get an update about the changing scenario. Meanwhile, the schedule will be announced depending on the response we get for the initiative," said a faculty with KITTS.

5

Towards Integrated HRM in the Tourism and Hospitality Industry

The importance of tourism and hospitality employment in both developed and developing countries is attested to by the World Travel and Tourism Council (WTTC), who suggest that travel-and tourism-related activities account for over 230 million jobs, or 8.7 per cent of jobs worldwide (WTTC, 2006). However, whilst the quantity of jobs is unquestionable, the *quality* of many of these jobs is of great concern to academics and policy-makers alike. Despite the rhetoric of policy-makers and business leaders that people are the industry's most important asset, many remain unconvinced that such a view is borne out by empirical evidence. For example, Douglas Coupland, the notable cultural commentator, has for many captured the *zeitgeist* when he talks pejoratively of 'McJob' which he describes as, 'Alow-pay, low-prestige, low-dignity, low-benefit, no-future job in the service sector.' Frequently considered a satisfying career choice by people who have never held one' (Coupland, 1993: 5; and see also Lindsay and McQuaid, 2004). MacDonald and Sirianni (1996) recognize the challenges of living and working in a service society which, according to them, is characterized by two kinds of service jobs: large numbers of low-skill, low-pay jobs and a smaller number of high-skill, high-income jobs, with few jobs being in the middle of these two extremes. Such a situation leads labour analysts to ask what kinds of jobs are being produced and who is filling them. This point is also true for the tourism and hospitality industry and it is important at the outset of this book to add a caveat about the generalizability (or otherwise) of the conditions of tourism and hospitality employment worldwide. Hence Baum (1995: 151) reflecting the diversity of employment within the sector notes that:

> In some geographical and sub-sector areas, tourism and hospitality provides an attractive, high-status working environment with competitive pay and conditions, which is in high demand in the labour force and benefits from low staff turnover...The other side of the coin is one of poor conditions, low pay, high staff turnover, problems in recruiting skills in a number of key areas, a high level of labour drawn from socially disadvantaged groups, poor status and the virtual absence of professionalism.

Organizations and managers in the tourism and hospitality industry face real challenges in recruiting, developing and maintaining a committed, competent, well-managed and well-motivated workforce which is focused on offering a high-quality 'product' to the increasingly demanding and discerning customer. This book seeks to address some of the key Human Resource (HR) issues that have to be tackled in order that organizations can maintain such an environment. To do so it will critically review some of the problems which lead many to characterize tourism and hospitality employment as generally unrewarding and unappealing, whilst also considering examples of good practice, important policy responses and models of HRM which may offer cause for greater optimism in the way people are managed within the tourism and hospitality industry.

Many academics, industrialists and policy-makers have attempted to define the nature of the tourism industry—and the place of the hospitality sub-sector within this broader conceptualization—yet there is still no one commonly accepted definition. Hence, there are inherent problems seeking to define what is a large and diverse sector, which means many of the activities may overlap, and could be described as encompassing tourism and hospitality. For example, Lucas (2004) in her recent work on employment relations in the hospitality and tourism industries chose to talk in broad terms about the Hotel, Catering and Tourism Sector (HCTS). This characterization of the HCTS recognizes that, in reality, many jobs in hospitality and tourism, 'share common attributes and are associated with both hospitality and tourism activities' (p. 4). Clearly, then, we should recognize the potential for a lack of precision in describing the tourism and hospitality industries.

In an attempt to avoid too much imprecision and, at the same time, capture the diversity of the sector this book uses the framework offered by People 1st, which is the Sector Skills Council (SSC) for the hospitality, leisure, travel and tourism sector, to exemplify the broad range of activities that may be seen in the HCTS. The reason for using People 1st is that SSCs are the government-licensed bodies in the UK responsible for improving skills within the industry. SSCs are employer led and amongst other things aim to be the voice of industry on skills matters and encourage best practice approaches to employment. Therefore, People 1st suggest that the sector as a whole is made up of 14 sub-sectors (People 1st, 2006):

- hotels;
- restaurants;
- pubs, bars and night-clubs;
- contract food service providers;
- membership clubs;
- events;
- gambling;
- travel services;
- tourist services;
- visitor attractions;
- youth hostels;
- holiday parks;
- self-catering accommodation; and
- hospitality services.

Moreover, within this broad classification of travel, tourism and hospitality there is massive diversity in the types of jobs generated, in relation to their technical and skills' demands, educational requirements, terms and conditions and the type of person that is likely to be attracted to employment in them. To illustrate this point we can consider Baum's (1997: 97-98) description of the range of people a person buying a package holiday is likely to interact with:

- the retail travel agent;
- insurance companies;
- ground transport to and from the airport;

- at least two sets of airport handling agents (outbound and return);
- airport services (shops, food and beverage outlets, bureaux de change) (outbound and return);
- the airline on all legs of the journey;
- immigration and customs services;
- local ground transportation;
- the hotel or apartment;
- tour services at the destination;
- companies and individuals selling a diversity of goods and services at the destination (retail, food and beverage, entertainment, cultural and heritage, financial, etc.);
- emergency services at the destination (medical, police, legal); and
- service providers on return (photography processing, medical).

Baum characterizes all of these possible intermediaries, and the interactions they will have with the holiday maker, as crucial in 'making or breaking the tourist experience'. Thus, while the physical product is important, for most tourists the quality of their experience is likely to be also reliant to a large degree on the interactions they will have with the variety of front-line staff in the travel, tourism and hospitality industry. These so-called 'moments of truth' (Carlzon, 1987) are therefore crucial for organizational effectiveness, success, competitiveness and profitability. Indeed, within an industry that is characterized by diversity and heterogeneity in terms of the purpose, size, ownership and demands of the enterprise, the only real point of homogeneity is delivering service to customers and the need to manage people in such a way that they offer a quality service. The corollary of this point would be the belief that such front-line staff would therefore be sufficiently well paid, trained and motivated to offer outstanding service. The reality however is that often such staff have the lowest status in the organization, are the least trained, and are the poorest paid employees of the company.

In recognizing the diversity both of the range of sub-sectors and types of jobs they are likely to generate, this book cannot consider all of these aspects in detail. Indeed, more is known about employment in certain sub-sectors than others. For example, the commercial hospitality industry encompassing hotels, restaurants and pubs, bars and nightclubs is the largest sub-sector with around 70 per cent of employees in the UK (People 1st, 2006). Unsurprisingly, then, the commercial hospitality industry is well served with extensive research on the nature of employment and HRM strategies (D'Annunzio-Green *et al.*, 2002; Lucas, 2004). On the other hand, little has been written on the events industry or the nature of HRM in youth hostels, for example. As a consequence many of the examples drawn on in this book are from the commercial hospitality industry, although, where possible, illustrations of organizational practice from travel and tourism organizations are also used. Ultimately, the main aim of the book is to attempt to understand the potentially diverse employment experience of those working in what we will broadly think of as the tourism and hospitality industries. Thus, how does the experience of an airline flight attendant differ from that of a pot washer in the kitchen in a small restaurant to a receptionist in the front desk of an international hotel or to a tour rep working on an 18-30-type holiday?

A further issue to consider is the manner in which the sector is heterogeneous in terms of the predominance of Small-and Medium-sized Enterprises (SMEs). People 1st (2006) note that within the UK hospitality, leisure, travel and tourism sector 76 per cent of establishments employ fewer than ten people and 50 per cent fewer than five. Heterogeneity is also seen in relation to the way that organizations adopt differing routes to competitive advantage, depending on which type of market they operate in. For example, full service carriers in the airline industry are likely to have very different approaches to HRM compared to low-cost airlines (Eaton, 2001; Spiess and Waring, 2005). The same is true for the hospitality sector, which may range from first class and luxury hotels providing extravagant, full 24-hour service to the more homely comforts of a bed and breakfast establishment; from fast food restaurants to Michelin starred restaurants. In turn, the jobs provided by these various organizations demand a variety of skills and attributes from those employees interacting with customers, which again will impact on HR strategies such as recruitment and selection and training.

The International Labour Organization (ILO, 2001) in their wide-ranging report on the global tourism and hospitality industry provides evidence that suggests that the industry globally is largely reliant on what Wood (1997) has described as so-called 'marginal workers', such as women, young workers, casual employees, students, relatively high numbers of part-timers and migrant workers. For example, within the UK women make up around 58 per cent of the broader hospitality, leisure, travel and tourism workforce (People 1st, 2006). More specifically, the hospitality sub-sector is indicative of the broader sector in having a higher proportion of part-time employees (52%) than most other industries with the all industry figure being 25 per cent (HtF, 2003). Young people are also prominent within the hospitality, leisure, travel and tourism sector. For example, 37 per cent of the total UK workforce is under 24 years and 58 per cent under 34 years (People 1st, 2006). Related to this last point a significant part of the tourism and hospitality workforce consists of student, seasonal and migrant workers. Students are an increasingly important segment of the labour market for hospitality and tourism organizations (ILO, 2001). They are prepared to work for low wages and be flexible in their working patterns (Canny, 2002), creating what Curtis and Lucas (2001) describe as a 'coincidence of needs' between employers and students. Thus, nearly three quarters of all students who are working are employed in the retail and hospitality industries and the vast majority of students who are working do so in front-line jobs such as sales assistants, waiters/waitresses and check out operators (Curtis and Lucas, 2001; Canny, 2002). The number of ethnic minority workers in the broader hospitality, leisure, travel and tourism sector is 11 per cent, slightly higher than the all industry figure of 9.6 per cent (People 1st, 2006). With regard to qualifications only 12 per cent of employees in hospitality, leisure, travel and tourism have a degree or equivalent compared to an all industry figure of 29 per cent, with 15 per cent of the workforce having no qualification compared to 11 per cent of the total workforce (People 1st, 2006).

Having briefly considered the nature of the hospitality and tourism industry and the characteristics of its workforce attention now turns to understanding HRM and the increasingly important role it is felt to play in organizational success.

HRM: AN OVERVIEW

There have been many attempts to define what exactly HRM might be and indeed Heery and Noon (2001) recognize that it is a subject of considerable academic analysis and that, ultimately, 'there is no common agreement on what HRM means' (p. 161). Resultantly, they offer 10 definitions, which they feel capture the complexity and dynamism of HRM as a subject of academic study:

- *A label* HRM is seen as simply being another name for personnel management and there is nothing distinct or special about HRM.
- *A convenient shorthand term* that allows for the grouping together of a whole series of sub-disciplines that are broadly concerned with people management: such as employee relations, industrial/labour relations, personnel management and organizational behaviour.
- *A map* to help guide students and practitioners to understand the concept and ideas associated with the management of people.
- *A set of professional practices* suggests that there are a range of personnel practices that can be integrated to ensure a professional approach to managing people. In this view a potentially key role is likely to be played by the Chartered Institute for Personnel and Development (CIPD), which is the professional association for those entering the HR and personnel profession.
- *A method of ensuring internal fit* again sees the need to co-ordinate approaches to people management, but here the co-ordination needs to be with other areas of the organization.
- *A method of ensuring external fit* where HRM activities have to be fully integrated with the demands of the external environment.
- *A competitive advantage* where HRM is the means by which an organization can gain competitive advantage, a view best captured by the cliché of 'our people are our greatest asset.'
- *A market-driven approach* is that decisions will often be market driven and the needs of the business determine

the manner in which employees are treated; some may be treated well, others less so well.

- *A manipulative device* sees it as inherently exploitative and manipulative.
- *A hologram* captures much of the above discussion in recognizing the fluid identity of HRM and the fact that it has multiple meanings.

Clearly what the above discussion points to is that HRM means many things to many people, depending on whether you are a manager, an employee or an academic and there is no one definition that will adequately capture the potential complexity of the topic.

That said, for the purposes of this book we will recognize HRM as being broadly about how organizations seek to manage their employees in the pursuit of organizational success. Reflecting this point the book utilizes the concise definition offered by Storey (1995: 5). Thus, HRM 'is a distinctive approach to employment management which seeks to achieve competitive advantage through the strategic deployment of a highly committed and capable workforce, using an integrated array of cultural, structural and personnel techniques'. The challenge of HRM then would seem to be how to recruit, deploy, develop, reward and motivate staff, leading to them being a source of competitive advantage. As the above discussion suggests, however, there is more than one route to seeking competitive advantage and this point is further considered in examining the notion of 'hard' and 'soft' HRM.

Hard vs. Soft

As well as providing the concise definition utilized above, Storey (1987) also provided one of the earliest and most enduring attempts to recognize different approaches to HRM. These different approaches are captured by the idea of hard and soft HRM, each of which are now briefly described. The *hard* version is seen to be an instrumental and economically rational approach to HRM. In this view people management strategies are driven by strategic considerations to gain competitive advantage, maximizing control while achieving the lowest possible labour cost. This approach is quantitative and calculative and labour is a commodity/resource, the same as any other. The focus is on HRM. On the other hand, the *soft* version is seen to be much more about adopting a humanistic and developmental approach to HRM. As a result an organization's people management approach is likely to be more consensual and based on a high level of managerial commitment to employees, which is intended to lead to mutual high commitment from employees, high trust, high productivity and so on. Employees are seen as being proactive, capable of being developed and worthy of trust and collaboration. This approach focuses on HRM.

What hard and soft approaches to HRM point to is that employers will vary their people management strategies. Clearly as well there are likely to be a number of external influences as HRM in practice 1.1 suggests. These external influences will reflect a variety of political, social, economic and technological aspects which will have an effect on HRM policies and practices. Hard and soft HRM point to the manner then in which organizations can vary their approaches to HRM and as a result the impact on employees may vary. A similar attempt to recognize that there may be different approaches to HRM is also seen in the debate over whether organizations should aim to achieve 'best fit' or 'best practice'.

HRM IN PRACTICE 1: HARD AND SOFT APPROACHES TO HRM IN THE AIRLINE INDUSTRY

The tourism and hospitality industry is particularly sensitive to economic cycles and political trouble and can be badly affected in times of uncertainty. For example, the global nature of the industry means that it is vulnerable to external events that cause fluctuations in tourist visits and spend. The global 2001-04 economic downturn, 9/11, the Iraq war and the outbreak of SARS in the Far East all led to a drop in revenue in the industry. These factors reduced the number of travellers internationally and left uncertainty and fragility in the tourism market. Many of these aspects are particularly pronounced in the airline industry and trade unions have often railed against the manner in which employees are used as 'shock absorbers' to protect the industry from the cyclical nature of the market. These hard approaches to HRM have seen major redundancy programmes in a number of airlines in recent years, especially after 9/11. On the other hand, a number of companies have sought a more soft approach to HRM which aimed at increasing the customer responsiveness of their front-line staff. British Airways, for example, had a series of initiatives in the 1980s and 1990s such as 'Putting People First' and 'Winning for Customers'. Amongst other things these initiatives sought to introduce team working, extensive training programmes, enhance quality procedures and multi-skill staff. As companies alternate between hard and soft approaches to HRM employees may become confused as to what the company message is. Ultimately, employees may well be a company's 'greatest asset', but in times of uncertainty and downturn are equally expendable as recent history suggests.

Best Fit vs. Best Practice

Boxall and Purcell (2000) suggest that attempts to understand the way in which organizations approach the management of their HR can be seen with regard to whether they aim for 'best fit' or 'best practice'. On the one hand, the best fit school argues for an approach to HRM, which is fully integrated with the specific organizational and environmental context in which they operate. On the other hand, best practice advocates argue for a universalistic approach to HRM where all firms who adopt a range of agreed HR policies and practices are more likely to create a high-performance/commitment workplace, as organizations aim to compete on the basis of high quality and productivity.

Best Fit

One of the earliest and most influential attempts to develop a model that recognized the need for a fit between the competitive strategy and HRM was that offered by Schuler and Jackson (1987). Schuler and Jackson developed a series of typologies of 'needed role behaviours' that enabled the link between competitive strategy and HRM practices to be made. The type of needed role behaviours within Schuler and Jackson's model was contingent on the overall strategies that an organization could adopt to seek competitive advantage and the HRM approached adopted to sustain this.

First, there is an *innovation* strategy, where organizations seek to develop products or services that are different from competitors, such that the focus here is on companies offering something new and different. Organizations adopting this approach seek to develop an environment where innovation is allowed to flourish. Resultantly, the employee needed role behaviour in such a scenario is characterized by things like a willingness to tolerate ambiguity and unpredictability, the need to be creative and risk taking. Given these characteristics the type of HRM strategy flowing from this approach is based on having a large number of highly skilled individuals who are likely to enjoy high levels of autonomy. Second, is the *quality enhancement* strategy wherein firms seek to gain competitive advantage by enhancing the product and/or service quality. The approach once again points to certain HRM practices to support a total-quality approach. These practices include the encouragement of feedback systems, teamwork, decision-making and responsibility being an integral part of an employee's job description and flexible job classifications. The intent of these practices is to create needed employee behaviour such as co-operative, interdependent behaviour and commitment to the goals of the organization. Lastly, the *cost reduction strategy* sees firms attempting to gain competitive advantage by aiming to be the lowest-cost producer within a particular market segment. The characteristics of firms seeking to pursue this strategy are tight controls, minimization of overheads and pursuit of economies of scale, in the pursuit of increased productivity. In following such a strategy organizations may use higher number of part-timers, seek to simplify and measure work *via* narrowly defined jobs that encourage specialization and efficiency, and offer short-term results oriented appraisal. Needed employee behaviours include, repetitive and predictable behaviour, low-risk taking activity and a high degree of comfort with stability.

This support for the importance of HRM practices 'fitting' the organizations own strategically defined market segment to create a fit between the functional areas of marketing, operations and HRM is also seen in the work of Lashley and Taylor (1998). Lashley and Taylor describe four basic archetypes within which tourism and hospitality organizations can be potentially located. These archetypes are the service factory, the service shop, mass service and professional services. These characterizations are based on the degree of customization and labour intensity involved in the service offer, in terms of the degree of customer contact required between employees and customers.

The service factory is relatively low labour intensity and low customization (i.e., high standardization). The service factory is most obviously exemplified by fast food operators, especially McDonald's. The service shop involves more customization, but relatively low labour intensity. The defining difference to the service factory lies in the degree of standardization within the process. Lashley and Taylor draw upon the example of TGI Fridays to argue that although there are high levels of standardization in the tangible aspects of the organization, such as the menus, layouts, décor and staff uniform, there is also some scope to customize the customers' eating and drinking experience. This customization is by virtue of their more extensive menu, and more importantly, greater spontaneity and authenticity in the intangible aspects of the service provided by front-line staff. The next classification is mass service where service processes involve a relatively high degree of labour intensity, though a limited amount of customization. Lashley and Taylor assert that the Marriott hotel brand typifies a mass service organization, as their four star offering is similar to others in relation to the tangibles reflecting the highly competitive nature of the mid to upper segment of the hotel market. As a result of this convergence of the tangibles the key lies in the intangibles and the scope available to organizations to differentiate themselves on the basis of service quality. Within this process of differentiation a key role is played by the staff *via* the relatively high level of contact with customers. The final grouping is professional services where there is a high level of service to individual customers and a high degree of labour intensity, as exemplified by hospitality management consultants.

The key point which emerges from the work of Lashley and Taylor is the likely relationship between the service operation type adopted by the organization and the style of HRM which best fits it. For example, it is apparent that in the four star hotel sector a broadly soft approach to HRM, as exemplified by high discretion in relation to the intangibles, moral involvement and a moderate trust culture, is suggested as being important to sustain a high quality, Total Quality Management (TQM) based approach to the service offering. At the other end of the spectrum, McDonald's are suggested as exemplifying a command and control style which is characterized by things such as low discretion for employees, limited responsibility and autonomy, and scripted service encounters. Importantly, Lashley and Taylor (1998: 161) see the command and control approach as being right for what McDonald's are aiming to offer their customers:

> ...the historic success of the McDonald's organization in delivering their market offer...is partly due to the ability to develop and maintain a close fit between the key characteristics of the strategic drivers and actual service delivery through utilization of an appropriate HRM style.

The key point remains that organizations in developing a certain product market strategy then ensure that their HR policies and practices are congruent and cost effective with this strategy.

Best Practice

Whilst arguments for best fit advocate a close fit between competitive strategies and HRM, those in favour of best practice approaches to HRM suggest that there is a universal 'one best way' to manage people. By adopting a best practice approach it is argued that organizations will see enhanced commitment from employees leading to improved organizational performance, higher levels of service quality and ultimately increases in productivity and profitability. Usually couched in terms of 'bundles', the HRM practices that are offered in support of a high commitment and performance model are generally fairly consistent. For example, Redman and Matthews (1998) outline a range of HR practices which are suggested as being important to organizational strategies aimed at securing high-quality service:

- *Recruitment and Selection*: Recruiting and selecting staff with the correct attitudinal and behavioural characteristics. A range of assessments in the selection process should be utilized to evaluate the work values, personality, interpersonal skills and problem-solving abilities of potential employees to assess their 'service orientation.'

- *Retention*: The need to avoid the development of a 'turnover culture', which may of course be particularly prevalent in tourism and hospitality. For example, the use of 'retention bonuses' to influence employees to stay.
- *Teamwork*: The use of semi-autonomous, cross-process and multi-functional teams.
- *Training and development*: The need to equip operative level staff with team working and interpersonal skills to develop their 'service orientation' and managers with a new leadership style which encourages a move to a more facilitative and coaching style of managing.
- *Appraisal*: Moving away from traditional top down approaches to appraisal and supporting things such as customer evaluation, peer review, team-based performance and the appraisal of managers by sub-ordinates. Generally, all of these performance appraisal systems should focus on the quality goals of the organization and the behaviours of employees needed to sustain these.
- *Rewarding quality*: A need for a much more creative system of rewards and in particular the need to payment systems that reward employees for attaining quality goals.
- *Job security*: Promises of job security are seen as an essential component of any overall quality approach.
- *Employee involvement and employee relations*: By seeking greater involvement from employees the emphasis is on offering autonomy, creativity, co-operation and self-control in work processes. The use of educative and participative mechanisms, such as team briefings and quality circles are allied to changes in the organization of work which support an 'empowered' environment.

In simple terms best practice is likely to entail attempts to enhance the skills base of employees through HR activities such as selective staffing, comprehensive training and broad developmental efforts like job rotation. Additionally, it also encourages empowerment, participative problem-solving; teamwork as well as performance-based incentives.

Models or Reality

Of course, ideal types and academic models may not always reflect the complex reality of what really goes on in tourism and hospitality organizations. Schuler and Jackson, for instance, freely admit the description of their three competitive strategies as pure types often does not reflect the reality of, for example, organizations pursuing two or more competitive strategies simultaneously. The same point can also be made with regard to hard and soft HRM; it is not uncommon for organizations to vary their approaches to employees depending on any given practice. For example, with regard to labour flexibility the use of numerical flexibility may well-reflect fairly hard approaches to HRM, whilst functional flexibility and multiskilling exemplifies a much softer approach. A further issue is the predominance of SMEs in tourism and hospitality. It is often suggested that their small scale means that they are unlikely to have the necessary means to employ the kind of HRM expertize to develop sophisticated soft approaches, for example. Nevertheless, they are still likely to require HR policies that require at least some thought with regard to their business circumstances.

Whilst some understanding of debate about soft and hard and best fit and best practice are important to place HR practices within a broader theoretical context, in reality, regardless of these various ideal types all organizations have to manage employees on a day-to-day basis. We can illustrate this in Figure 5.1, which outlines the notion of an HRM cycle.

Figure 5.1 is useful in allowing us to appreciate that these broad aspects of attracting, maintaining and developing a workforce are constant and that organizations and managers, both specialist HR and line managers, are wrestling with HR issues on a day-to-day basis. However, whilst a number of the functional aspects of HRM are unlikely to differ, the manner in which organizations actually develop their overall strategy will. In these circumstances models that allow for recognition of differing strategic intent in HRM are still useful in allowing us to appreciate why and how companies differ in their approaches to HRM in tourism and hospitality. It would be naïve to imagine we could talk in very broad terms about HRM in tourism in hospitality. The reality is far too complex and as we have already noted the employment experience for employees can vary enormously depending on the type of

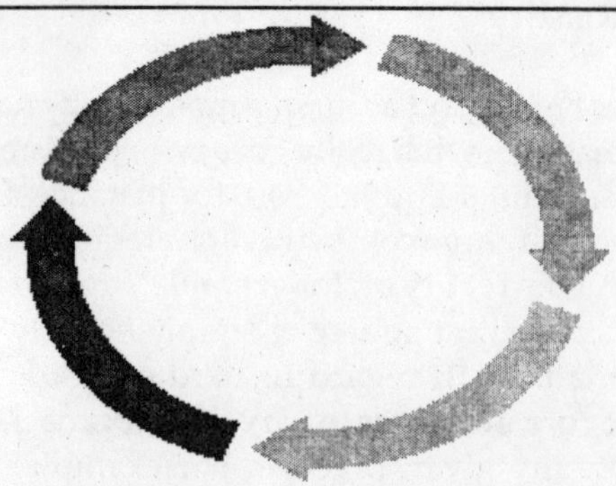

- **Attract an effective workforce**
  - HR planning/labour markets
  - Recruitment and selection
- **Maintain an effective workforce**
  - Rewards and welfare
  - Labour relations (e.g. the role of trade unions)
  - Grievance and disciplinary procedures
- **Develop an effective workforce**
  - Training and development
  - Appraisal

Figure 5.1: The HRM Cycle.

organization they work in and the job or role they have within their organizations. With this recognition, we should consider the key question: so what does HRM in hospitality and tourism look like? Reflecting some of our earlier discussion of hard and soft and best fit and practice we can also crudely distinguish between those who argue for a pessimistic view of HRM in the sector and those who suggest that increasingly organizations are seeking a much more progressive approach to managing their employees.

Pessimistic Views of HRM in Tourism and Hospitality

Generally tourism and hospitality has often struggled with negative perceptions about employment practices and conditions and this perception has often been matched by the reality. Keep and Mayhew (1999) for example in their review of the skills issue in the tourism and hospitality industry suggest the industry has a number of personnel problems, including:

- generally low wages, unless skill shortages act to counter this (e.g. chefs);
- unsocial hours and shift patterns that are not family friendly;
- over representation of women and ethnic minorities in low-level operative positions, with better paid, higher status and more skilled jobs filled by men, pointing to undeveloped equal opportunities policies in the sector;
- poor or non-existent career structures and use of casualized seasonal employment;
- over reliance on informal recruitment methods;
- lack of evidence of good practice personnel/HRM practices;
- little or no trade union presence;
- high levels of labour turnover; and
- difficulties in recruitment and retention of employees.

Recognizing this reality of poor employment practices, Riley *et al.* (2000) argue that economics is the key determining factor for HRM policies and practices in tourism and hospitality. Of course, this point is likely to be true of any industry, but as Riley *et al.*, point out it carries a particular resonance in tourism and hospitality, due to the nature of the sector. That is not to say that organizations and managers in the industry are not well aware of new managerial thinking on HRM. However, they also find themselves wrestling with 'traditional problems', which are underpinned by 'fundamental labour economic imperatives' (p. 120). Importantly, these problems limit managerial actions and this leads Riley *et al.*, to argue the behaviour of managers is determined 'by the structures and forms under which they live' (p. 119). This economic imperative creates a short-term perspective on managerial decision-making and strategy in relation to HRM, and also means that management are more likely to deploy a weak internal labour market. An obvious impact of this is that HRM concerns of tourism and hospitality organizations are constantly directed to short-term responses to issues such as recruitment, selection and basic training, rather than more long-term areas which could conceivably offer more development and career progression for existing employees.

Another reason for continuing pessimism is the general attitude of employers and particularly the extent to which they are willing to recognize the extent of the HRM problem in the sector. The DfEE (2000) registers with some incredulity the awareness of low pay, for example, existing alongside the naïve view of employers of tourism and hospitality as a 'good' employing sector. Thus, although in a number of locations labour shortages were clearly reflective of an unwillingness of employers to offer competitive pay and terms of conditions of employment, the DfEE (2000: 35) notes how, "we were struck by the extent to which employers described pay and working conditions as reasonable or even 'good' while at the same time reporting extensive recruitment problems, skills gaps and labour turnover.' This disjuncture between the views of employers and employees is also noted by the ILO in a recent report on the international tourism industry. They recognize how:

> Employers' representatives generally consider that the turnover in the industry should be attributed to the essentially transient nature of part of the workforce, namely students, young mothers and young people as a whole, as well as the general difficulty in retaining staff. Employees, on the other hand, frequently cite low pay as a reason for changing employment, though a lack of career structure and benefits would appear to be of even greater importance (ILO, 2001: 6).

This inability by industry to recognize the most glaring of issues is long standing and can also be seen in relation to things like a degree of hostility and opposition from the employers associations in the industry, such as the British Hospitality Association (BHA), to governmental initiatives such as the minimum wage and working time directive. The BHA still remains unsure of the benefits of such initiatives, despite support from others who argue these initiatives are likely to have a potentially positive impact on the industry (e.g. see Lucas, 2004).

Given the above discussion it is unsurprising to see a long history of support for the proposition that tourism and hospitality remains a poor employing sector. From Orwell's *Down and Out in Paris and London* in the 1930s to recent work by the likes of Price (1994), Kelliher and Perrett (2001), Kelliher and Johnson (1997) and McGunnigle and Jameson (2000), the dominant paradigm has tended to stress the negative aspects of working in the sector. For example, McGunnigle and Jameson surveyed a selected number of hotels from the top 50 hotel groups ranked by ownership of bedroom stock, which were considered to be most likely to exhibit good practice HRM. Despite this they concluded, 'This study suggests that there is little adoption of HRM philosophy in corporately owned hotels in the UK sample...[and hospitality]...has a long way to go before it can claim that it is encouraging a 'culture of commitment' (*ibid.*, p. 416). Similarly, Kelliher and Perrett (2001), drawing explicitly on Schuler and Jackson's typology, develop a case study analysis of a 'designer restaurant'. Such a restaurant might be though of as potentially developing a more sophisticated approach to HRM as they sought to differentiate themselves from chain establishments such as Hard Rock Café and TGI Friday's. However, although the restaurant had moved to a more sophisticated approach to HRM in areas like planning, training and development and appraisal, and ostensibly sought an 'innovation' strategy, 'there was little real evidence that human resources were seen as a source of competitive advantage' (p. 434). Instead, the HRM approaches adopted by the restaurant were much more reflective of immediate environmental constraints, such as the difficulties in recruiting and retaining staff.

In sum, any number of reasons may account for poor personnel practice in the tourism and hospitality industry. Economic determinism, the predominance of SMEs, a low-skills base, employer antipathy to a more progressive approach to HRM, labour market characteristics, organizations ensuring best fit HRM practices to support a high volume, low-cost strategy; all are plausible reasons for a view of HRM which is not necessarily premised on high-skills, high-wages and a high-quality route to competitive advantage. That said, it would be equally wrong to paint a wholly pessimistic picture. It was recognized earlier in the chapter that there are also examples of good practice HRM, particularly in certain sub-sectors of the industry and in market segments where organizations are likely to seek differentiation on the basis of offering high-quality services.

Best Practice in Tourism and Hospitality

Some of the most important work to emerge in recent years on the question of the extent of good practice in the HCTS is the work of Hoque (2000). Based on his work on the hotel sector, he argues that arguments which portray the industry as backward and unstrategic are now outdated, at least where larger hotel establishments are concerned. Indeed, he suggests that 'it is perhaps time researchers stopped highlighting the example of 'bad management' and branding the industry as under-developed or backward, and started identifying approaches to hotel management capable of generating high performance" (2000: 154). The research conducted by Hoque consists of a questionnaire-based survey of 232 hotels and a number of follow-up interviews conducted in targeted hotels, based on the results of the survey.

Based on this research he discusses three key issues. First, the extent to which hotels have experimented with new approaches to HRM. Secondly, the factors that influence HRM decision-making and whether these factors are any different in the hotel industry compared to elsewhere. Finally, he reviewed the relationship between HRM and performance in the hotel industry. Hoque is able to claim that, compared to a sample of over 300 greenfield-site manufacturing establishments, the hotels in his sample where utilizing a number of practices that were very similar to best practice. Indeed, in illustrating the manner in which academic models can, in reality, overlap it is also worth noting that there is significant overlap between Schuler and Jackson's quality enhancement and innovation approaches with much of the 'best practice' approaches. This point about such overlap is further illustrated in HRM in practice 1.2.

Hoque's work remains useful in offering a description of organizational practices that support a professional, high-quality approach to service. That said, there are a number of criticisms that can be levelled at the research (Nickson and Wood, 2000). As Hoque himself recognizes his sample of hotels is large by industry standards, averaging 125 employees per unit compared to an industry 'standard' of 81 per cent of establishments employing fewer than 25 people, and thus as Hoque (2000: 51) himself recognizes 'patently unrepresentative of the industry as a whole'. Furthermore his reliance on city-centre hotels with a high proportion of corporate clients is equally unrepresentative. Lastly, the reliance on managerial voices in his research, to the exclusion of those on the receiving end of many of the initiatives described (i.e. employees), may be considered an important omission. To be fair, Hoque's exclusive reliance on managerial voices is not unique and is shared by much of the literature on HRM. The key point emerging from the work of the likes of Redman and Matthews and Hoque is what good practice HRM is likely to look like in the tourism and hospitality industry.

HRM IN PRACTICE 2 : THE HRM QUALITY ENHANCER HOTEL

The hotel in Hoque's (2000) research, which is termed the HRM quality enhancer hotel, employed 140 staff and was part of a large international chain. In relation to their approach to HRM a number of practices were prominent in the hotel. Recruitment and selection emphasized the need for employees to have an aptitude for customer care, although this tended to be 'spotted' at interview rather than through psychometric or behavioural tests. The hotel used extensive induction programmes to lessen the potential of employee turnover. The use of cross-functional teams aimed to generate co-operation and team building and staff were encouraged to view the hotel as a unit rather than a collection of discrete functions. Allied to this extensive multi-skilling and cross-functional flexibility was encouraged, this 'cross-exposure' allowed staff to see a number of the other parts of the hotel. There was extensive decentralization, which sought to encourage responsible autonomy, for example through a well-understood empowerment scheme operating in the hotel. Consultation *via* a representative consultative committee allowed employees to voice their views on the running of the hotel. Further to this consultation the hotel also operated an annual attitude survey. Employees were appraised on a yearly basis. The appraisal system was used for succession planning and the hotel was also working towards linking appraisal with a merit-based remuneration system. Employees were also encouraged by a strong internal labour market which promoted from within, whenever possible. Finally, throughout the hotel there was an overriding emphasis on quality and the need to offer 'outstanding customer service'.

In sum, whilst all tourism and hospitality employers are, for a variety of reasons, unlikely to aspire to the deluxe version of best practice they should at least aim to avoid the real howlers as suggested by Boxall and Purcell. The remainder of the book considers how they might do this in considering policies and practices in a variety of organizational and occupational settings.

NELSON MARLBOROUGH INSTITUTE OF TECHNOLOGY (NMIT): A CASE STUDY

NMIT is a high quality tertiary education provider located in the Nelson/Marlborough region at the top of New Zealand's South Island.

The Nelson/Marlborough region is one of the most beautiful and desirable areas in New Zealand to live and study. Each year, NMIT attracts around 3,600 equivalent full time students who come to enjoy the scenery, beaches, sunny climate, culture, relaxed lifestyle and education opportunities offered.

With campuses in Nelson and Blenheim, NMIT offers more than 80 programmes at certificate, diploma or degree level across a broad range of areas.

Student life is vibrant. There is always something to entertain you, as well as support services to help you ease your way into your studies with as little stress as possible. Our tutors are enthusiastic and committed to helping you achieve your goals and we work together with local business and industry representatives to ensure you get the most up-to-date training available.

NMIT is a government-owned and funded organisation established in 1905. Follow these links to find information about our charter, profile, council and policies.

A comprehensive knowledge and understanding of the environment in which the tourism industry operates is essential for gaining employment at the supervisory level and to effectively operate your own business.

Cultural Tourism

Culture is a way of living and visitors come to experience Nelson's unique culture.

Te Puna Wai

Hoglund

Visits to boutique accommodation for the discerning tourist, local wineries, restaurants and cafes, arts and crafts will take students out of the classroom for most of the time. A visit to the Wakatu Marae to experience authentic Maori culture is a highlight for students in tourism. The opportunity to participate in the preparation and consumption of traditional hangi kai is an experience not to be forgotten.

Tourism Marketing

It doesn't matter how great your product is, if your target market doesn't know about you and your offerings then you haven't got a sale. It's all in the Brand!! If you fail to plan then you plan to fail. A good marketing plan is an essential business tool.

Customer Relations

Develop essential skills and knowledge to analyse customer service and develop a customer service strategy for a tourism business, keeping in mind the interaction required with local communities.

Industry Practice

The real learning happens out there in the work place. Students undertake work-based training in a commercial tourism operation to consolidate and enhance skills and knowledge. By getting known to industry, good students have a foot in the door for employment after they graduate.

Information Technology

Effective communication with target markets *via* the internet is essential if tourism operators are to reach independent tourists and secure their business with sales.

Appraise the usefulness of information technology systems available to the tourism industry and modify a system used in the industry.

Tourism Industry Management

To bring it all together students undertake a detailed feasibility study based on a new tourism business of their choice.

Environmental Tourism Management

The brand 100 per cent Pure Clean Green New Zealand' — truth or fallacy? If we are serious about tourism in this country, then we must develop products and services that are environmentally sustainable in the long-term. If we don't then we *will destroy the goose that laid the golden egg.*

Students investigate existing tourism businesses in NZ and overseas to determine for themselves how 'Green' we really are and to develop sound principles and practises to sustain the environment in which tourism operates.

A visit to 'Western Ranges Horse Treks' adjacent to Kahurangi National Park exposes students to rustic energy efficient resources in a natural setting.

Tourism Business Skills

Apart from a few large corporations and medium sized operators, tourism in NZ is based on small businesses employing less than 5 staff. Consequently people working in the industry need a broad range of skills in marketing, management, finance and people.

Managing finance effectively is the key to a profitable business. You'll contribute to financial decision-making through defining, measuring and allocating costs, as well as being able to manage the financial resources for a small business.

Human Resource Management for the Tourism Industry

Staff are the greatest asset to any business tourism industry. Business productivity and profits are directly linked to staff performance. Good managers are skilled in getting the best out of their staff.

Programmes by Subject

At NMIT, all courses are offered as part or full study programmes. Options range from single semester to three years and include certificates, diplomas and degrees. Interested in short-term study options? Check out short courses available this semester.

Below you will find information about the content of individual programmes, the entry requirements, the qualifications you can gain and career pathways or click here to download the 2008 Prospectus.

Offering Detail

Short Courses—Hospitality and Cookery

- Short Courses—Hospitality and Cookery Home.
- Request an information pack.

Bar Managers Course

Start	Finish	Location	Room	Time	Fee#: (NZ/Aus)	Apply (International)
28 Jan. 08	28 Jan. 08	Nelson			$154.30	
25 Feb. 08	25 Feb. 08	Nelson			$154.30	
31 Mar. 08	31 Mar. 08	Nelson			$154.30	
05 May, 08	05 May, 08	Nelson			$154.30	
16 June, 08	16 June, 08	Nelson			$154.30	
21 July, 08	21 July, 08	Nelson			$154.30	
18 Aug. 08	18 Aug. 08	Nelson			$154.30	
22 Sep. 08	22 Sep. 08	Nelson			$154.30	
20 Oct. 08	20 Oct. 08	Nelson			$154.30	
17 Nov. 08	17 Nov. 08	Nelson			$154.30	
08 Dec., 08	08 Dec. 08	Nelson			$154.30	

Bar Managers Course—SDL Option

Start	Finish	Location	Room	Time	Fee#: (NZ/Aus)	Apply (International)
14 Jan., 08	19 Dec., 08	Nelson			$137.70	

Bartenders Course

A 18 hou course designed to give students the skills and knowledge to be a Bartender.

Start	Finish	Location	Room	Time	Fee*: (NZ/Aus)	Apply (International)
28 Feb., 08	14 Mar., 08	Nelson			$148.90	
19 May, 08	4 June, 08	Nelson			$148.90	
19 Nov., 08	4 Dec., 08	Nelson			$148.90	

Food Safety

Start	Finish	Location	Room	Time	Fee*: (NZ/Aus)	Apply (International)
28 Feb., 08	14 Mar., 08	Nelson			$148.90	
19 May, 08	4 June, 08	Nelson			$148.90	
19 Nov., 08	4 Dec., 08	Nelson			$148.90	

Introduction to Espresso

Start	Finish	Location	Room	Time	Fee*: (NZ/Aus)	Apply (International)
25 Feb., 08	11 Mar., 08	Nelson			$220.50	
14 July., 08	29 July., 08	Nelson			$220.50	
13 Oct., 08	29 Oct., 08	Nelson			$220.50	

Lifestyle and Nutrition

The purpose of this course is to introduce nutrition and provide participants with the knowledge to make informed nutrition and life style choices for themselves and their families.

Start	Finish	Location	Room	Time	Fee#: (NZ/Aus)	Apply (International)
12 Feb., 08	19 Feb., 08	Nelson	T Block	6.00PM	$130.00	
06 May, 08	13 May, 08	Nelson			$130.00	
15 July, 08	22 July, 08	Nelson			$130.00	
08 Sep., 08	15 Sep., 08	Nelson			$130.00	
11 Nov., 08	18 Nov., 08	Nelson			$130.00	

Note: Fees listed on this site are indicative only and may vary with course selection. Exact fees can be confirmed as part of your enquiry or application.

* *Programme fees*: Include GST, but an additional compulsory student association fee also applies.

\# *Course fees*: Include GST and the compulsory student association fee.

School of Tourism, Hospitality and Amp; Well-being

Aspiring adventure guides can choose the Diploma in Adventure Tourism, delivered by experienced tutors with a love of the outdoors. Adventure Tourism is one of the fastest growing sectors of the industry and who better to learn it from than people who have been successful guides, operations managers and company owners.

The Diploma in Tourism Management provides you with skills and knowledge to work at a supervisory or management level in all sectors of the industry—own your own business or manage somebody else's in an environmentally sustainable way.

The Certificate in Travel will enable you to work around the world in retail or wholesale travel. You can follow a career working in information centres, manage travel desks across the sectors of accommodation, transport and ancillary services; be employable by central reservations such as hotel chains, car and campervan rentals, inbound and outbound tour operators, cruise operators, or manage an office of a tourism business.

The Nelson region has a vibrant arts, food and wine culture and visitors come seek out artists, craftspeople, wineries and food experience. There is a potent arts and tourism culture which is unique to Nelson.

In addition a new 12 week programme in Cultural Tourism designed for international students celebrates our way of life in New Zealand and the Nelson region.

This celebration of our region is also reflected in other programmes offered in the School of Tourism and Hospitality. Chefs can train over two years, full-time or part-time to complete international qualifications in cookery. Students gain the Certificate in Cookery or the Certificate in Professional Cookery.

Front of house staff train on the Certificate in Professional Restaurant, Wine and Bar Service programme where they also have opportunities for work experience in excellent local restaurants.

The School also offers part-time courses in preparation for General Managers Certificate, Bartending, Food Safety and Espresso.

CONFEDERATION OF TOURISM, HOTEL AND CATERING MANAGEMENT (CTHCM): A CASE STUDY

The Diploma and Advanced Diploma Management Programmes offer supervisor to management level qualifications which are recognised by universities and employers involved in the hospitality and tourism industries. Centres can run any of the programmes below.

Overview

The CTHCM Diploma and Advanced Diploma programmes are recognised by major organisations in the hospitality and tourism industries as suitable for employment at supervisory and management level. CTHCM Management Programmes have been awarded Institute of Hospitality Endorsement, (formerly the HCIMA). All learners on CTHCM Diploma programmes are eligible for Affiliate Membership of the Institute of Hospitality, and learners who successfully complete the CTHCM advanced Diploma programmes are eligible to apply for Associate membership. The qualifications are recognised by a number of British universities. Centres can run each module separately as single subjects providing students still sit the same exam dates. Please contact CTHCM for more information.

Centre Benefits

- Institute of Hospitality, (formerly the HCIMA), endorses CTHCM Management Programmes.
- Student exam and membership fees are suitably priced.
- The Diploma and Advanced Diploma programmes have three exam rounds a year to suit centre semesters and university entrance.
- Student results are issued within eight weeks of the exam week.
- Centres receive guidance and support through schemes of work and previous exam questions for lecturers.
- Successful Diploma and Advanced Diploma students are issued with professional certificates.

- CTHCM is a member of the Federation of Awarding Bodies, the membership body which represents organisations that award vocational qualifications in the UK.
- Common modules at Diploma and Advanced Diploma level make the qualifications cost-effective for colleges to run.
- University recognition adds value to CTHCM qualifications.
- Endorsement by the Royal Institute for the Protection of Health (RIPH) means holders of the CTHCM Food Hygiene, Health and Safety module can sit the RIPH Food Hygiene certificate. It is a legal requirement for workers to have this in the food industry.
- London Clubs International endorses the Casino modules as part of the Diploma in Hotel and Casino Management.

Hotel Management

The hospitality industry is one of the largest industries in the world. Each year progressively more meals and bed nights are purchased, which is why the hotel industry is experiencing rapid growth. Customers are becoming ever more demanding in their requirements for high standards of service and facilities. It is only through organised and structured training that the industry can meet these expectations.

Diploma in Hotel Management

The Diploma in Hotel Management aims to provide students with a broad understanding of the operational aspects of the international hotel industry, and a knowledge of the underlying principles involved. This programme has been devised on the basis that students will attend a course of study of not less than 450 hours. Private study will be required over and above this figure. Each of the modules has a 2 and a half hour examination, set and marked by CTHCM.

Syllabus

- Food and Beverage Operations.

- Food Hygiene, Health and Safety.
- Front Office Operations.
- Facilities and Accommodation Operations.
- Hospitality Finance.
- Introduction to Business Operations.
- Marketing.
- The Tourism Industry.
- Business Computing.
- Understanding the Global Hospitality Industry.

Option in Casino Management

Students wishing to prepare for careers in the more specialised field of Casino Management may choose to undertake this specially developed derivative programme. The course combines seven key hospitality based modules of the Hotel Management Diploma with three specialised modules in Casino Management.

Syllabus

- Front Office Operations.
- Facilities and Accommodation Operations.
- Hospitality Finance.
- Introduction to Business Operations.
- Marketing.
- The Tourism Industry.
- The Hospitality Industry.
- Casino Management 1.
- Casino Management 2.
- The Psychology of Gambling.

London Clubs International believes that the Casino modules available as part of the CTHCM Diploma in Hotel and Casino Management will provide a valuable foundation for those who have an interest in pursuing a career in the casino business in a regulated environment.

Advanced Diploma in Hotel Management

The Advanced Diploma in Hotel Management aims to provide an understanding of the managerial, decision-making and leadership aspects of the international hotel industry and to develop independent research and study skills which will be required when working at senior managerial level in the industry. The scheme has been devised on the basis that students will attend a course of study of not less than 450 contact hours. Private study will be required over and above this figure. Each of the modules has a 3 hour examination, set and marked by CTHCM.

Syllabus

- Food and Beverage Management.
- Strategic Hospitality Management.
- Facilities Management.
- Management Accounting.
- Human Resource Management.
- Management Research Report.

Tourism Management

Travel and tourism is the fastest growing industry in the world. It has been estimated by the World Tourism Organisation that around one job in ten depends upon tourism, which includes holiday-makers and business visitors. It is only through organised and structured training that the industry can meet these expectations.

Diploma in Tourism Management

The Diploma in Tourism Management aims to provide students with a broad understanding of the operational aspects of the international tourism industry, together with a knowledge of the basic principals which underpin the industry. This Diploma has been devised on the basis that students will attend a course of study of not less than 450 hours. Private study will be required over and above this figure. Each of the modules has a two and a half hour examination, set and marked by CTHCM.

Syllabus

- Travel Geography.

- The Tourism Industry.
- Business Computing.
- Travel Agency and Tour Guiding Operations.
- Introduction to Tourism Economics.
- Special Interest Tourism.
- Destination Analysis.
- Introduction to Business Operations.
- Finance for the Travel Industry.
- Marketing.

Option in Travel Agency Management

Students wishing to prepare for careers in the more specialised field of Travel Agency Management may choose to undertake this specially developed derivative programme. The course combines seven key tourism modules of the Tourism Management Diploma with three modules from our IATA approved Fares and Ticketing courses.

Syllabus

- Travel Geography.
- The Tourism Industry.
- Business Computing.
- Travel Agency and Tour Guiding Operations.
- Introduction to Business Operations.
- Finance for the Travel Industry.
- Marketing.
- Fares and Ticketing Level 1.
- Fares and Ticketing Level 2.
- Computer Reservations (GDS).

Advanced Diploma in Tourism Management

The Advanced Diploma in Tour Operation and Management aims to provide an understanding of the managerial, decision-making and leadership aspects of the international tour operation industry and to develop the independent research skills which will be required when working as a senior manager in the industry. The scheme has been devised on the basis that students will attend a course of study of not less than 450 contact hours. Private study will be required over and above this figure. Each of the modules has a 3 hour examination, set and marked by CTHCM.

Syllabus

- Tour Operation.
- Management Accounting.
- Strategic Tourism Management.
- Sustainable Tourism and Destination Management.
- Human Resource Management.
- Management Research Report.

The Confederation of Tourism, Hotel and Catering Management is committed to developing and improving its programmes under the careful scrutiny and supervision of the hotel and tourism industries. We reserve the right to amend our programmes at any time.

HUMAN RESOURCE MANAGEMENT FOR THE TOURISM AND HOSPITALITY INDUSTRIES POSTGRADUATE: UNIVERSITY OF STRATHCLYDE

The Department of Hospitality and Tourism Management is part of the Strathclyde Business School. It has 15 academic staff.

The Department is an international leader in hotel, hospitality and tourism education, undertaking research of international quality in its field in its field, with a high international reputation in industry circles. The Department is a leading institution for tourism and hospitality research and home to a number of academics who are leaders in their field.

About HRM for Tourism and Hospitality Industries

The aim of the MSc/PgDip in Human Resource Management for the Tourism and Hospitality Industries is both to facilitate access to specialist managerial positions, and to advance the academic standing of those wishing to pursue a career in the fields of education and training within the tourism and hospitality context.

The course was developed by the Department of Hospitality and Tourism Management (formerly The Scottish Hotel School) in response to the growth of academic interest in tourism and hospitality related issues and the increasingly sophisticated employment needs of the tourism and hospitality industries.

The course aims to reflect the highest academic standards in a rapidly developing field, and to provide an excellent student learning experience in a friendly and multicultural environment. The course seeks a balance of applications from Scotland, Europe and overseas. Students are encouraged to participate in the active scholarly life of the Department.

Target Market

The course allows students already holding a qualification in tourism or hospitality management to undertake an in-depth study of human resource issues relating to the industry. It will also appeal to managers with industry experience who wish to improve their career progression prospects.

The course builds on the generic analytical, social, technical and learning skills required to work at managerial level in this dynamic sector of the economy by helping students develop a wide competence in human resource management.

The MSc dissertation requirement is an exciting opportunity for students to upgrade their academic skills and pursue their particular interests by undertaking a piece of work which will contribute substantially to the body of knowledge in this rapidly developing field and may be suitable for publication in academic journals.

Course Structure

The taught part of the course consists of ten modules (six compulsory, four optional). In addition to compulsory classes, students can select options from the entire range of postgraduate tourism and hospitality classes offered by the Department of Hospitality and Tourism Management.

Successful completion of ten modules leads to the award of the Postgraduate Diploma. In addition to the modules, MSc students also undertake a dissertation of 15,000 to 20,000 words.

Compulsory Modules

- Human Resource Management in Tourism and Hospitality.
- International Human Resource Management for the Tourism and Hospitality Industries.
- Education and Training in Hospitality and Tourism.
- International Tourism.
- Tourism Policy and Organisations.
- Research Methods.

Options

- Strategic Management for the Hospitality and Tourism Industries.
- Tourism Products Marketing.
- Hospitality Finance and Control (two semesters).
- Hotel Operational Management.
- Tourism Project Appraisal.
- Tourism in Developing Countries: Issues and Policies.
- Tourism Planning in Developing Countries.

Further Information

Study Modes

The course is available full-time or part-time (over two academic sessions), with exams in January and May. The dissertation should be submitted by September.

Assessment

Assessment is by a mix of written assignments (essays, reports) and formal exams (typically 40/60 split).

Start Date and Duration

The course starts in late September and takes nine months for the Diploma, 12 months for the MSc.

Entry Requirements

A good honours degree from a UK university or equivalent is normally required. Professional experience may be taken into account.

Fees

Full information on current fee levels can be found at http://www.strath.ac.uk/registry/students/finance/.

How to Apply

Application forms are available from:
Registry—Business
Online applications may be made *via* the University website at:
http://applicants.strath.ac.uk/
Contact Details—For further information please contact Jithrendran Kokkranikal at jithu@strath.ac.uk

HRM for the Tourism and Hospitality Industries 08/09 (PG Diploma)

Full-time, Admission Code: SHPD4
Our current entry requirements are published at the end of each course description in our Prospectus.

HRM for the Tourism and Hospitality Industries 08/09 (MSc)

Full-time, Admission Code: SHMSC1
Our current entry requirements are published at the end of each course description in our Prospectus.

How to Apply

Application forms are available from:
Registry—Business
Online applications may be made *via* the University website at:
http://applicants.strath.ac.uk/

Glossary of Terms

360-Degree Appraisal: Sometimes called multi-source evaluation. Involves an individual being evaluated by their superiors, peers, subordinates and others (for example, customers).

Ã la Carte: Menu of dishes prepared to order and priced individually.

AA: Automobile Association.

Absenteeism: Failure of employees to report to work when they are scheduled to do so.

Academic Employee: An academic rank or qualified academic rank employee in the professional Services Negotiating Unit.

Academic Rank: Rank held by those members of the professional staff having the title of professor, associate professor, assistant professor, instructor, librarian, associate librarian, senior assistant librarian and assistant librarian.

Academic Staff: The staff comprised of those persons having academic rank or qualified academic rank.

Academic Year Obligation: An annual obligation of service for the academic year, not to exceed 10 months.

Access: Concerned with who will have access to the HRIS. For example, will there be decentralised access and data entry capability or will access and data entry be centralised and tightly controlled?

Accident-Prone: The proposition that certain employees have specific characteristics that make them more likely to have accidents, and that these same employees cause or are involved in most accidents.

Account Number: The account that will be charged to cover employee salary and fringe benefit costs.

Accreditation (HR): The process of certifying the professional competence of HR specialists.

Achievement Motivation: The desire to be successful in competitive situations or to perform in terms of a standard of excellence.

Acquisition: Purchase of a firm or company by another firm or company.

Across-the-Board Increases: General pay increases awarded to all employees irrespective of performance.

Acting Appointment: An employee appointed to fill a vacancy during a temporary absence such assabbatical or medical leave.

Action Learning: Based on learning by experience. Uses real problems from the work situation for trainees to solve.

Active Listening: Asking lots of questions and carefully listening to the answers.

Activity Phase (Training): Concerned with selecting the training methods and learning principles to be employed in a training programme.

Adaptability: Relates to the extent that HRM policies foster employee and organisational readiness for, and acceptance of change.

Added Value: Often refers to the analysis undertaken by management of the cost and contribution made by employees involved at each stage in the process of producing a product or providing a service.

Administrative Expert: Refers to the efficiency of HR managers and the effective management of HR activities (such as selection, etc.) so that they create value.

Administrative Services Unit (ASU): A negotiating unit in NYS service composed of classified service employees, primarily office and administrative support staff, currently represented by the Civil Service employees' Association, Inc. (CSEA).

Adobe Acrobat: Software that allows you to view electronic documents, which have been stored in pdf format (see *pdf*).

Adventure Training: Adventure or wilderness training presents managers with physical and mental challenges such as abseiling, canoeing and bushwalking. The aim is to promote self-awareness, confidence and teamwork.

Advertised Recruitment: Communicating to the public an

organisation's HR requirements using the media (such as newspaper advertisements).

Advocates: Employer or union representatives who argue a case before an industrial tribunal or court.

Aesthetic Value: Appreciation of the harmonious visual impact of a setting.

Affirmative Action (AA): Programmes that require firms to make special efforts to recruit, hire and promote women and members of minority groups.

Ageing Population: Occurs when the number of older people increases relative to the number of young people in the population.

AIDS (Acquired Immune Deficiency Syndrome): A disease that undermines the body's immune system, leaving the person susceptible to a wide range of fatal diseases.

Air Rage: Offensive and violent behaviour by commercial airline passengers. Examples include food throwing, sexual harassment, indecent behaviour, insulting language, abusive conduct and physical assault.

Alcoholism: A treatable disease characterised by uncontrolled and compulsive drinking that interferes with normal living patterns.

Alert-Box: A window that appears on the screen to warn the user or to report an error.

Alien: An individual born in, and a citizen of, a country other than the country in which he or she is living.

Allowable Matters: These are provisions allowed to remain in awards by the Workplace Relations Act. No other items can be covered by an award.

Americans with Disabilities Act (ADA) of 1990: The ADA prohibits discrimination on the basis of disability in employment, programmes and services provided by State and Local Governments, goods and services provided by private companies, and in commercial facilities. For more information, contact HRM.

Ante: Refers to the maximum amount, which may be paid to an incumbent.

Anti-discrimination: Elimination of any practice that makes distinctions between different group based on age, sex, etc. and that results in one group being advantaged and the other group disadvantaged.

APEC: Asia Pacific Economic Community.

Appendix A: A list of professional services negotiating unit positions not eligible for permanent appointment found in Appendix A of Article XI in the SUNY Policies of the Board of Trustees. In lieu of permanent appointments, appointees to Appendix A titles must be given 5-year term appointments after an initial 1-year probationary appointment.

Application Form: Basic source of employment information covering qualifications, experience and other job-related data.

Application: A programme that performs a specific task such as word processing, database management or web browsing.

Appointing Authority or Appointing Officer: The officer, commission or body having the power of appointment to subordinate positions. In SUNY, each campus President is an appointing authority.

Appointment: The act of placing a person in a position.

Appraisal Schemes: An individual's performance is reviewed by their manager. Their past performance is examined and future goals are set.

Apprenticeship Training: A combination of classroom and on-the-job training.

Aptitude Tests: Tests of special abilities (such as clerical, linguistic, musical and artistic abilities) that are required in specific jobs.

Arbitration: The submission of a dispute to a third party for a binding decision. Assessment centre Technique that uses interviews, tests, simulations, games and observations to evaluate an individual's potential.

Assessment Phase (Training): Establishes what training is needed, by whom, when and where so that training objectives can be established.

At-Risk' Compensation: Rewards that are payable only when a performance target is met. Attitude survey Systematic method of determining what employees think about their job, supervision and the organisation.

Attraction: Any visitor service or product which tourists would enjoy visiting or using. An attraction may not be an "attractor" but can still be an attraction. To be considered an attraction, a product must be: A. Findable (clearly located on maps and street addresses, and directions provided). If tourists can't find the facility, it is not a tourist attraction. B. Hours of operation clearly denoted in any and all promotional materials (if a tourist arrives only to find the attraction closed, it is not an attraction). Examples of attractions include everything from a theme park that attracts over a million visitors a year, to a produce stand by the side of the road.

Attractor: A significant tourist attraction, which compels visitation. The primary "must sees" in an area. The top reasons a tourist would choose to visit this area.

Australian Council of Trade Unions (ACTU): National trade union organisation which represents the Australian trade union movement.

Australian Workplace Agreements (AWA): Agreements made directly between an employer and an employee.

Automatic Progression: Sometimes called incremental salary scales. Salary increases occur automatically each year on a specified date, irrespective of performance.

Autonomous Work Teams: Represents job enrichment at the group level. This is achieved by creating self-managed work teams responsible for accomplishing defined performance objectives.

Autonomy: The extent to which the job provides the employee freedom to plan, schedule and decide about work procedures.

Avoidable Turnover: A standard method of computing employee turnover that focuses on that part of employee turnover that can be reduced.

Award Restructuring: Process designed to simplify, update and remove anomalies from industrial awards.

Awards: Written determinations setting out the legally enforceable terms and conditions of employment in a firm or industry.

Background Investigation: Process of checking job applicant information prior to an employment offer being made.

Backpacker: A visitor in NZ for the purpose of a holiday or special event who stays in a backpackers lodge/hostel.

Bargaining Agent: The organization chosen by employees in a negotiating unit to have exclusive representation rights for them in collective bargaining.

Bargaining Zone: The parameters between which the union and management are prepared to negotiate comprises the bargaining zone.

Bargaining: Another term for negotiation.

Base Salary: Standard salary that an employee receives for doing a job. It is used as the basis for calculating other allowances and benefits.

Behaviour Modelling: Process of learning from other people's experience by simulating (copying) their behaviour.

Behaviour Observation Scale (BOS): Performance appraisal system that uses critical incidents to develop a list of desired behaviours needed to perform a specific job successfully.

Behaviourally Anchored Rating Scale (BARS): A performance appraisal method that combines elements of the traditional rating scale and critical incidents method.

Benchmark Job or Key Job: A job that is similar or comparable in content across firms.

Benchmark: The identification of best practices among competitors and non-competitors that make them superior performers.

Benchmarking: Benchmarking measures standards of performance against others doing similar work.

Benchmarking: The process of comparing performance and processes within an industry to assess relative position against either a set industry standard or against those who are "best in class" (Synergy, 2000).

Benefits: All financial rewards that are not paid directly in cash to the employee; for example, annual and maternity leave, life insurance.

Best Practice(s): A term used to designate highest quality, excellence, or superior practices in a particular field by a tourism operator.

Biographical Information Blank (BIB): A specially designed application form that is used to obtain comprehensive information about an employee's background, attitudes, hobbies, sports, early life experiences, and so on.

Blog: Blogs are web logs kept by individuals, groups or organisations to record thoughts, ideas, work notes or outcomes on the Web chronologically. Readers can comment on blog posts- and post-discussion comments.

Blue Circle Salaries: Salaries that are below the range minimum for the job.

Body Language: Non-verbal signals (such as facial expressions) that can indicate what a person is really thinking or feeling.

Bonus: A discretionary reward provided after the achievement of a goal.

Bookmark: A way of storing web addresses so you can find them easily. Bookmarks can be found on Netscape—they are called "favourites" on Microsoft Internet Explorer.

Bottom Line: Refers to a final result, such as the net profit after taxes.

Boundaryless Careers: Careers that involve switching jobs, specialisations, companies, industries and location. They may involve upwards, downwards and sideways moves.

Broadbanding: Collapses numerous job grades with narrow salary bands in a salary structure into a few broad job grades with wide salary bands.

Browse, Browsing: A way of finding information by looking through a set of web pages containing lists of resources grouped by subject.

Browser: Software such as Microsoft Internet Explorer or Netscape Navigator that provides a way of accessing information on the World Wide Web.

Bulletin Board: An area on a computer where people can read or write messages. Certain bulletin boards are private, requiring an access code.

Bullying: Examples of workplace bullying include persecuting or ganging up on an individual; making unreasonable demands or setting impossible work targets; restrictive and petty work rules;

constant, intrusive surveillance; abusive language; physical assault; and open or implied threats of dismissal or demotion.

Burnout: A state of mental, emotional and physical exhaustion that results from substantial and prolonged stress.

Business Game: Simulation that represents actual business situations.

Business Process Re-engineering (BPR): It refers to the methods by which a company or service undertakes a thorough review of all its operations.

Business Travel: Travel for commercial, governmental or educational purposes with leisure as a secondary motivation.

Business Travel: Travel of 1-365 days duration for the purpose of attending a convention or training, conducting official/ government or private business.

Business Units: Often have their own Trading Accounts and operate with relative autonomy from the rest of the company or service.

Cafeteria Benefits: Employees choose their own benefits up to a certain cost per employee.

Calendar Year Obligation: An annual obligation of service for a full year, (i.e., 12 months).

Canvass: An inquiry as to whether an eligible candidate for a classified service vacancy would be willing to accept appointment, if offered.

Career Counselling: Involves the giving of information and advice to employees to facilitate their career planning and development.

Career Path: Flexible line of progression through which an employee moves during their employment with an organisation.

Career Pathways: Progressive steps of development within a specific area of work.

Career Planning and Development: Giving employees assistance to develop realistic career goals and the opportunities to realise them.

Career Plateau: Point in an individual's career where the probability of further advancement is negligible.

Career Transition: Involves a significant change in an employee's career via transfer, demotion, promotion, overseas assignment or switch from one occupation to another.

Career: All the jobs that an employee has held in their working life.

Casual Employee: Unclassified service employee whose employment relationship does not justify assignment to a negotiating unit.

Central Processing Unit (CPU): The brain of the computer. It causes data to be read, stored, written or otherwise processed.

Central Tendency: A common error that occurs when every employee is incorrectly rated near the average or middle of the scale.

Certified Agreements (CA): Agreements that are the product of negotiations between an employer and a union(s) and that are subsequently registered by an industrial tribunal.

Change Agents: People who act as catalysts for change.

Charter of Professional Standards: Statement of an organisation's ethical values and standards that guides the professional conduct of its employees.

Chat Room: A Web-site where users with a common interest can communicate in real time.

Classification Method: A job evaluation method by which classes or grades are defined to describe a group of jobs.

Classified Service: Comprise all positions not included in the unclassified service. The positions in the classified service shall be divided into four classes, to be designated as the exempt class, the non-competitive class, the labour class, and the competitive class.

Click: A single press and release of a mouse button.

Closed Shop: Exists when a job applicant cannot be hired by an employer unless he or she is a member of a designated union.

Coach Tour: A guided bus tour for a group of holiday makers that follows a scheduled itinerary. Visitors purchase all arrangements from the Inbound Tour Operator prior to arrival in NZ.

Coaching: On-the-job approach to management development in which the manager is given an opportunity to teach on a one-to-one basis.

Collateral: Promotional materials distributed to travel trade partners, for the purpose of educating sellers about and/or assisting in the sale of suppliers' products.

Collective Bargaining: The process through which representatives of management and the union meet to negotiate a labour agreement.

College Year Obligation: An annual obligation of service for any period less than the full year.

Comments Box: Feature of the Intuit: Virtual Training Suite for Further Education allowing users to annotate the Web-sites stored in their Links Basket.

Commission: An individual incentive system whereby an employee is paid either a percentage or flat sum amount on the revenue of sales volume they generate.

Commitment: Relates to the extent that HRM policies enhance employee identification with and attachment to their job and the organisation.

Common Law: 'Case law' developed in the court system. It is the body of previous judgements that guides how the other sources of legal obligations should be interpreted.

Communication: The process of transferring meanings from a sender to a receiver.

Community-based Operations: Informal or formal business activities (e.g. street vending, shebeens, day care centres) based within a community.

Compa Ratio (Salary Index): The ratio between the average salary for a particular job point or grade and the mid-point of the salary range for that point or grade.

Compensation: What employees receive in exchange for their work. Includes pay and benefits (total compensation) or just pay (cash compensation).

Compensatory Approach: Involves considering all the selection data (favourable and unfavourable) before a selection decision is made.

Competence: Relates to the extent that HRM policies attract, retain, motivate and develop employees with the abilities, skills, knowledge and competence to achieve the organisation's strategic business objectives.

Competencies: Demonstrable and assessable skills that distinguish effective from ineffective job performance.

Competency Profiling: Job analysis method that focuses on the skills and behaviours needed to successfully perform a job.

Competency-Based Training (CBT): Skills approach to employee development. Focus is on performing specific tasks to a predetermined standard.

Competitive Advantage: A special edge that allows organisations to better deal with business challenges.

Competitive Analysis: Review of the competitive forces in an industry, including the threat of new entrants, bargaining power of buyers and suppliers and the threat of substitute products or services.

Competitive Class: The competitive class shall include all positions for which it is practicable to determine the merit and fitness of applicants by competitive examination.

Compulsory Unionism: An arrangement whereby union membership is a necessary condition of employment.

Computer-based Training: Uses computers as a learning vehicle to provide interactive drills, problem-solving, simulations and gaming. The emphasis is on self-managed learning.

Conciliation: Occurs when a dispute involves a third party (a conciliator) who tries to facilitate agreement between unions and management.

Conduct Guide: A formal statement of expected professional conduct and ethical rules.

Congruence: Relates to the extent that HRM policies generate (or sustain) and promote the simultaneous achievement of employee goals and the organisation's strategic business objectives.

Conscript Mindset: Employees are externally motivated (that is, they are coerced by management) to perform.

Consent Agreement: Occurs when the parties to an industrial dispute reach agreement without third party involvement. If ratified by an industrial tribunal, it becomes a consent award and is binding on the parties in the same way as an arbitrated award.

Consent Awards: These occur when the parties to an industrial dispute reach agreement without third party involvement, and the agreement is then ratified by an industrial tribunal. A consent award is binding on the parties in the same way as an arbitrated award.

Consolidators: Based in some offshore markets, consolidators buy air fares in bulk from airlines and sell these to retail agents for on-sale to consumers.

Consumer Show: A product showcase for the general public. Differs from a "Trade Show" as a trade show generally targets industry professionals. Consumer Shows target the consumer. Often there is a charge to get into the show.

Content Theories: Attempt to explain motivation in terms of factors that initiate employee behaviour.

Contingent Permanent: An appointment, transfer, or reinstatement to a temporarily vacant position of a person meeting all merit and fitness requirements for such appointment. Except in the case of the return of a prior incumbent, contingent permanent appointees have all rights and benefits of permanent appointees.

Contingent Worker: Temporary or part-time employee, continuous reinforcement occurs when rewards are given after each desired behaviour.

Continuing Appointment: An appointment to a position of academic rank which shall not be affected by changes in such rank and shall continue until resignation, retirement, or termination.

Continuous Improvement (Kaizen): Requires employees to constantly seek ways of improving the quality of the product or service.

Contract: Legal agreement, enforceable by law, that sets forth the relationship between parties regarding the performance of a specific action.

Contribution-based Pay: Pay plan designed to directly link rewards to the contributions made by an individual employee.

Contributory Superannuation: Scheme where the employee (along with the company) is required to make a regular contribution (typically 5 per cent of monthly base salary) to their retirement plan.

Convention and Visitors Bureau: These organizations are local tourism marketing organizations specializing in developing conventions, meetings, conferences and visitations to a city, county or region.

Copyright: Many Web pages on the Internet will be protected by copyright. Only the owner of the copyright, usually the creator of the piece, is allowed to produce or reproduce the work or to allow anyone else to do so. Always check copyright information before you use images, written material or other resources on the Web in your course work.

Corporate Culture: The values, beliefs, assumptions and symbols that define the way in which the organisation conducts its business.

Correlation Coefficient: A statistical procedure showing the strength of the relationship between two variables; for example, between an employee's test score and on-the-job performance.

Corruption: Includes fraud, bribery, graft and the payment of secret commissions and kickbacks.

Cost Centre: A unit in which managers are held responsible for all associated costs; for example, administrative and service departments where inputs are measured in financial terms, but outputs are not.

Cost-Benefit Analysis: Involves an evaluation of the tangible and intangible costs and benefits resulting from a decision.

Cost-Effectiveness: Relates to the extent that HRM policies reduce personnel-related costs, help correctly size the organisation, eliminate unnecessary work, reduce compensation and benefit costs, reduce labour turnover, etc.

Cost-of-Living Allowance (COLA): Designed to protect the expatriate's standard of living from cost-of-living differences between the host country and the home country and to offer some protection against exchange rate fluctuations.

Counselling: A private conference between a supervisor and an employee at which the employee's performance deficiencies are discussed. The motivation for such counselling sessions is to improve the employee's performance and eliminate the performance deficiencies.

Counselling Memorandum: A written follow-up to an employee following corrective counselling which confirms the reason for the counselling, a summary of the effect of the employee's deficiencies, a summary of the employee's response to the counselling, and the corrective actions expected.

Country of Residence: Consists of the country where she/he has lived for most of the past year (12 months), or for a shorter period if she/he intends to return within 12 months to live there.

Craft Unions: Unions that include workers who have a common skill; for example, carpenters or plumbers.

Criterion Validity: A type of validity based on showing that scores on the test (predictors) are related to job performance (criterion).

Critical Incident Method: A performance appraisal technique that requires a written record of highly favourable and highly unfavourable employee work behaviour.

Critical Incidents: Examples of employee behaviour that illustrate effective or ineffective job performance.

CRM: Customer Relationship Management.

Cross-cultural Communications: Occur when a person from one culture (for example, an Australian) communicates with a person from another culture (for example, a Korean). Misunderstandings may occur because of differences in language, values, attitudes and beliefs.

CRS: Computerised Reservation System.

Cultural Heritage: Those aspects that are unique to a particular culture (e.g. ingredients, preparation methods, dishes, or service of foods).

Cultural Tourism: Travel for the purpose of learning about cultures or aspects of cultures (NEAP, 2000).

Culture Shock: The inability to adjust to a different cultural environment.

Cursor: A movable, blinking bar of light on a computer screen marking the next point of character entry or change.

Cut-off Score: The score on a test below which an applicant will not be considered for employment.

Data: Facts, numbers, letters, and symbols stored in a computer.

Data: Numerous facts that are part of an information system.

Databanks: Stored collection of raw, unanalysed facts.

Database Management: Systematic approach to storing, updating and retrieving information stored as data items.

Database: A collection of information specific to an operation, business or enterprise.

Database: A collection of organised data to be used for an application, e.g. payroll information.

Day Visitors: Visitors who arrive and leave the same day for leisure, recreation and holidays, visiting friends and relatives and business and professional.

Deadline: The time limit set for the completion of the negotiation.

Deadlock: Occurs when neither side in a negotiation will make a concession.

Decision Making: Choosing from alternatives.

Defined Benefit Plans: Retirement plans that specify the actual benefit payable upon retirement.

Defined Contribution Plans: Retirement plans that specify employer and employee contributions, but do not specify what the actual benefit at retirement will be.

Delayering: Delayering is the removal of middle layers of management resulting in a 'flatter' management organisation.

Delegation: Giving decision-making responsibilities to subordinates.

Delphi Technique: Obtains predictions from a panel of experts about some specific future occurrence. The collective estimates are feedback to individual panel members until general agreement is reached.

Demarcation: An exclusive right that restricts a specific type of work to members of a particular union. In practice, it operates as a form of job protection.

Demographic Profile: Characteristics used in research such as age, gender, occupation, income, marital status, place of residence, etc.

Demotion: The process of moving a worker to a lower level of duties and responsibilities, which typically involves a pay cut.

Department of Civil Service: The State's agency responsible for the classification and allocation of classified service positions, the recruitment and selection of candidates for classified service employment, and the development and maintenance of statewide agency personnel systems.

Deregulation: Removal or relaxing of barriers to travel such as restrictions on the nature of outbound travel, amount of money taken out of the country, visa requirements and costs, air service agreements.

Desk Rage: Offensive and/or violent employee behaviour occurring in an office environment.

Destination Marketing Organization (DMO): A company or other entity involved in the business of increasing tourism to a destination or improving its public image.

Destination Marketing: Marketing a city, state, country, area or region to consumers and trade.

Development: Involves those activities that prepare an employee for future responsibilities.

Dial-up: This is a service that allows a computer to use a telephone system to communicate with other computers. This is probably how you connect to the Internet at home.

Diary/Log: The employee keeps a written record of the duties they perform.

Digital Material, Digitise: Digital material refers to any material processed by a computer. It includes both those resources that were created in a digital format and those that have been "digitised" (for example a textbook that has been changed into digital format).

Direct Deposit: Making direct deposit of an employee's salary to the employee's bank account *via* electronic transfer rather than issuance of paychecks.

Direct Discrimination: Refers to any overt bias towards a person based on characteristics such as age, sex, race, etc. Direct discrimination is often the product of stereotypes about a particular group. It can be expressed through a refusal to hire, dismissal, providing unfavourable working conditions or limited opportunities.

Disability Insurance: Insurance designed to protect employees during long-term disablement (and loss of income) through illness or injury.

Disciplinary Action: Invoking a penalty against an employee who fails to meet organisational standards or comply with organisational rules.

Discrimination: Any practice that makes distinctions between different groups based on characteristics such as sex, race, age, religion and so on, which results in particular individuals or groups being advantaged and others disadvantaged.

Disk Storage: Determines how much data can be kept in a computer for access and processing.

Dismissal: Dismissal is when you are removed from employment.

Distribution of Learning: Relates to the scheduling of training activities. In most cases, spacing out training produces more rapid learning and better retention.

Diversity Management: Activities involved in integrating non-traditional employees (such as women and minorities) into the work force and using their diversity to the firm's competitive advantage, as well as considering other work force characteristics that need to be addressed to ensure fair and effective utilisation of employees.

Diversity: Human characteristics that make people different from one another.

Divestiture: Selling selected operating units for either strategic or financial reasons.

Division of Labour: Process of dividing work and assigning tasks to workers.

DOC/DoC: Department of Conservation.

Domestic HRM: HRM as practised within the geographical boundaries of one country. Its focus is the management of people in a single-country context.

Domestic Supply of Tourism Commodities: Domestic supply of tourism commodities is defined as the total production in Canada of the tourism commodities which are mainly produced by tourism industries. Not all of domestic supply is purchased by visitors, so that supply exceeds tourism demand for the National Tourism Indicators (NTI). For example, visitors purchase only a small proportion of food and beverage services, with most going to local consumption. Also, supply does not include imports. For example, the sale of a ticket on a non-Canadian airline is excluded from supply.

Domestic Tourism: Travel within the country of residence.

Dominant or Traditional Employees/Group: Employees who come from the majority group. In Australia, the dominant racial/ ethnic group are people, particulary men, of Anglo-Celtic ancestry.

Door Rate: Retail price for accommodation/activity.

Dormitory Income Fund Reimbursable (DIFR): Budgetary term to describe funding for positions and budgets supported by income generated from dormitory (Residence hall) fees. Positions may be established as PSR (Personal Service Regular) or TS (Temporary Service) even though funded by revenues.

Double-click: Clicking a mouse button twice in quick succession.

Download: Process of transferring a file or programme from a remote location on to your own computer.

Downsizing: A reduction in a company's work force to improve its bottom line.

DTS: Domestic Travel Study.

Dual Career: Situation where both spouses or partners have career responsibilities and aspirations.

Duration Code: Identifies the expected duration of the position (e.g., calendar year).

DVD: Digital Versatile Disk: stores digital data (e.g. audio, video, text for use on computers, televisions, etc.

Early Retirement: Occurs when an employee retires from an organisation before normal retirement age.

Earmark: The term used when a position has been designated for restudy when vacant to determine its proper classification before being refilled.

ECAT: E-Commerce Action Team.

Economy Class Syndrome: Blood clots caused by cramped airline seating.

Ecotourism: "Responsible travel to natural areas that conserves the environment and improves the welfare of local people," according to the International Ecotourism Society.

Education: Activities designed to improve the knowledge, skills and abilities of an individual.

Effective Date: The day an action is to commence.

Effectiveness: Determining appropriate objectives; 'doing the right things'.

Efficiency: Minimum use of resources to achieve the organisation's objectives; 'doing things right'.

eLearning: Learning with the support of electronic materials (e.g. *via* computers, the Internet and DVDs).

Electronic Books: Also known as ebooks, these are electronic copies of books. Ebooks may be available in electronic format only, or they may have a print equivalent.

Electronic Journal/Magazine: A journal which is available electronically. It may be available in electronic format only, or it may have a print equivalent. Some ejournals are available free of charge, others require payment or a subscription (see *pay-to-view*).

Electronic Recruiting: Recruiting via the Internet (external) and intranet (internal). Sometimes called *cybercruiting*. Employability having marketable skills (skills that are attractive to employers).

Eligible List: A certified list of candidates for a competitive title ranked in order of their respective final examination ratings, including seniority and veterans credits.

email: Short for electronic mail, this allows users to send messages *via* computers and networks. Email is normally sent and received very quickly.

Employee Assistance Programmes (EAPs): Company-sponsored programmes that help employees to cope with personal problems that are interfering with their job performance.

Employee Champion: Requires the HR manager to be the employee's voice in management decisions.

Employee Motivation: See *motivation*.

Employee Obligations: Those duties and obligations defined in law that an employee must fulfil.

Employee Relations (ER): Concerned with the relationship between an organisation and its employees. Sometimes ER is regarded as the same as Industrial Relations (IR). The focus of ER is more on workplace relations than the traditional IR emphasis on institutions and the making of rules governing the employer-employee relationship.

Employee Retirement Income Security Act (ERISA): Employee Retirement Income Security Act.

Employee Turnover: See *turnover*.

Employees' Retirement System (ERS): Employees' Retirement System. A define benefit retirement programme available to all State employees.

Employer Associations: Represent employer interests at industrial tribunals and provide a range of IR advisory services, including award interpretation, dispute handling and how to countre union activity.

Employer Obligations: Those duties and obligations defined in law that an employer must fulfil.

Employment Contract: An informal (oral) or formal (written) agreement between an employer and employee specifying the legal obligations of each.

Employment Process: Includes recruitment, application flow, hiring, job placement, compensation, promotion, transfer, termination, shift assignments, geographical and departmental assignments, and all other such activities.

Employment Relations: Attempt to integrate HR and IR. Views industrial relations and HRM as its constituent parts.

Employment Tests: Attempt to assess the match between the application and the job requirements. Examples include typing, welding and driving tests.

Empowerment/Enablement: Empowerment/Enablement are strategies aimed to give people more control and responsibility for their work.

Empowerment: Giving employees a reasonable amount of authority and the means and decision guidelines for exercising it.

Enterprise Award: An award that applies to a single employer or enterprise and its employees.

Enterprise Bargaining: Direct negotiation that takes place between an employer or enterprise and its employees and/or its nominated representatives.

Enterprise Flexibility Agreements (EFAs): Collective non-union agreements directly negotiated between employers and their award employees.

Enterprise Unions: Unions that only represent the interests of employees working for a single employer or enterprise.

Entrepreneurial Skills: Skills related to identifying business opportunities and receiving a sustainable income from these opportunities.

Environmental Awareness: Consideration of the impact of practices and operations on the natural environment (e.g. using products that do not harm the environment).

Environmental Influences: Refers to opportunities and threats that may be present in the organisation's external and internal environments.

Equal Employment Opportunity (EEO): Means giving people a fair chance to succeed by avoiding discrimination based on unrelated job factors such as age, race, sex or nationality.

Equal Employment Opportunity Commission (EEOC): Federal agency responsible for administration of several statutes which prohibit discrimination; has power to subpoena witnesses, issue guidelines that have the force of law, render decisions, provide technical assistance to employers, provide legal assistance to complainants, etc.

Equal Opportunity: Concept that all individuals should have equal consideration and treatment in employment regardless of their sex, race, religion or other non-job-related factors.

Equity Theory of Motivation: A theory that assumes that people have a strong need to balance their inputs of labour and their rewards.

Error Message: A text message displayed when the computer detects a problem.

Essay Description: A written statement describing an employee's strengths, weaknesses, past performance and future development prepared by the rater.

Ethics: Deals with what is good and bad or right and wrong, or with moral duty and obligation. Ethical behaviour may require higher standards than that established by law.

Ethics: Set of unwritten rules by which society or an industry abides.

Ethics: Usually a reference to New York State Ethics Commission which was established by the Public Officers' Law.

Ethnicity

- American Indian or Alaskan Native—a person having origins in any of the original peoples of North America who maintains cultural identification through tribal affiliation or community recognition;
- Asian or Pacific Islander—a person having origins in any of the original peoples of the Far East, Southeast Asia, the Indian Sub-continent, or the Pacific Islands;
- Black—a person, not of Hispanic origin, having origins in any of the black racial groups of Africa;
- Hispanic—a person of Mexican, Puerto Rican, Cuban, Central or South American, or other Spanish culture or origin, regardless of race; or
- White—a person, not of Hispanic origin, having origins in any of the original peoples of Europe, North Africa, or the Middle East.

Evaluation Phase (Training): Concerned with measuring how well a training activity met its objectives.

Executive Leasing: Similar to temporary help except that the focus is on supplying management and professional personnel.

Executive Recruiters: Firms specialising in locating qualified candidates for top management jobs.

Executive Search: Sometimes called 'head-hunting'. Executive search firms specialise in identifying top-level executives for key positions and approaching them directly.

Exempt Class (Classified): All positions for the filling of which competitive or non-competitive examination may be found to be not practicable.

Exempt Employees (Professional): Employees in jobs that are purely management, administrative, or professional that perform without close supervision and consequently, they are exempt from coverage under the Fair Labour Standards Act. Rules regarding overtime and wages do not apply.

Exit Interview: An employee's final interview following separation. The purpose of the interview is to find out the reasons why the employee is leaving (if the separation is voluntary) or to provide counselling and/or assistance in finding a new job.

Expatriate Packages: Total compensation and benefits given to personnel on a foreign assignment. Include base salary, foreign service premium, hardship allowance, housing assistance, education allowance, relocation allowance and other special allowances and benefits associated with a foreign assignment.

Expatriate: Someone who lives and works in a foreign country.

Expectancy: Employee's perceived probability that exerting a given amount of effort will lead to performance.

Exposure: Employee behaviour designed to make management aware of the employee's abilities and achievements.

External Equity: Payment of employees at rates comparable with those paid for similar jobs elsewhere.

Extinction: Withdrawal of a positive reinforcer so that the undesired behaviour gets weaker and eventually disappears.

Extra Longevity Rate: Salary resulting from the addition of two extra increments provided to employees who have rendered continuous and satisfactory service for ten years after having attained the normal maximum pay of their salary grade.

Extra Service: Work performed by an employee in addition to the regular full-time position.

Factor Comparison System: Job evaluation technique that involves comparing (ranking) jobs on a range of factors such as know-how, responsibility, etc. Each factor ranking for each job is converted to points. The total number of points for the factors equals the job size.

Fair Labour Standards Act (FLSA) : Law enacted to establish a minimum wage, to limit work hours, and to discourage oppressive child labour. Referred to as the Wage Hour Act because it ensures fair treatment of employees with respect to wages and hours. Act defines exempt and non-exempt employees. For more information go to Fair Labour Standards Act Handbook or Fair Labour Standards Act Regulations.

Familiarization Trip: A complimentary or reduced-rate travel programme for travel agents, airline or rail employees or other travel buyers, designed to acquaint participants with specific destinations or suppliers and to stimulate the sale of travel. Familiarization tours, also called fam tours, are sometimes offered to journalists as research trips for the purpose of cultivating media coverage of specific travel products.

Family Medical Leave Act (FMLA): For more information, go to Family Medical Leave Act Handbook (FMLA) or Family Medical Leave Act Regulations.

FAQ (Frequently Asked Questions): FAQs are commonly used on the Web to offer novice users help on a particular topic.

Faveurites: A way of storing web addresses so you can find them easily (Favourites can be found on Microsoft Internet Explorer—they are called "Bookmarks" on Netscape).

Featherbedding: A type of restrictive work practice that involves the use of too many employees for the actual work to be performed.

Fee: A method of payment that allows periodic payments of varying amounts based upon the completion of some measurable unit of work/accomplishment.

Feedback: The extent to which the job permits the employee to obtain clear and direct knowledge about how well they are doing. Fixed interval schedule Frequency of reinforcement is determined by an interval of time (for example, hour, day, week, month, year).

File: A collection of related data or records. A file is used to store data, or programme, on disk for later use.

Financial Exigency: An imminent financial crisis which threatens the survival of the institution as a whole and which cannot be alleviated by less drastic means than layoffs.

Fiscal Year: The States fiscal year is from 4/1-3/31; SUNY's fiscal year is from 7/1-6/30.

FIT (Free Independent Travellers): Visitors coming to NZ on holiday who do not purchase pre-packaged travel or pay for anything other than international airfares prior to arriving in NZ. Whilst in NZ, they organise their own travel as they go, do not travel as part of a tour group or on a coach tour.

Fixed Ratio Schedule: Occurs when an employee is rewarded after producing a fixed number of items or performing an activity a fixed number of times.

Flame: Abusive message posted to a newsgroup as part of an on going argument or discussion.

Flat Organisation Structure: Organisation structure with a wide span of control, few managerial levels and a short chain of command.

Flexibility: It describes changes in the size of the workforce, depending on short-term changes in market conditions.

Flexitime: Allows employees to follow different schedules of work each day of the workweek.

Flexitime: System that allows employees to choose their own starting and finishing times within a broad range of available hours.

Focus Groups: Groups of employees who are brought together to confidentially discuss specific HR topics such as a company's pay-for-performance programme, restructuring, quality of management, and so on.

Food Commodities: Food items (e.g. meat, vegetables, dairy, eggs, fish).

Foreign Independent Travel or Foreign Individual Travel (FIT): An international pre-paid unescorted tour that includes several travel elements such as accommodations, rental cars and sightseeing. A FIT operator specialises in preparing FITs documents at the request of retail travel agents. FITs usually receive travel vouchers to present to on-site services as verification of pre-payment.

Foreign Service Premium: Paid to the expatriate as compensation for being located outside of their home country.

FOREX: Foreign Exchange Earnings.

FoRST: Foundation of Research, Science and Technology.

Freedom of Information Act: Establishes that any person has the right to request access to federal agency records or information.

Freeware: Software distributed *via* the Internet that can be downloaded and utilised for free.

Fringe Benefits Tax: Australian federal government tax designed to tax organisations on the benefits provided by them to their employees.

Fringe Benefits: Indirect or non-cash compensation items such as life insurance, medical benefits, sick leave and the like.

FTE (Full Time Equivalent): A full-time position budgeted from 7/1 to 6/30. The term equates an employee to a full-time equivalent. For example, a part-time employee who works one half of the time required of a full time employee would be counted as .50 FTE.

FTE: Full Time Equivalent employee.

Full Text: When it is possible to view a complete document, rather than simply a summary or abstract of it.

Functional Areas: The operating areas in the hospitality industry, including front of house (reception), accommodations services, food preparation, and food and drink service.

Functional Competency: Concerned with job-specific competencies. For example, can the person satisfy the skills, knowledge and experience requirements of the job to perform at a satisfactory level?

Functional Job Analysis: Job analysis method that uses standardised statements and terminology to describe the nature of jobs and to prepare job descriptions and job specifications.

Gainsharing: An incentive system that shares the gains from productivity improvements with the employees who made the improvements.

Gate Rate: Retail price for accommodation/activity.

Gateway: A search tool that provides links to Websites, organised by subject area. These links have been assessed against specified quality criteria and also provide short descriptions of sites.

GBA: General Booking Agreement.

GDP (Per Cap): Gross Domestic Product (earned per capita).

Gender: The social construction of males and females. It describes what is seen as appropriate rules and behaviour for men and women.

General Union: A union that represents workers without regard to their skill, qualifications, occupation or industry (for example, the Australian Workers Union).

Genetic Screening: Biological testing that can determine whether a job applicant is genetically susceptible to certain diseases, such as cancer and heart disease or to specific chemical substances.

Geotourism (1998): Tourism that sustains or enhances the geographic character of the place being visited—its environment, culture, aesthetics, heritage, and the well-being of its residents.

Glass Ceiling: Occurs when people can see higher-level positions but are blocked by an unseen barrier, such as discrimination.

Glass Walls: A hypothetical barrier that faces women (and minorities) in moving across functions in an organisation.

Go Slows: Occur when workers refuse to work at their normal pace in order to pressure management into making a concession. Often implemented by working strictly according to the rules.

Goal Setting: The process of defining an objective or target to achieve. Gives a sense of purpose or direction to an action.

Goal: Also called an *objective* or *target*. A goal is a desired result. It may be quantitative or qualitative. A goal should be measurable and have a deadline.

Government Employment Agencies: Sometimes called *personnel consultants*. Typically specialised in the recruitment of clerical and secretarial personnel.

Governor's Office of Employee Relations (GOER): An abundance of information on collecting bargaining units, training, benefits, etc.

Grading: Employee's performance is matched with a specific grade definition such as superior, good, acceptable, marginal and unsatisfactory.

Graduate Student Employee Union: Union that represents State graduate and teaching assistants.

Graphic Scales: Rating scale that evaluates employee performance using specific employee behaviour or characteristics (for example, quality and quantity of output, reliability, etc.).

Graphology: The study of handwriting for the purpose of measuring personality.

Grievance Procedure: A formal, systematic process that permits employees to complain about matters affecting them and their work.

Grievance: Any dispute or difference arising between the employer and an employee or the union.

Gross Lettings: This refers to all room lettings, i.e., both paid and complimentary listings are included.

Group Incentives: Incentives designed to recognise group as opposed to individual performance.

Group Interviews: Meetings in which several job applicants interact in the presence of one or more company representatives.

Group Tour and Group Leader: Group Tour—a travel agent type company which plans motor coach trips. Group Leader—A small, informal group, such as a church group, scout troop, or social group. Usually one person plans the activities for the group. Some travel shows target these planners such as GLAMER.

Group Travel: Often used to mean coach tour travellers, but can also refer to holiday-makers who travel with a group of two or more couples, a family group, a school or special interest group, etc.

GSA: General Sales Agreement.

Halo Effect: A problem that occurs during performance appraisal, when a supervisor's rating of a subordinate on one factor biases the rating of that person on other factors.

HANZ: Hospitality Association of New Zealand.

Harassment: Behaviour designed to make a person feel unwelcome, offended, humiliated and/or intimidated.

Hardship Allowance: Paid to compensate the expatriate for hardship resulting from physical isolation, cultural and language differences, extremes of climate, political instability and other inconveniences.

Hardware: Physical parts of a computer; for example, the hard drive.

Hardware: The actual electronic (and mechanical) devices that make up a computer system. This includes both the computer itself, the monitor (with the screen), the keyboard and any other parts.

Health and Safety Committee: Joint employer-employee committee responsible for examining OHS matters in the workplace.

Health and Safety Representative (HSR): Employee charged with representing the OHS interests of a work group.

High-context Cultures: Cultures where non-verbal communications (such as body language and gestures) and indirect language are used to transfer meaning. China and Japan are examples of high-context cultures.

HIS: Hospitality and Service Industry Training Organisation.

Hits: Different definitions depending on context. *Search hits.* The number of results retrieved from an Internet search. *Site hits.* The number of times a server is accessed for different Web object. This is sometimes used to compare the usage of different sites, but is an unreliable indicator as one page with five graphics will register six hits when viewed, whilst a page with no graphics will display one hit.

HIV/AIDS Testing: Medical tests designed to determine the presence of AIDS in job applicants or existing employees.

HIV/AIDS: Human immunodeficiency virus that causes a breakdown in the body's immune system and can lead to the development of AIDS.

Holiday Pay: Additional compensation for time worked by an employee during regularly scheduled hours on a date observed as a holiday by the State.

Holiday Travel: Travel of 1-365 days duration, for the purpose of a holiday, a honeymoon, skiing/snowboarding, or as an incentive/reward for good work.

Home Page: The default document World Wide Web users see when connecting to a Website for the first time. Websites often use the term to describe the first (or most important) page on their particular site.

Home-country National: An expatriate who is a citizen of the country where a multinational company is headquartered; for example, an American working for a company with its headquarters in the United States.

Homosocial Reproduction: Sometimes called 'comfort cloning'.

Occurs when existing groups of people replicate themselves through selecting people like themselves to join their group.

Honesty Tests: Tests designed to evaluate a candidate's honesty and integrity.

Horizontal Loading: Job enrichment through the addition of tasks of a similar nature.

Hospitality: A general term used in travel & tourism describing the "hospitality industry"; Refers to the general greeting, welcoming, food service, etc.

Hospitality Products: Incorporates all services supplied by the hospitality industry (e.g. accommodation, food and drink, conferencing).

Host-Country National: A local employee of the foreign location working for a multinational; for example, a Singaporean working in Singapore for a US multinational.

Hostile Work Environment: Occurs when an employee is subjected to unwanted harassment in the workplace.

Hotel Package: A package offered by a hotel, sometimes consisting of no more than a room and breakfast; sometimes, especially at resort hotels, consisting of (ground) transportation, rooms, meals, sports facilities and other components.

HR Audit: Involves a systematic analysis and evaluation of the efficiency and effectiveness of the HRM function and its contribution to the achievement of the organisation's strategic business objectives.

HRIS Security: Concerned with the protection of HRIS data from invasion and abuse by unauthorised parties.

HRM Activities: Refers to HR activities such as job analysis, HR planning, recruitment, etc.

HRMS (Human Resource Management System): Information system for management of employee and position data. For campuses using HRMS, it forwards information to PayServ to effect payments.

HTML (Hypertext Markup Language): Which is the standard computer language for creating Web pages. So if you see a file called "Bristol-University.html" the chances are it is a hypertext document for the Web about Bristol University.

HTTP (Hypertext Transmission Protocol): The standard language that World Wide Web clients and servers use to communicate. You will often see HTTP at the beginning of a URL (Web address).

Human Capital: The knowledge, skills and abilities of an organisation's employees.

Human Relations Movement: Recognises that employees seek more than financial rewards from their jobs. Focus is on group norms and behaviour.

Human Resource Development (HRD): Includes training and development, career planning and performance appraisal. Its focus is on the acquisition of the required attitudes and knowledge to facilitate the achievement of employee career goals and organisational strategic business objectives.

Human Resource Information System (HRIS): Use of computers to systematically generate relevant and timely information for the making of HRM decisions.

Human Resource Management (HRM): Involves the productive use of people in achieving the organisation's strategic business objectives and the satisfaction of individual employee needs.

Human Resource Planning: The process of systematically reviewing human resource requirements to ensure that the required number of employees, with the required skills, are available when they are needed.

Human Resource Strategy: A firm's deliberate use of human resources to help it to gain or maintain an edge against its competitors in the marketplace.

Humanistic (Soft): HRM recognises the need for the integration of HR policies and practices with the organisation's strategic business objectives, but places emphasis on employee development, collaboration, participation, trust and informed choice.

Hygiene Factors: Lower-order employee needs that are met by pay, working conditions, interpersonal relations, supervision, company policy and administration.

Hyperlink: You can navigate around Web pages using hyperlinks *via* mouse clicks. Hyperlinks are usually blue, underlined text although other colours are sometimes used. Hyperlinks usually change colour (often to purple) once you click on them.

I-9: Form required of all appointees to verify their U.S. citizenship, or if they are aliens, their eligibility for employment in accordance with the U.S. Citizenship and Immigration Services.

IATA: International Air Transport Association.

ICOMOS: International Council of Monuments and Sites.

IMP (International Media Programme): A Tourism New Zealand programme to attract quality media to cover New Zealand.

Impromptu Travel: No arrangements booked in country of destination prior to travel (Another name for FIT travel).

In-basket Exercises: See *in-basket training.*

In-basket Training: A simulation in which the participant is asked to establish priorities for handling a number of business papers, such as memoranda, reports and telephone messages, that would typically cross a manager's desk.

Inbound Tour Operator: NZ based tourism operators who put together itineraries and process reservations (including accommodation, transport, activities and attractions) on behalf of offshore tour wholesalers and retail agents.

Inbound Travel/Tourism: Short-term arrivals into a country by nationals/residents of other countries.

Incentive: A reward to be given if a specified goal is achieved.

Incentive Compensation: Compensation that is linked to performance by rewarding employees for actual results achieved instead of seniority or hours worked.

Incentive Tour: A trip offered as a prize, usually by a company to stimulate employee sales or productivity.

Income Fund Reimbursable (IFR): Budgetary term to describe funding for positions and budgets support by income generated from fees. Positions may be established as PSR (personal service regular) or TS (Temporary Service) even though funded by revenues.

Increment (Classified): An established salary increase between steps of a given salary grade, marking a steady progression from the minimum of the grade to the maximum.

Independent Travel: Travellers who make their own arrangements and devise their own itineraries, i.e. both FIT and SIT travellers but not group or coach tour travellers.

Indirect Discrimination: Occurs when policies, procedures and practices that appear to be neutral (that is, non-discriminatory) produce adverse outcomes for people with specific characteristics.

Individual Incentives: Incentives directly linked to individual (as opposed to group or team) performance.

Industrial Democracy: Type of employee participation that involves a redistribution of decision-making power from management to employees (often *via* a trade union).

Industrial Relations: Involves employees and their unions, employers and their associations and governments and the industrial tribunals that make regulations governing the employment relationship.

Industrial Relations Commission (IRC): Federal industrial tribunal charged with preventing and settling industrial disputes.

Industrial Tribunal: Refers to government tribunals charged with preventing and settling industrial disputes.

Industrial Unions: Sometimes called general unions. Include all types of workers ranging from unskilled to skilled.

Information: Data that have been analysed and processed.

Infrastructure Costs: Cost of rent, maintenance, electricity, water and other overheads in the calculation of selling prices of meals or dishes.

Inquiry: A request for more information about an attraction or destination.

Institutional Services Unit (ISU): A negotiation unit in state service composed mostly of classified service employees responsible for providing therapeutic and custodial care in the State's institutions, currently represented by the Civil Service employees' Association, Inc. (CSEA).

Instrumental (Hard): HRM Stresses the rational, quantitative aspects of managing human resources. Performance improvement and improved competitive advantage are highlighted.

Instrumentality: The degree to which an employee believes that performing at a specific level will bring about a desired result.

Insubordination: The intentional and wilful refusal to accept the valid authority of a supervisor...the refusal to act on a direct order.

Integrated Competence: The foundational, practical and reflexive competences necessary to achieve an outcome.

Intellectual Capital: The knowledge that exists within an organisation.

Intellectual Disability: Refers to an impairment of a person's mental functioning. A person is determined to have an intellectual disability if they have an IQ score of less than 70-5 and have difficulties with adaptive skills (e.g. following and understanding directions). Intellectual disabilities may result from genetic factors (e.g. Down Syndrome), physical factors (e.g. injuries, accident, infection) or environmental factors (e.g. inadequate nutrition).

Intelligence Tests: Measure an Individual's Intelligence (IQ) (that is, ability to reason).

Interactive: An interactive Website is one in which an action of the user generates a response either from another human being at the other end of the connection or with a computer programme.

Interest Tests: Aim to measure how an applicant's interest patterns compare with the interest patterns of successful people in a specific job.

Interim Appointment: An employee who is appointed following the departure of one employee and the installation of a permanent employee.

Internal Equity: Payment to employees according to the relative values of their jobs within an organisation.

International HRM: HRM as practised by multinational organisations. Its focus is the management of people in a multi-country context.

Internet: A global network of electronic information sources. It enables people to send mail, access reference material, share documents electronically and send computer software directly from one computer to another.

Internet Explorer: The name of a Web browser (a means of accessing information on the World Wide Web). Internet Explorer is provided by Microsoft.

Interviews: The job analyst interviews the job holder about the duties performed.

Intranet: A system of computers that enables employees within an organisation to communicate with each other.

IP Address: An IP (Internet Protocol) Address is something that identifies the computer you are using.

ISP (Internet Service Provider): An ISP is a company that provides Internet access for individuals, organisations and companies.

IT (Information Technology) Department: Responsible for the methods and equipment that provide information about all aspects of the operation of an organisation.

Itinerary: A travel schedule provided by a travel agent for his/her customer. A proposed or preliminary itinerary may be rather vague or specific. A final itinerary however provides all details (flight numbers, departure times, reservation confirmation numbers) and describes planned activities.

ITOC: Inbound Tour Operators Council.

ITOs: Industry Training Organisations or Inbound Tour Operator.

IVA (International Visitor Arrivals): Research on the number of international arrivals to NZ.

IVS (International Visitor Survey): Research on the behaviour of international visitors to NZ.

Job: A group of tasks that must be performed if an organisation is to achieve its objectives.

Job Analysis: A systematic investigation of the tasks, duties and responsibilities of a job and the necessary knowledge, skills and abilities a person needs to perform the job adequately.

Job Analysis Questionnaire: Questionnaire specially designed to collect information about job content, how the job is done and the personal requirements needed to do the job successfully.

Job Analysts: People who collect information about job content, how the job is done and the personal requirements needed to do the job successfully.

Job Characteristics Model: An example of comprehensive job enrichment. It combines both horizontal and vertical loading to stimulate employee motivation and satisfaction.

Job Characteristics Theory: See Job Characteristics Model.

Job Description: A written statement explaining what a job holder does, how the work is performed and where and when it is performed.

Job Design: Specification of the content of a job, the material and equipment required to do the job, and the relation of the job to other jobs.

Job Dissatisfaction: Employee dissatisfaction caused by poor pay, working conditions, supervision and/or company policy and administration.

Job Enlargement: The horizontal expansion of a job by adding similar level responsibilities.

Job Enrichment: The vertical expansion of a job by adding planning and decision-making responsibilities.

Job Evaluation: The systematic determination of the relative worth of jobs within the organization, which results in a pay system within the organization.

Job Grading: Job evaluation method that sizes jobs using a series of written classifications.

Job Hierarchy: A list of jobs in order of their importance to the organisation, from lowest to highest.

Job Posting: Advertising of job openings to current employees *via* bulletin boards, newsletters or personal letters.

Job Pricing: Placing a dollar value on the worth of a job.

Job Ranking: Job evaluation method that sizes jobs by placing them in rank order.

Job Rotation: Increases task variety by moving employees from one task to another.

Job Satisfaction: The degree to which employees have positive attitudes about their jobs.

Job Sharing: A concept that allows two or more people to share a single full-time job.

Job Specialisation: Involves the use of standardised work procedures and having employees perform repetitive, precisely defined and simplified tasks.

Job Specification: A written statement of the qualifications, skills and know how a person needs to perform a given job successfully.

Joint Venture: A form of strategic alliance or co-operative arrangement where ownership is shared and a separate enterprise formed. This may strengthen existing businesses through shared expertise, capital, removal of competition and creation of economies of scale. International tourism joint ventures between foreign organisations and local partners facilitate introduction of foreign products into local markets.

Jungle Tourism: Jungle tours have become a major component of green tourism in tropical destinations. A jungle is a sub-climax tropical forest consisting of a tangled growth of lianas, trees and scrub which may form an almost impenetrable barrier to the tourist. Jungle tours are a relatively recent phenomenon of Western international tourism.

Jurisdictional Classification: Means the assignment of positions in the classified service to the competitive, non-competitive, exempt, or labour classes.

Keyboard: The set of keys you press to input text and commands to the computer.

Key-informant Survey: This involves interviewing people who are likely to have some insight into a problem: operating managers; sales staff; managers; suppliers and consultants.

Keying: A social convention by which social 'reality' is transformed and seen as something else, such as the presentation of a fight as mere horseplay. In tourism, a peculiar, inverted variety of keying is frequently employed: the 'as if' situation in which participants are induced to playfully make believe that presented settings, activities or events are 'real', when as tourists they may be well aware that such occurrences are contrived.

Keywords: Used throughout this tutorial to indicate words you can use as search terms.

Kitchen/Restaurant Brigade: The specific titles and ranks of a team of workers in the kitchen or restaurant.

Knowledge Management: Deals with an organisation's ability to collect, store, share and apply knowledge in order to enhance its survival and success.

Knowledge Worker: A worker who transforms information into a product or service.

Labour Class: The labour class shall comprise all unskilled labourers in the service of the state and each of its civil divisions except those whose positions can be examined for competitively.

Labour Costs: The cost of the people and the time they take to prepare a meal or dish, as calculated in the selling price of the meal or dish.

Labour Market: The geographical area from which employees are recruited for a particular job.

Large-group Incentives: Designed to cover large groups of employees. Typically use broad achievement measures such as profit or sales.

Lateral Career: Career path where an employee undertakes a series of lateral moves (often in different functions) instead of moving upward within the organisation.

Lay Off: Separation of the employee from the organisation because of economic or business reasons.

Layoff: A layoff separates employees from the payroll due to budget constraints.

Lean Organisation: Organisation with relatively few managers overall and a low ratio of staff managers to line managers.

Learning Curve: A graphical representation of the rate at which a person learns something over time.

Learning Organisations: Organisations where the focus is on the acquisition, sharing and utilisation of knowledge to survive and prosper.

Legislation: The laws governing operations (e.g. health and safety).

Leisure Tourist: Leisure tourists, in contrast with business travellers, travel for pleasure and thus are not under any obligations to frequent specific destinations or facilities. They tend to be price and fashion conscious, concentrate their touristic activities to specific (vacation) times, and are influenced by marketing and publicity. Leisure tourism is heavily influenced by living standards, discretionary income levels and vacation entitlements.

Length of Stay: This refers to the period of time which people spend in a destination. Many definitions require that visitors to a destination stay at least 24 hours or overnight, and less than one year, to be considered a tourist. Destination areas often look for means to extend tourists' length of stay in order to increase positive economic impacts.

Leniency Bias: Occurs when employees are rated more highly than their performance warrants.

LGNZ: Local Government New Zealand.

Library Catalogue: A searchable database of items held in a library's collection.

Lifelong Employment: Situation where an employee is 'guaranteed' a job for their entire working life.

Line Manager: A manager who is authorised to direct the work of subordinates and is responsible for accomplishing the organisation's objectives.

Line Number: The unique number assigned to a position to identify it for payroll, accounting and budget certificate purposes.

Line of Sight: The relationship between employee control and influence over the end result. The more direct the relationship, the stronger the line of sight.

Link: A connection between two documents, image maps, graphics etc. on the Web.

Links Basket: Feature of the Intuit: Virtual Training Suite allowing users to collect links to Websites mentioned in the tutorial.

Local Area Network (LAN): Computer network connecting a group of computers within one work site, allowing them to exchange data and share hardware and software.

Local Employee: Someone who lives and works in their home country.

Local Nationals: Citizens of the host country in which the business is located; for example, a Singaporean working for an Australian company in Singapore.

Lockout: Refusal by management to let workers enter a plant or building to work.

Log of Claims: A list of demands covering pay and conditions of work typically made by a union on an employer.

Longevity Rate: Salary resulting from the addition of one extra increment provided to employees who have rendered continuous and satisfactory service for five years after having attained the normal maximum pay of their salary grade.

Long-haul Travel: Air travel of 8 or more hours duration.

LOS/LoS (Length of Stay): The amount of time a tourist spends in a particular place.

Lost Time: Employee absence not covered by allowable leave credits results in a lost-time pay deduction.

Lost-time Injury: A severe job-related injury that causes an employee to be absent from the job.

Low-context Cultures: Cultures where verbal communications are explicit and direct. What is said is what is meant. Australia and the United States are examples of low-context cultures.

Macro Region: Grouping of Regional Tourism Organisations into a larger regional marketing entity.

Mailing List: An email address which will distribute on to all subscribed members any email sent to it.

Mainframes: Biggest, fastest and most expensive class of computer.

Management: Art of getting things done through people.

Management by Objectives (MBO): Involves setting specific measurable goals with each employee and then periodically reviewing the progress made.

Management Confidential: Persons designated as managerial or confidential are excluded from coverage of the Taylor Law. Such persons are not eligible to be represented by an employee organization for the purpose of collective negotiations. They cannot belong to or hold office in an employee organization that represents or seeks to represent public employees employed by the public employer. Criteria for designation as managerial are: (*a*) formulates policy; (*b*) may reasonably be required on behalf of the employer to assist directly in preparation for and conduct of collective negotiations; and (*c*) has a major role in administration of agreements or in personnel administration not routine or clerical and requiring exercise of independent judgement. Confidential employees assist or act in confidential capacity to managerial persons who have a labour relation's responsibility.

Management Development: Any attempt to improve current or future management performance by imparting knowledge, changing attitudes or increasing skills.

Management Position Description Questionnaire: Job analysis method that uses a behaviourally oriented, structured questionnaire to describe, compare, classify and evaluate management positions. Management recruitment consultants Concentrate on advertised recruiting for professional and managerial positions.

Management Style: Reflects the particular approach used by a manager to achieve goals through other people.

Managerial Prerogatives: The decision-making rights considered by management as essential for the efficient and effective operation of the organisation.

Managing Diversity: See *diversity management.*

Mandatory Retirement: Designated age at which all employees must retire from the organisation (usually 65 years).

Market Postures: Determine where an organisation seeks to be in the pay market—above market, market average or below market.

Marketing Tool: A leaflet, pamphlet, card menu or invitation that is used to promote a product, service or event.

Markov Analysis: A mathematical technique used to forecast the availability of internal job candidates.

Marxist Approach: Sees industrial conflict as an aspect of class conflict. The solution to worker alienation and exploitation is the overthrow of the capitalist system.

Maximum Room Nights: This is calculated based on the total room inventory for all gazetted hotels.

Medical Examination: Examination to determine whether an applicant is physically fit to perform a job.

Medium-haul Travel: Air travel of between 4 and 8 hours duration.

Mentor: A person (generally an experienced manager) who helps a younger employee to advance his or her career by offering advice, giving instruction and opening up career opportunities.

Mentoring: A developmentally oriented relationship between senior and junior colleagues or peers that involves advising, role modelling, sharing contacts and giving general support.

Menu: A list of options from which the user selects an action to be performed by entering a letter or moving the cursor.

Merger: Combination of two or more firms to form one new company, which often has a new corporate identity.

Merit: Concerned with excellence, superiority and/or being the best qualified.

Merit Grid: Technique used to allocate rewards linked to performance.

Merit Pay: Any salary increase awarded to an employee based on their individual performance.

MFE: Ministry for the Environment.

MICE: Meetings, Incentives, Conventions and Events.

Micro-computer: Smallest and least expensive class of computer. Generally called a Personal Computer (PC).

Micro-processor: The logic, mathematic and central functions contained in a computer chip.

Microsoft Internet Explorer: The name of a Web browser (a means of accessing information on the World Wide Web) provided by Microsoft.

Middle Managers: Managers who are concerned with implementing the plans and policies of top managers.

MIDI Files (Musical Instrument Digital Interface): this is a way of communicating instructions for playing music from one electronic device to another, for example from a synthesizer to a computer to a musical instrument. Pronounced "middy".

Minicomputers: Computers that are more powerful than a microcomputer but less powerful than a mainframe computer.

Minimum Qualifications: Education, training, and/or experience requirements denoting the minimum standards that all candidates are required to possess to give reasonable assurance that they can perform satisfactorily.

Minimum Wage: The minimum hourly rate an employee may be paid for employment in the United States by federal statute.

Mise-en-Place: Basic preparation prior to or after cooking and serving.

Mission: General purpose or reason for an organisation's existence.

Mission Statements: The operational, ethical and financial reasons for an organisation's existence.

Motivation: That which energises, directs and sustains employee behaviour.

Motivator Factors: Higher-order employee needs for achievement, recognition, an interesting job, responsibility and advancement.

Motivators: Job-centred factors such as achievement and responsibility which, when present in a job, moderate employees.

Mouse: A device for a computer incorporating a ball, which is rolled around a flat surface. The movement is translated into movement of a cursor around the computer monitor screen.

Multimedia: The combination of plain text, pictures, sound and even moving video clips.

Multimedia Training: Training that combines audio-visual training methods with computer-based training.

Multi-Skilling: It is the increase of the skills base of the workforce, usually bringing in new technology.

Multi-source Evaluations (360-Degree Appraisals): Seek performance feedback on employees from their colleagues, superiors, customers and subordinates. Popular in companies with teams, TQM and employee involvement programmes.

Multi-tasking: It requires for staff to take on a wider range of tasks, usually involving on-the-job training.

Nature Tourism: Travel to unspoiled places to experience and enjoy nature.

Navigation Bar: The main set of links on a Website that connects to the main sections of the site. Also called the "navbar."

Needs Hierarchy: Sequence of five human needs, as proposed by Maslow—physiological, safety, social, esteem, and self-actualisation needs.

Negative Reinforcement: Also called avoidance learning. Involves the withdrawal or withholding of punishment when the desired behaviour occurs.

Negotiating Unit: The grouping of employees for the purpose of collective negotiations. When it is agreed or determined which employees shall make up a unit, the employees then select the employee organization they want to represent them in negotiations.

Negotiation: The process by which one party (for example, a union) seeks to get something it wants (for example, a pay increase) from another party (for example, an employer) through persuasion.

Netiquette: The cultural and social rules on the Internet. Ignoring them may result in being flamed or embarrassed in public.

Netscape: The name of a Web browser (a means of accessing information on the World Wide Web).

Networking: Using informed contacts inside and outside an organisation.

NewRTOs: Proposed 'new generation' RTOs.

Newsgroups: Internet bulletin boards that provide specialist discussion forums covering a vast range of topics.

Non-Competitive Class: Positions that are not in the exempt or the labour class and for which it is found by the commission having jurisdiction to be not practicable to ascertain the merit and fitness of applicants by competitive examination.

Non-Contributory Superannuation: Scheme where all contributions to the retirement plan are made by the organisation.

Non-Traditional Employees: Employees who are not part of the dominant group because of sex, race/ethnicity, disability or some other characteristic.

NTO (National Tourism Organisation): The body responsible for marketing the nation to tourists.

NZTB (New Zealand Tourist Board): Trading as Tourism New Zealand.

NZTE: New Zealand Trade and Enterprise.

Objective (Bargaining): The goal or target solution. It gives a sense of direction or purpose to the negotiation.

Objectives: Measurable targets to be achieved within a certain time frame.

Observation: The job analyst observes an employee working and records the duties performed.

Occupancy Rate: A tourism business occupancy rate refers to the number of airline seats or the units of hotel room space sold. This demand is usually measured as a percentage of available seats or space occupied for a given period of time. It is calculated by dividing the number of occupied rooms/seats by the total number available for sale during the same period.

Occupational Health and Safety (OHS): Concerned with the provision of a safe and healthy work environment.

Occupational Union: A union that represents workers from one occupation (for example, nurses or teachers).

OECD: Organisation for Economic Co-operation and Development.

Office of the State Comptroller: The Office of the State Comptroller in New York State is responsible for the audit and control function, for payroll auditing, for legal opinions, and for managing the NYS defined benefit retirement programmes.

Off-the-Job Training: Employment training that takes place away from the workplace.

Off-the-Shelf: Commercially available HRIS software.

Online: Connected to the Internet, usually *via* a personal computer and telephone line.

On-the-Job Training: Employment training that takes place at the job site and tends to be directly related to the job.

Open-Competitive List: A certified list of appointment eligibles containing the names of candidates who passed an open competitive examination for a title ranked by examination scores. Transfer lists, preferred lists, reemployment rosters, and promotional lists, if any take precedence.

Operant Conditioning: Also called learning by reinforcement or behaviour modification. Focuses on rewards and punishments and the effect that they have on employee behaviour.

Operational: Aspects pertaining to the operations occurring within the hospitality industry.

Operational Services Unit (OSU): A negotiating unit in NYS service composed of craft workers, maintenance and repair personnel and machine operators, currently represented by the Civil Service Employees' Association, Inc. (CSEA).

Operators: Terms that allow you to link keywords together to expand or refine a search (commonly AND, OR, NOT). You might also hear them referred to as "Boolean operators".

Optimal Turnover: Employee turnover that sees unwanted (i.e. low performing) employees depart and valued (i.e. high performing) employees stay.

Optional Retirement Programme (ORP): Refers to defined contribution retirements programmes approved for SUNY in 1964. Currently the authorized providers include ING, MetLife, TIAA-CREF and VALIC.

Options: Provide the opportunity for employees to be given shares, or to buy a specified number of shares at or below current market price.

Organisation Chart: Shows the relationships between jobs and those given authority to do those jobs.

Organisation Incentives: Cover all employees in an organisation and can take the form of a bonus, standard incentive or 'at-risk' incentive.

Organisational Competency: Concerned with what and how a person can contribute to the achievement of the organisation's objectives.

Organisational Culture: See corporate culture.

Organisational Structure: Refers to the organisation's framework or design.

Orientation (Expatriate): The introduction of the expatriate and their family to the culture, living conditions, etc., of the host country.

Orientation (New Hire): The introduction of new employees to their job, their colleagues and the organisation.

OTSP/OTSp (Office of Tourism and Sport): Now know as the Ministry of Tourism, te Manatu Tapoi (TMT).

Outbound Travel: Short-term departures by nationals/residents of a country.

Outbound Tourism: Outbound tourism is defined as tourism involving residents of a country travelling to another country. Outbound tour operators offer package tours abroad. They either operate the tours themselves, or they commission the services of an inbound operator to handle local arrangements at the destination. The country from which the tourists originate is known as the generating market or country.

Out-of-Title Work: Duties performed by an incumbent of a position, which are not appropriate to the class to which the position has been assigned.

Outplacement: Special assistance given to terminated employees to help them to find jobs with other organisations.

Outsourcing: It occurs when management invites external contractors to undertake work that was previously done by in-house staff.

Overtime Service: Hours worked in excess of the required 40 or 37 1/2 hours in the basic workweek as the case may be. Overtime in excess of 40 hours must be paid at a time and one-half rate. Employees whose basic workweek is 37½ hours accrue compensatory time for hours worked in excess of 37½ hours but not in excess of 40 hours in a basic workweek.

Package Tour: A saleable travel product offering an inclusive price with several travel elements that would otherwise be purchased separately. Usually has a predetermined price, length of time and features but can also offer options for separate purchase.

Package Traveller: Travellers who buy pre-packaged travel arrangements such as international airfares, accommodation, transport, activities/attractions prior to arriving in NZ for a holiday.

Paid Lettings: This refers to room lettings that are paid for by hotel guests.

Panel Interview: An interview in which a group of interviewers question the applicant.

Partial Reinforcement: Occurs when rewards are given occasionally after each desired behaviour; that is, the desired behaviour is not rewarded each and every time.

Participation Rate: Refers to the numbers of a particular group in the work force. For example, the increased participation rate of women in the work force is one of the most significant demographic changes to occur in recent times.

Password: A string of characters from the computer keyboard selected by a user to authenticate them when they log on.

Passwords prevent unauthorised access to personal accounts, restricted files, subscription services etc.

PATA: Pacific Asia Travel Association.

Pattern Bargaining: Occurs when the same (or essentially the same) pay and conditions are negotiated for several firms (often in the same industry).

Patterned Interview: An interview using a set sequence of questions that every candidate is asked.

Pay: The monetary compensation paid an employee for services.

Pay Compression: Occurs when workers perceive that the pay differential between their pay and that of employees in jobs above or below them is too small.

Pay for Performance: Pay system that rewards employees on the basis of their performance.

Pay Mode: The methodology used to compensate an employee. For full-time positions the pay mode is annual. For part-time employees it is usually biweekly.

Pay Policy: A firm's decision to pay above, below or at the market rate for its jobs.

Pay Secrecy: Occurs where salaries are kept confidential between the employer and the employee.

Payroll Deduction: An after-tax deduction from an employee's pay check for payment of taxes, insurance premiums, unions dues, health insurance premiums, etc.

PayServ: NYS Payroll System administered by OSC.

Pay-to-View: In the context of the Internet, this refers to sites that charge users subscription fees to view Web content.

PC (Personal Computer): A general term for a microcomputer designed for use by a single user at a time.

Pdf (Portable Document Format): Which is a file format for electronic documents. So if you see a file called "Annual-Report.pdf" the chances are it will be an electronic version of an annual report! To read pdf documents you need to have Adobe software on your computer, but this can be freely downloaded from the Web and you may have it on your machine already. Pdf documents have the advantage that they always appear with the same format, look and feel, whatever the equipment people use to view them. Because of this, they are often used by publishers who want some control over how their publications will appear to people who see them (contrast this with the Web, where the look and feel of a Web page usually depends on how you have your computer set up—in other words, the same Web page can look very different from different computers).

Peer Review: A performance appraisal system in which workers at the same level in the organisation rate one another.

Performance: Relates to the achievement or non-achievement of specific results designated to be accomplished.

Performance Appraisal: Concerned with determining how well employees are doing their jobs, communicating that information to employees and establishing a plan for performance improvement.

Performance Appraisal Record: Document used to record the performance ratings and supervisor comments on an employee's performance.

Performance Evaluation: A method of evaluating the behaviour of employees in the workplace, normally including both the quantitative and qualitative aspects of job performance.

Performance Indicators: Performance Indicators measure the improvements in throughputs, outputs and outcomes.

Performance Management: Aims to improve organisational, functional, unit and individual performance by linking the objectives of each. Incorporates job design, recruitment and selection, training and development, career planning and compensation and benefits, in addition to performance appraisal.

Performance Range: Salary administration technique used to better align performance with rewards.

Performance Related Pay (PRP): Links an individuals performance with their pay. Different schemes have been set-up to measure.

Performance Review Discussion: Where the manager and subordinate mutually review the employee's job responsibilities, performance improvement and career goals.

Performance Standards: The benchmarks against which performance is measured.

Permanent Appointment (Classified): An appointment to an unencumbered position of a candidate who has met all of the merit and fitness requirements for such appointment, including passing the necessary competitive examination and being reachable for appointment from an eligible list, if necessary. An appointment other than a Contingent Permanent, temporary, or Provisional appointment. After completion of a probationary term a permanent appointment continues until retirement, layoff, termination for incompetence or misconduct, resignation, or death.

Permanent Appointment (Professional): An appointment of a professional employee in a professional title, except those titles listed in Appendix A of the SUNY Policies of the Board of Trustees, which shall continue until a change in such title, resignation, retirement, or termination.

Personal Service Regular (PSR): A budgetary term to identify the type/source of funding. May include positions funded from IFR and DIFR as well as state positions (FTE) authorized in the NYS executive budget. PSR positions must be classified to appear on the SOP and appointees to them must be paid on an annual salary basis.

Personality Tests: Measure basic aspects of a person's personality or temperament (such as level of motivation, assertiveness, sociability, etc.).

Personnel Consultancies: Privately owned employment agencies.

Personnel Management (PM): Emphasis is on the administration of activities such as selection, training, welfare and industrial relations. As such, it is regarded as reactive and non-strategic.

Person-trip: A Person-trip for non-residents begins each time a non-resident traveller enters Canada. The person-trip concludes when the traveller leaves Canada. For residents, each time a person departs from Canada a person-trip begins. It ends when the traveller returns to Canada.

Physical Disability: Refers to an impairment of the body (e.g. someone who is missing a limb or who is paralysed). It can also include impairments to physical abilities resulting from diseases or conditions such as arthritis, back injuries and muscular dystrophy. Sometimes, people also refer to sensory disabilities (e.g. visual or hearing impairments) as physical disabilities.

Piecerate: Incentive system in which compensation is based on the number of units produced or sold. Employees are paid according to their level of output as opposed to a fixed amount per day, week or month.

Placement: Assignment of an employee to a new or different job.

Plagiarism: Plagiarism is using other peoples' ideas and words without clearly acknowledging the source of the information.

Plan: Action step that identifies how an objective or goal is to be achieved.

Plateauing: A career condition that occurs when job functions and work content remain the same because of a lack of promotional opportunities within the firm.

Plug-in: Plug-in applications are computer programmes that can enhance the use you get from your Web browser. For example, they can help you hear music and sounds over the Web, see videos and TV over the Web, see cartoon animations over the Web, read documents in a set format from the Web etc.

There are now hundreds of possible plug-ins, many available for free, though you will need to download them on to your machine (this is usually very easy). Once this has been done your Web browser will automatically incorporate it and use it when necessary. Popular plug-ins include: Adobe's Acrobat, a document presentation and navigation programme that lets you view documents just as they look in the print medium; Real Networks' streaming media player; Macromedia's Shockwave for interactive animation and sound. Most users wait until they need a particular plug-in before they download it.

Pluralist Approach: Regards conflict as inevitable because employers and employees have conflicting interests. Trade unions are seen as a legitimate counter to management authority.

Point System: An approach to job evaluation in which numerical values are assigned to specific job factors and the sum of those values provides a quantitative assessment of a job's relative worth.

Policies: Policies of the Board of Trustees of the State University of New York. Applies to all State employees in the SUNY Unclassified/professional Service (M/C & UUP).

Policy: A general statement that guides decision -making.

Polygraph: Lie detector that records changes in a person's physiology (such as heart rate, blood pressure) in response to a structured set of questions.

Population Ageing: The effect of slowing birth rates and longer life expectancy on the median age of the population.

Portability: The ability of an employee to transfer without penalty their accrued retirement benefits from one superannuation plan to another superannuation plan.

Position: An assigned group of duties and responsibilities, temporary or permanent, requiring the full-time or part-time employment of one person. It may be occupied or vacant.

Position Analysis Questionnaire: Job analysis method that uses a structured questionnaire for quantitatively assessing jobs.

Position Classification: Inventory Job analysis inventory that can be used to classify occupations and assess person—job fit.

Positive Reinforcement: Encourages a desired behaviour by repeatedly pairing the desired behaviour with rewards.

Post-exit Questionnaire: Survey questionnaire used with departed employees to find out why they left the organisation, their feelings about the company, their supervision, and so on.

Pre-booked Travel: Domestic airfares, accommodation, activities/ attractions or transport paid for prior to arrival in NZ.

Predictor: A selection criterion, such as the level of education or scores in an intelligence test.

Preferred List: A certified list of employees laid off from a title ranked by their seniority date. Preferred list candidates have absolute preference for positions based upon the "rule of one". Appointing officers must either reinstate the number one eligible willing to accept appointment or leave the position vacant.

Prejudice: Where a manager demonstrates a positive or negative bias.

Preventive Health Programmes: Programmes designed to promote employee health and fitness. Examples include physical fitness, stress reduction, weight loss and smoking cessation.

Printer: A device for producing paper copies of data.

Printout: Refers to anything printed out by a computer, or any computer-generated hardcopy.

Pro-active: When managers anticipate problems and take corrective measures to minimise their effect.

Probationary Period: Every permanent appointment from an open competitive list and every original permanent appointment to the non-competitive, exempt, or labour class shall be subject to a probationary period of not less than 26 weeks. If the probationer's service is less than satisfactory, employment may be terminated any time after the completion of eight weeks.

Process Theories: Attempt to explain motivation in terms of the thought processes that employees go through in choosing their behaviour.

Processing Speed: Speed at which a computer can process information and produce a report.

Productivity: The overall output of goods and services produced, divided by the inputs needed to generate that output.

Profession: An occupation having a common body of knowledge, a code of ethics and a procedure for certifying its practitioners.

Professional Association: Group of specialists who join together to advance their profession and enhance their own personal development.

Professional Employee: An employee in the professional services negotiating unit, other than an employee with academic rank or qualified academic rank.

Professional Ethics: Rules and principles that define right and wrong professional conduct.

Professional Literature: Literature relating to a particular academic discipline or professional occupation.

Professional Obligation: The professional obligation of an employee consistent with his or her academic rank or professional title shall include teaching, research, university service, and other duties and responsibilities required of him or her during the term of the professional obligation. Except for part-time or temporary employment where the obligation may be less, the term of professional obligation will be calendar year, or academic year, or college year.

Professional Staff: All persons occupying positions designated by the Chancellor as being in the unclassified service.

Professional Title: The title of a position in the professional services negotiating unit, other than a position of academic or qualified academic rank, as shown on the budget certificate for the position on file with the State Director of the Budget.

Professional, Scientific Services Unit (PS&T): A negotiating unit in NYS service composed primarily of professional classified service personnel, often with professional experience or a college degree prerequisite; currently represented by the Public Employee Federation (PEF).

Profit Centre: A unit where performance is measured by the difference between revenues and expenditures.

Profit Share: Reward programme that gives employees additional income based on the profitability of a work unit division or the entire organisation.

Profit Sharing: A plan whereby employees share in the company's profits.

Programme: A collection of instructions needed to solve a particular problem or to guide the computer in its operation.

Programmed Instruction: Based on the principles of operant conditioning. It involves presenting questions or facts, getting the trainee to respond, and then giving the trainee immediate feedback on the correctness of their answer.

Promote: Advance to a higher level or position generally resulting in increasing demands in terms of skills, abilities, and responsibilities.

Promotion: The movement of a person to a higher level position in the company.

Promotion from Within: Policy that gives preference to existing employees when filling a job vacancy.

Promotional List: A certified list of appointment eligibles containing the names of candidates who successfully passed a promotional examination for a title ranked by examination scores. Promotional lists take precedence over open-competitive lists but are subordinate to preferred lists.

Protected Class: Legally identified groups (by race, colour, sex, and national origin) that are specifically protected by statute against employment discrimination.

Provisional Appointment: A stopgap appointment to an unencumbered permanent position which may be made when no appropriate eligible list of at least three persons willing to accept appointment is available to fill a vacancy in the competitive class.

Psychological Contract: Unwritten expectations of an employee or an employer.

Public Employee Relations Board (PERB): A State agency with responsibility for providing oversight of collective bargaining for state employees including making unit determinations, rendering decisions in disputes, etc.

Public Employees Federation (PEF): Union that represents classified service professionals in New York State service.

Punishment: Occurs when negative consequences are experienced after the undesired behaviour is demonstrated.

Qualified Academic Rank: Rank held by those members of the academic staff having titles of lecturer or titles of academic rank preceded by the designation "clinical", or "visiting" or other similar designations. Service in qualified academic rank does not count in meeting the service requirements for tenure.

Qualitative HR Planning: The use of the opinions of experts to predict future HR requirements.

Quality: In tourism, the product is often intangible and quality is not apparent until after it is consumed. Quality has been defined as zero defects or defections, but still may be defined by the customer. The International Organisation for Standardisation defines quality as 'the totality of features and characteristics of a product oı service that bear on its ability to satisfy stated or implied needs'. Others believe that quality is a combination of outcome and processes, including internal and external conditions, and is obtained when the expectations and needs of customers are met.

Quality Circles: Small groups of employees who meet regularly to identify and solve work-related problems.

Quality of Work Life: Involves the quality of supervision, working conditions, pay and benefits and the nature of the job.

Qualmark: Classification and grading system for the New Zealand tourism industry, using 5 star system.

Quantitative HR Planning: Use of statistical and mathematical techniques to forecast demand and supply of labour.

Quicktime: Software developed by Apple that allows users to play back audio and video on their computer. You can download Quicktime Player freely from the Apple Website (see *plug-in*).

Quid Pro Quo: Involves a negotiator requesting a trade-off for every concession asked for; that is, something is always demanded for something.

Racial Vilification: A particular form of discrimination sometimes called racial harassment.

Rack Card: The typical tourism brochure sized 4" x 9" and used primarily in tourism racks. Also known as a "teaser."

Rack Rate: The official cost posted by a hotel, attraction or rental car, but not used by tour operators.

Rank: The salary grade level assigned to a position.

Ranking: The manager compares their subordinates' performance then ranks each in order from 'best' to 'worst'.

Rater Errors: Errors in the evaluation of an employee's performance resulting from leniency, strictness, bias, central tendency, prejudice, recency effect and the like.

Reachable: A person ranking by test score among the top three on an eligible list who are willing and able to accept appointment to a position in the competitive class.

Reactive: When managers wait until a problem occurs before taking action.

Real Player: Software that allows users to play back audio and video from your computer. You can download a free-version of the software from the Internet (see *plug-in*).

Realistic Job Preview: A method of conveying job information to an applicant in an unbiased manner, including both positive and negative factors.

Reasonable Notice: The amount of notice to be given to an employee before actual termination. What constitutes reasonable or sufficient notice is dependent on the particular circumstances of each case.

Reassignment: The change, without further examination, of a permanent employee from one position to a position in the same title under the jurisdiction of the same appointing authority.

Recall: An employee eligible to earn overtime compensation who is recalled to work overtime, after having completed his/her scheduled work period and left the scheduled work station, is considered to have worked a minimum of one-half day for the purpose of computing overtime compensation.

Recency Effect: The use of most recent events to evaluate employee performance instead of using a longer, more comprehensive time frame.

Reclassify: To reassign a position to a different class based upon a re-examination of the duties and responsibilities of the position.

Recognition Programmes: Make use of various rewards such as cash, merchandise, travel, certificates and the like.

Record: A collection of related data items, e.g. the personnel record of an individual.

Recruitment: The process of seeking and attracting a pool of qualified applicants from which candidates for job vacancies can be selected.

Recruitment Methods: The specific means by which potential employees are attracted to an organisation.

Recruitment Sources: Where qualified individuals are located.

Red Circle Salaries: Salaries that are above the range maximum for a job.

Redundancy: Employee termination resulting from the permanent elimination of some jobs because organisational or technological change has removed the need for those particular skills.

Re-entry Shock: The reverse culture shock experienced when the expatriate returns to their home country.

Re-entry: The repatriation or return of an expatriate to their home country after an international assignment.

Reference Check (Background Investigation): Investigation of the background of job candidates. Includes contacting previous employers, verifying dates of employment, salary and job title, as well as reports from credit agencies, letters of reference, and so on.

Reinforcement: The strengthening or weakening of a behaviour through the use of rewards or punishments.

Relationship Capital: The value of an organisation's relationships with its suppliers, customers and competitors.

Relationship Effect: This occurs where the nature of the superior/subordinate relationship influences a performance rating.

Reliability: The extent to which a measure (for example, a test) is consistent and dependable.

Renewal Capital: The intellectual property (patents, trademarks, copyrights, licences) of an organisation that have marketable value.

Repatriation: The return of the expatriates to their home country on the completion of an overseas assignment.

Replacement Chart: A visual representation of which employee will replace the existing incumbent in a designated position when it becomes vacant.

Resident: A person living in a given country, whether he is a national or not.

Resignation: Voluntary departure of an employee from a job.

Resignation Rate: A standard method of computing employee turnover that focuses on that part of employee turnover due to resignations.

Resource Discovery Network: (see *RDN*)

Restrictive Work Practices: Any practice designed to restrict the efficient and effective operation of an organisation. Examples include featherbedding, demarcations and limits placed on output.

Restructuring: Involves a major change to an organisation *via* downsizing, flattening, elimination of departments, and so on.

Retailer: Firms such as travel agents and airlines, that promote and sell travel to consumers.

Retirement: Permanent separation of an employee from the company (usually at a specified age; for example, age 60).

Retrenchment: Termination of the employment of any academic or professional employee during any appointment other than a temporary appointment as a result of financial exigency, reallocation of resources, reorganization, or curtailment of programmes or functions.

Reverse Discrimination: Occurs when a more qualified candidate from the majority group is denied an opportunity in preference to a less qualified candidate from a minority group.

RMA: Resource Management Act.

Role Ambiguity: Occurs when employees are uncertain of what they are expected to do in a job.

Role Conflict: A condition that occurs when an individual is expected to achieve opposing goals.

Role-Playing: A training technique where the trainee assumes a role in order to learn how others feel and think.

Role-Plays: Training activities in which participants assume the roles of specific people in situations (such as the roles of interviewer and job applicant), act out the event and then review the implications of their behaviour.

RTO (Regional Tourism Organisation): The entity responsible for marketing a region to tourists.

Rucker Plans: Gainsharing plans that calculate employee gains using a value-added formula.

Rule of Three: The "rule of three" requires that appointment or promotion to classified service positions in the competitive class from an eligible list must be made by the selection of one of the three highest ranking eligibles willing to accept appointment.

Rust-out: Stress produced from having too little to do.

Salaried Operations: Involves all employees being treated equally as staff rather than as staff and wages (or union) personnel.

Salary: Pay, which is usually stated as a monthly or annual figure and is monetary compensation for employee contributions without regard to the specific hours required of them to complete their responsibilities.

Salary Formula: The straight line (least squares) formula used to calculate the organisation's salary line.

Salary Line: Graphically depicts the salaries currently being paid for jobs, related to job size.

Salary Policy Line: A graphical representation of the organisation's predicted salary mid points.

Salary Range: Sets the minimum and maximum scheduled amounts paid for a job at a particular job size.

Salary Reviews: Management reviews of present salaries to determine if an increase is to be given and, if so, how much and when.

Salary Structure: Presents all salary ranges over the whole spectrum of job sizes.

Salary Survey: The vehicle for relating an organisation's salaries to those for similar jobs in other organisations.

Scanlon Plan: A gainsharing plan designed to link employee rewards to the firm's performance.

Schedule of Positions (SOP): Part of the position/expenditure control system. All positions established in PSR must be lined out (list by line item number) on the Schedule of Positions before OSC will approve expenditures from them.

Scientific Management: Explanation of employee motivation based on the work of Frederick Taylor. Emphasises the division of labour, task specialisation, time measurement and the use of monetary rewards.

Screen: The display surface of a computer monitor.

Scroll Bars: Controls what is displayed in the window; the position of the scroll bar button indicates the position of the information displayed in the total workspace. For example, if the scroll bar button is in the middle of the scroll bar, there is a equal amount of information off-screen on either side.

Scroll, Scrolling: Scrolling allows you to view consecutive lines of information on your computer screen. You will often need to scroll down a Web page to read all the data available.

Search Engine: An Internet search tool that is created automatically by a robots (also known as "spiders" or "crawlers"). Search engines usually catalogue millions of Web pages, so are a good place to go if you want to find a specific piece of information.

Search Tool: These are tools that allow you to search the Web. Common tools include search engines, Web directories and subject gateways.

Searching: A way of finding information on the Internet by entering one or more keywords into a search tool.

Seasonality: The influence of the time of the year on patterns in travel. The volume of travel to NZ is far greater during our summer and lower over winter.

Secondary Boycott: The practice of a union attempting to encourage third parties (such as suppliers and customers) to stop doing business with a firm.

Security Services Unit: A negotiating unit in NYS service composed of security personnel such as correction officers, campus public safety officers, and institution safety officers, currently represented by Council 82.

Security Supervisors Unit: A negotiating unit in NYS service composed of supervisors of corrections and safety employees, mostly lieutenants, currently represented by Council 82.

Selection: The process of choosing from a group of applicants those individuals best suited for a particular position.

Selection Criteria: Key factors in making a decision to hire or not to hire a person. May include qualifications, experience, special skills, abilities or aptitudes. Selection criteria should be job-related.

Selective Menu: A menu that offers a guest a limited choice of items per course.

Self-actualisation: Becoming what one is capable of becoming.

Self-evaluation: Occurs where the employees evaluate their own performance.

Self-fulfilling Prophecy: Occurs when expectations about someone cause them to behave in a way consistent with the expectations.

Self-regulation (OHS): Applies where employers are held responsible for providing a safe and healthy work environment. Emphasis is placed on education and information rather than detailed government regulation.

Seniority: Refers to an employee's length of continuous service with the State or at a campus; sometimes may also refer to an employee's time in title or rank, or appointment type, or length of service in a position or positions represented by a particular bargaining unit.

Seniority System: Where the length of time that an employee has worked with an organisation is given recognition and priority for promotions and salary increases.

Seniority-based Pay: Occurs where pay levels and increases are determined by length of time on the job and not performance.

Separation Rate: A standard method of computing employee turnover. Includes both avoidable and unavoidable separations.

Server: A computer which provides a service to other client computers.

Service Excellence: Service that exceeds the needs and expectations of the customer.

Sex: Relates to having male or female physical characteristics.

Sex Discrimination: Occurs when an individual is disadvantaged in employment because of sexual prejudice.

Sexual Harassment: Behaviour involving sexually suggestive remarks, unwanted touching and sexual advances, requests for sexual favours, or other verbal or physical conduct of a sexual nature.

SFRITO: Sports, Fitness, Recreation Industry Training Organisation.

Shift Pay Differential: Additional compensation over an employee's basic annual salary which may be authorized by the Director of Classification and Compensation subject to approval by the Director of the Budget. The pay differential may be prescribed for those employees on a night shift, four or more hours of which fall between 6:00 p.m. and 6:00 a.m.

Shockwave: A technology developed by Macromedia that enables Web pages to include multimedia objects. To view a Shockwave object, you need the Shockwave plug-in, a programme that is freely available from Macromedia's Web site (see *plug-in*).

Shop Stewards: Elected union officials who represent union members to management when workers have complaints.

Short-haul Travel: Air travel of less than 4 hours duration.

Sick Leave: Provides pay for an employee when they are absent from work because of illness.

Sick Leave Exchange Programme (SLEP): Programme that allows eligible M/C and UUP represented employees to exchange sick leave credits to reduce health insurance premiums.

Simulation: A training device designed to reproduce a real-world situation in a risk-controlled learning environment.

SIT (Semi-Independent Travellers): Visitors coming to NZ on holiday who do not purchase a fully pre-planned travel package. They may organise their own travel arrangements prior to or after arriving in NZ.

Skill-based Pay: A system that compensates employees on the basis of job-related skills and the knowledge they possess.

Skills Inventory: A company-maintained record of employees' abilities, skills, knowledge and education.

Skills Variety: The degree to which a job holder requires a variety of activities, skills and talents to perform the job.

Small-group Incentives: Incentives designed to reward work teams, project groups or departments.

SME(s): Small and Medium Enterprises.

Social Loafing: Occurs when an employee expends less effort and performs at a lower level when working in a group than when working alone.

Social Security: A federal retirement and disability income programme.

Socio-technical Enrichment: Focuses on the relationship between technology and groups of workers. The aim is to integrate people with technology.

Software: Programme of instructions that makes computers perform.

Spam: Used to describe unsolicited email advertising. Named after a sketch on Monty Python.

Specialisation: Occurs when a very limited number of tasks are grouped into one job.

Split Halves Method: A method of determining the reliability of a test by dividing the results into two parts and then correlating the results of the two parts.

Sponsor: A sponsor is a person who creates career development opportunities for others.

STA: Student Travel Association.

Staff Personnel: People in an organisation who provide advice and specialised support services to line personnel.

Stakeholder: Any individual group or organisation that is affected by or has a vested interest in an organisation's policies and decisions.

Statutes: Acts of parliament that legislate the minimum conditions of employment that must apply in any employer-employee relationship.

Stock Option Plan: The opportunity for employees to buy a specified amount of stock (shares) in the company in the future at or below the current market price.

Strategic Choice: Refers to managers being pro-active (as opposed to reactive) in facilitating the organisation's successful adaptation to changes in its environment.

Strategic Compensation: Involves compensation practices being aligned with the achievement of the organisation's strategic business objectives.

Strategic HRM: Focuses on the linking of all HR activities with the organisation's strategic business objectives.

Strategic Intent: Sustained obsession to achieve a challenging long-term objective.

Strategic Partner: Refers to HR managers being an essential part of the management team running an organisation and contributing to the achievement of the organisation's objectives by translating business strategy into action.

Strategic Planning: The determination of overall organisational purposes and goals and how they are to be achieved.

Strategic Recruitment: The linking of recruiting activities to the organisation's strategic business objectives and culture.

Strategic Selection: The linking of selection activities to the organisation's strategic business objectives and culture.

Strategy: Defines the direction in which an organisation intends to move and establishes the framework for action by which it intends to get there.

Strategy (Negotiating): The overall game plan designed to achieve the negotiating objectives.

Strategy Formulation: Involves selecting an organisation's mission, key objectives and business strategies.

Strategy Implementation: Involves designing an organisation's structure and control systems and evaluating the selected strategies in achieving the organisation's key objectives.

Stress: A condition of strain that affects one's emotions, thought processes and physical condition.

Stressors: Stressors are conditions that cause stress.

Strictness Bias: Occurs when employees are rated lower than their performance justifies.

Strike: Refusal by employees to work until their demands are met by the employer.

Strikebreakers: Non-union employees hired to replace striking union workers; also called scabs.

Structural Capital: The knowledge that is captured and retained in an organisation's systems and structures.

Structural or Systemic Discrimination: A form of hidden or indirect discrimination that is the product of social conditioning and that has become embedded within the system; for example, the view that it is 'natural' for women to be secretaries and men to be engineers.

Structured Interview: Uses a predetermined checklist of questions that usually are asked of all applicants.

Subordinate Evaluations: Sometimes called upward appraisals. Involve the subordinate evaluating the performance of their superior.

Substance Abuse: Concerned with alcohol, tobacco and other drug addiction.

Succession Planning: A career development activity that focuses on preparing high-potential employees to fill management positions.

Successive Hurdles Approach: Involves the screening out of candidates at each stage of the selection process.

Summary Dismissal: Dismissal based on an employee's serious breach of the employment contract (for example, physical and verbal abuse, drunkenness, neglect of duties and dishonesty).

Superannuation: Benefit paid as a pension and/or lump sum to help employees to meet their financial needs in retirement.

Supervisors: Lowest level of managers, responsible for managing operating employees.

Supplier: New Zealand based tourism companies, includes accommodation providers, activities/attractions, event organisers, retail shops, tour and transport operators.

Surfing: A favourite pastime for many Internet users! It means to move from place to place on the Internet searching for topics of interest. It's usually used to describe a rather undirected type of Web browsing where the user jumps from page to page, as opposed to specifically searching for specific information.

Sustainable Tourism: This is, according to the World Tourism Organisation, "envisaged as leading to management of all resources in such a way that economic, social and aesthetic needs can be fulfilled with maintaining cultural integrity, essential ecological processes, biological diversity, and life support systems."

SWOT Analysis: Review of an organisation's strengths and weaknesses and the opportunities and threats in its environment.

Sympathy Strike: Strike mounted by workers not directly involved in an industrial dispute to support strikers who are directly involved.

System: The combination of hardware and software making up a computer.

Systematic Approach to Training: Three-step approach to training that involves: (*a*) assessment of training needs; (*b*) conduct of the training activity; and (*c*) evaluation of the training activity.

TAANZ (Travel Agents Association of New Zealand): Association for NZ based travel agents.

Table d'hote: A set meal at a fixed price.

Tactics (Negotiating): Moves or ploys used to facilitate the successful negotiating strategy.

Tall Organisation Structure: Organisation structure with a narrow span of control, many managerial levels and a long chain of command.

Task Identity: Means doing an identifiable piece of work, thus enabling the worker to have a sense of responsibility and pride.

Task Significance: Means knowing that the work one does is important to others in the organisation and outside it.

Tax Equalisation: Ensures that the expatriate does not suffer a loss or windfall gain because of differences between home-country tax and the host-country tax obligations. This is achieved by the expatriate being taxed at the home-country tax rate irrespective of the host-country tax rate.

Tax Protection: Ensures that the expatriate does not suffer a loss in spendable income because of higher host-country taxes (by reimbursing the expatriate if the actual host-country taxes exceed the hypothetical home-country tax obligation).

Teachers' Retirement System (TRS): A defined benefit retirement programme available to SUNY professional service employees.

Team Appraisals: Appraisals that are specially designed to evaluate how well a team has performed.

Team Building: Brings together employers and employees, with the goal of increasing performance by strengthening relationships within the workplace.

Technical Assistant or Specialist Casual: A temporary employee appointed on a non-recurring basis that works less than 20 hours per week and is appointed for a period of 6 weeks or less per year unless working on a specific task or project.

Temporary Appointment (Classified): An appointment to a position which is established for only a temporary, short duration, or an appointment to a permanent position which is temporarily vacant.

Temporary Appointment (Professional): An appointment which may be terminated at any time. temporary appointments ordinarily shall be given only when service is to be part-time, voluntary, or anticipated to be for a period of one year or less, or when an employee's initial appointment is made to a position vacated by a professional employee who is serving a probationary appointment in another position. A temporary appointment is also appropriate whenever an employee on an approved leave vacates a position.

Tenure: Status granted to an employee, usually after completion of a probationary period, assuring him or her of the permanency of his or her employment.

Term Appointment: Except as provided in Section 6 of title D of Article XI of the SUNY Policies of the Board of Trustees, a term appointment shall be an appointment for a specified period of not more than three years which shall automatically expire at the end of the period unless terminated earlier because of resignation, retirement, or termination.

Test-retest Method: Determines selection test reliability by giving the test twice to the same group of individuals and correlating the two sets of scores.

Theory X: The assumption that employees dislike work, are lazy, seek to avoid responsibility and must be coerced to perform.

Theory Y: The assumption that employees are creative, seek responsibility and can exercise self-direction.

Third-country National: A citizen of a country differing from the home or host country; for example, a Singaporean working for an Australian company in Hong Kong.

TIA/TIANZ (Tourism Industry Association of New Zealand): Association that represents members in the tourism industry, mainly small and medium sized businesses.

Time Accrual System (TIMA): A system that is used to maintain employee accrual balances.

TLAs: Territorial Local Authorities.

TMT: The Ministry of Tourism, te Manatu Tapoi (also known as OTSp).

TNZ: Tourism New Zealand (also known as NZTB).

Tool Bars: Bars usually running along the top of the application allowing the user to carry out functions, e.g. menu bar, title bar, formatting toolbar.

Total Compensation: The package of quantifiable rewards an employee receives for their labour; includes three components: base compensation, incentives and indirect compensation/benefits.

Total Quality Management (TQM): Usually involves the introduction of continuous monitoring. It refers to initiatives designed to improve the quality of products and services to meet customer's requirements.

Tourism: The definition of tourism used in the National Tourism

Indicators (NTI) is that adopted by the World Tourism Organization and the United Nations Statistical Commission: "the activities of persons travelling to and staying in places outside their usual environment for not more than one consecutive year for leisure, business and other purposes."

Tourism Commodity: Tourism Commodity is one for which a significant part of its total demand in Canada comes from visitors.

Tourism Demand: Tourism Demand is defined as the spending of Canadian and non-resident visitors on domestically produced commodities. It is the sum of tourism domestic demand and tourism exports.

Tourism Domestic Demand: Tourism Domestic Demand is the spending in Canada by Canadian visitors on domestically produced commodities.

Tourism Employment: Tourism Employment is a measure of employment in tourism and non-tourism industries. It is based on an estimate of jobs rather than "hours of work". Thus, someone who works 10 hours a week counts for as much, by this measure, as someone who works 50 hours a week.

Tourism Exports: Tourism Exports is spending by foreign visitors on Canadian-produced goods and services. It includes spending that may take place outside of Canada, for instance, the purchase of an airline ticket from a Canadian international carrier, to travel to Canada.

Tourism Industry: Tourism Industry is an industry that would cease to exist or would continue to exist only at significantly reduced levels of activity in the absence of tourism.

Tourism Receipts: Tourism Receipts (TR) measures the total revenue received by Singapore from tourism activity. It includes all payments and prepayments for goods and services made by visitors, transit passengers, air and sea crew and foreign students (staying for one year or less) during their stay in Singapore. Visitors' payments to our national carriers (SIA & Silk Air) for international transport are also included.

Tourist: Temporary visitor staying at least twenty-four hours in the country visited for a purpose classified as either holiday (recreation, leisure, sport and visit to family, friends or relatives), business, official mission, convention, or health reasons.

Tracking Research: Ongoing research conducted at regular intervals to track changes in specific factors, for example, potential customers' intention to travel to NZ.

Trade Show: A product showcase for a specific industry. Generally it is not open to the public. Differs from a "Consumer Show" in that a trade show targets the professional industry, while a consumer show targets consumers.

Trade Unions: Formal organisations that represent individuals employed in one organisation, throughout an industry or in an occupation.

Traditional Career Path: A vertical line of career progression from one specific job to the next, more senior job.

Training: Represents activities that teach employees how to better perform their present jobs.

Training Needs Analysis: Identifies training needs and translates them into training objectives.

Transaction Processing: Discrete actions undertaken by a computer that are common and repetitive; for example, payroll calculation.

Transfer: A transfer involves an employee's reassignment to a job with similar pay, status, duties and responsibilities. Whereas a promotion involves upward movement, a transfer entails horizontal movement from one job to another.

Transfer of Training: Relates to the transfer of training to the work situation. The greater the transfer, the more effective the training.

Transformational Research: An information-gathering approach designed to help organisations to create an improved employment relationship.

Travel Agent: The individual who sells travel services, issues tickets and provides other travel services to the travel services to the traveller sat the retail level.

TRCNZ: Tourism Research Council New Zealand.

TRENZ (Tourism Rendezvous New Zealand): Annual exhibition at which tourism operators to market their products and services to wholesalers.

Tripartite Approach (OHS): Approach to OHS involving the active participation of employers, unions and government.

TRM: Trade Relations Management.

Trust: A measure of how willing employees are to share information, cooperate with one another and not take advantage of each other.

TSA (Tourism Satellite Account): Official calculation of the contribution of tourism to the New Zealand economy.

Turnover: The loss of employees by the organisation. It represents those employees who depart for a variety of reasons.

Turnover Analysis: Involves an examination of why employees leave an organisation.

Tutorial (Web): Web based exercises to work through to understand a particular topic/subject area.

Unclassified Service: The unclassified service shall include the following: all positions in the state university in the professional service as defined in sub-division 3 of Section 355a of the education law; all persons, other than persons covered under above, whose principal functions are teaching or the supervision of teaching in a public school, academy or college.

Under-development: Within development theory, the concept of under-development suggests that wealthy capitalist countries have held back the development of so-called Third World countries. Tourism in Third World destinations is controlled for the economic benefit of foreign owners, reinforces dependency, lacks involvement of local decision-makers, leads to negative socio-cultural impacts, and results in the promotion of staged attractions to capture an international tourism market.

Unfair Dismissal: Occurs where a dismissal is harsh, unjust or unreasonable, but need not involve a fundamental breach of the employment relationship.

Union Preference: Situation where job applicants who are union members have to be given preference in employment over non-union members.

Unitarist Approach: Industrial relations is grounded in mutual cooperation, individual treatment, teamwork and the sharing of common objectives. Trade unions are regarded as competitors for the employee's commitment and co-operation.

Unstructured Interview: Uses few, if any, planned questions. It enables the interviewer to pursue, in depth, the applicant's responses.

Upward Appraisals: Appraisals where the subordinate evaluates the performance of a superior.

Urban Recreation: The concept of urban recreation covers recreational activity that takes place in an urban environment in contrast to a rural setting. Participants in such activities are either urban residents themselves, day visitors from rural areas, or tourists. The major activities are shopping, visits to heritage sites, museums, movie theatres, operas, sport and music events, and indoor sports activities.

URL (Uniform Resource Locator): A unique address that allows you to access a Website. An example is http://www.bristol.ac.uk. Also called a Web address.

User: The person who is using or operating a computer system or terminal.

User Interface: The set of prompts, commands, messages provided to a user to enable him/her to use a computer programme or package.

USP (Unique Selling Proposition): Your point of difference, the thing that makes your product/service uniquely marketable to customers.

Valence: The value or importance that an employee places on a potential result or reward that can be achieved.

Validity: The extent to which something measures what it claims to measure.

Value-added: Activity that increases worth or utility.

Vapourware: Occurs when there is a discrepancy between what software claims to do and what it can actually accomplish.

Variable Interval Schedule: Rewards are administered at varied intervals.

Variable Pay Component: That part of pay that is not guaranteed and is at risk; that is, it is paid only if the performance target is met.

Variable Ratio Schedule: Rewards are administered only after an employee has performed the desired behaviour a number of times.

VDU (Visual Display Unit): A combined monitor and keyboard. Also referred to as a "terminal".

Vertical Career: Traditional career path where an employee enters the organisation at a junior level and progresses upward to more senior positions over a period of time.

Vertical Loading: Job enrichment through increased opportunities for responsibility, decision-making, recognition, personal growth and achievement.

Vestibule Training: Training that takes place away from the production area on equipment that closely resembles the actual equipment used on the job.

Vesting: Provision in a retirement plan that gives employees a right to specific benefits after a stated number of years of service.

Veterans Credits: Qualifying disabled veterans who pass competitive examinations are given ten points additional credits on their examination scores in open-competitive examinations and five points in promotional examinations. Non-disabled qualifying veterans receive five points and two points respectively. Veterans also have right of preference in retention in the event of a Reduction in Force (RIF) in the competitive class.

VFR: A trip for the purpose of Visiting Friends or Relatives for 1-365 days.

VIN (Visitor Information Network): Officially recognised network of information centres.

Virtual Training Suite: The parent service of this tutorial, a national Web service run by Intuit.

Virus: Rogue programme which can transfer itself from one disk to another (without the owner of the receiving disk knowing about it). The virus programme can then be triggered into action by certain commonplace commands or actions performed by the user. Some virus programmes may simply flash messages or pictures on the screen, but others may corrupt programme and data files.

Visitor: Any person visiting a country other than that in which he has his usual place of residence for any reason other than following an occupation remunerated from within the country visited.

Visitor Arrivals: Includes all who go through immigration clearance regardless of length of stay. This excludes the following:

(*a*) All Malaysian citizens arriving by land.
(*b*) Returning Singapore citizens residing abroad.
(*c*) Non-resident air and sea crew (except for sea crew flying in to join ship).
(*d*) All visitors arriving and leaving Singapore on the same ship/vessel and stayed in Singapore for less than 24 hours are not required to complete Disembarkation/Embarkation (D/E) cards, if passenger manifest is submitted.
(*e*) All organised tour groups leaving Singapore for Johor Bahru, Batam and Bintan, returning on the same day are not required to complete Disembarkation/Embarkation (D/E) cards, if passenger manifest is submitted.
(*f*) Air transit passengers
VISITOR DAYS = Number of Visitor Arrivals x Average Length of Stay.

Visitor Expenditure: Includes expenditure incurred during a visitor's stay in Singapore, or pre-payment by non-package tour visitors (this took effect from 1995). This excludes:

(*a*) *International Air and Sea Fare*: It is made up of the following components:
 (*a*) Shopping.
 (*b*) Accommodation.
 (*c*) Entertainment.
 (*d*) Sightseeing.
 (*e*) Food & beverage.
 (*f*) Local transportation.
 (*g*) Medical/dental treatment.
 (*h*) Miscellaneous.

Visitors: Visitors are persons who undertake tourism as defined above. They are referred to as either tourists (those who stay overnight or longer in the place visited), or same-day visitors.

Visitors Centre: Travel information centre located at a destination to make it easier for visitors to plan their stay; often operated by a convention and visitors bureau, chamber of commerce or tourism promotion organisation.

Volunteer Mindset: Employees are internally motivated (that is, they are self-motivated) to perform.

Wage: Pay for services rendered by employees, which is directly related to time (hours) worked.

Wage and Salary Surveys: Studies made by an organisation to discover what other employers in the same labour market are paying for specific key jobs.

Web Address: A unique address that allows you to access a Web site. An example is http://www.bristol.ac.uk. Also called a URL (Uniform Resource Locator).

Web Directories: These are search tools where human editors organise Websites under subject headings.

Web-based Training: Refers to training that is delivered *via* the Internet.

Weblog: See *blog*.

Website: The Web address or location of an organisation; for example, the Website for the Australian Human Resources Institute is www.ahri.com.au.

Wholesaler: Firms that purchase products or ground arrangements from New Zealand suppliers or inbound operators, and package products for sale. Wholesalers deal primarily with retailers, but sometimes also sell directly to the public.

Wiki: The term Wiki comes from wikiwiki, which means 'very quick' in Hawaiian. They provide a service which enables anyone to publish on a website without the use of special knowledge or software for editing HTML, the code of the Web. They may or may not be moderated and so the quality and accuracy of their content is variable.

Wildcat Strikes: Spontaneous work stoppages that take place in violation of the labour contract and are officially against the wishes of the union leaders.

Window: A rectangular area on the screen that contains the interface between the user and a particular programme. Several windows can be open at the same time, enabling a user to run programmes simultaneously. Thus a user might have a document displayed in one window, while running an application in another.

Win-lose Bargaining: Sees the negotiation as a competitive conflict with one party winning and the other party losing.

Win-win Bargaining: Sees the negotiation as a cooperative problem-solving exercise that will benefit both parties.

WOM/WoM (Word of Mouth): What customers say to others about your product/service.

Work Climate: Refers to the overall 'feeling' of the work environment as conveyed by the physical layout and surroundings, employee social interaction and employee-management relationships.

Workers Compensation: A legally required benefit that provides medical care, income continuation and rehabilitation expenses for people who sustain job-related injuries or sicknesses.

Work-family Conflict: The conflicting demands made on an individual by home and work.

Workplace Relations: Refers to employer-employee relations in a specific workplace (for example, at a factory site or branch office) as distinct from the total organisation or industry.

Workplace Violence: Violent behaviour occurring in the workplace.

Worksafe Australia: Peak Australian occupational health and safety organisation.

Workstation: Individual computer system with keyboard, graphics monitor and mouse. PCs can be referred to as workstations but this term usually refers to more powerful, non-DOS systems.

World Tourism Organisation (WTO): The World Tourism Organisation, a UN-related institution based in Madrid that collects data on tourism and lobbies on behalf of the industry.

World Travel and Tourism Council (WTTC): The WTTC is made up of chief executives from all sectors of the tourism industry, including accommodation, catering, cruises, entertainment, recreation, transportation and travel-related services. Its central goal is to work with governments to realise the full economic impact of tourism. Its millennium vision is to make tourism a strategic economic and employment priority, to move towards open and competitive markets, to pursue sustainable development, and to eliminate barriers to growth.

World Wide Web: One of the most commonly used parts of the Internet (along with email and ftp)—a vast network of information resources held on Websites and Web pages, all of which have been built using the Hypertext Transfer Protocol (HTTP).

Wrongful Dismissal: Occurs when an employee's employment is terminated by an employer for reasons that are in breach of the employment contract.

WTO: World Tourism Organization.

WTTC: World Travel & Tourism Council.

WWW: WWW is common shorthand for the "World Wide Web" (See above for a definition).

Xenophobia: Xenophobia is an irrational fear or contempt of strangers or foreigners. This ancient cultural and political phenomenon is also present in contemporary tourism, mainly manifesting itself in the hostile attitudes of residents towards tourists. Xenophobia should be considered in domestic and international tourism in terms of economic, social and cultural distance, which is accentuated by the type and the number of tourists and the rate of tourism development.

YHA: Youth Hostels Association.

Yield Management: The concept of maximising the revenue by raising or lowering prices in respect to demand is known as yield management. The necessary conditions for a successful application of yield management include a fairly fixed capacity, high fixed costs, low variable costs, fluctuations in demand and similarity of inventory capacity. Yield management was popularised with the deregulation of the US airline industry and it is extensively used by this and other tourism sectors.

Yield Percentage: To demonstrate the variable effect of both average price rates and occupancy rates, tourism managers develop a comparison focusing upon the yield rates during a given period of time. Managers can increase the yield rate (see yield management) by raising rates when demand is high.

Zoning: Zoning seeks to regulate land uses by separating them based on incompatibility, or allowing like/compatible uses to co-exist. A basic principle of tourism zoning is the conservation of specific environmental features such as wetlands, archaeological and historic sites, important stands of vegetation and unusual geological features. Related to this is the maintenance of visual diversity. Also important is the achievement of successful functional groupings of resort facilities and activities, such as accommodation, commercial and cultural facilities, and recreation facilities in suitable areas. Buffer zones containing mixtures of tourism facilities and less fragile environmental preservation requirements may also be designated.

Bibliography

A Host of Opportunities: *An Introduction to Hospitality Management.* Chicago: Irwin, 1996.

A.B.C. Lateline, (1992). June.

Abbey, James R. (1998). *Hospitality Sales and Advertising*. Lansing: Educational Institute of the American Hotel and Motel Association.

Adams, J.S. (1965). *Inequity in Social Exchange* in L. Berkowitz (Ed.), *Advances in Experimental Social Psychology* (Vol. 2, 267-299). New York: Academic Press.

Adler, N.J. (1991). *International Dimensions of Organizational Behaviour*. Boston: PWS-Kent Publishing Company.

AFL-CIO (1994). *The New American Workplace: A Labour Perspective,* Washington, DC, AFL-CIO.

Aikens, Charlotte A. (1910). *Hospital Housekeeping.* Detroit Mich: D.T. Sutton.

Aikens, Charlotte A. (1911). *Hospital Management; A Handbook For Hospital Trustees, Superintendents, Training-school Principals, Physicians, and all Who are Actively Engaged in Promoting Hospital Work.* Philadelphia: Saunders.

Aikens, Charlotte Albina (1906). *Hospital Housekeeping.* Detroit Mich: D.T. Sutton.

Aikens, Charlotte Albina (1913). *Hospital Housekeeping.* Detroit Mich: D.T. Sutton,.

Airports and Tourists. Global Culture (2007).

Albert Pick and Company (Chicago) (1920). *Equipment for Cafeterias, Lunch Rooms, Restaurants and Dining Rooms, Kitchen Equipment.* Chicago: The Company.

Alch, M.L. (2000). Get Ready for the Net Generation. *USA Today,* 129, 26-27.

American Dietetic Association (1944). Food Administration

Section. *Care of Food Service Equipment.* Minneapolis, Minn.: Burgess Publishing Co.

American Dietetic Association (1947). Food Administration Section. *A Guide to the Selection and Training of Food Service Employees.* Minneapolis: Burgess Pub. Co.

American Hotel and Motel Association, Educational Institute. *Hospitality Skills Training Series.* East Lansing: The Institute, 1995.

Anderson, G.F., & Hussey, P.S. (1999). *Health and Population Aging: A Multinational Comparison.* [Online]. International Health Policy. Available http://www.cmwf.org/programmes/international/aging_chartbook.asp [2003, March 4th].

Anderson, Kenneth (1993). *International Dictionary of Food & Nutrition.* New York: Wiley.

Anderson, Kenneth (1993). *International Menu Speller.* New York: Wiley.

Angelo, Rocco M. (1998). *An Introduction to Hospitality Today.* Orlando: Educational Institute, American Hotel & Motel Association.

Applebaum, E. and Batt, R. (1994). *The New American Workplace: Transforming Work Systems in the United States,* London, ILR Press.

Applebaum, E.; Bailey, T.; Berg, P. and Kalleberg, A.L. (2000). *Manufacturing Advantage: Why High Performance Work Systems Pay Off,* London, Cornell University Press.

Armstrong, M.A. (1999), *Handbook of Human Resource Practice,* Kogan Page.

Armstrong, Michael (2006). *A Handbook of Human Resource Management Practice,* 10th edition, London: Kogan Page.

Aron, A. and Aron, E.N. (1999). *Statistics for Psychology.* (2nd ed.). New Jersey: Prentice-Hall International, Inc.

Ashton, D. and Green, F. (1996). *Education, Training and the Global Economy,* Cheltenham, Edward Elgar.

Ashton, D. and Sung, J. (2000). *Skill Recognition Systems: The US, UK and European Experience,* Paper Prepared for the ILO/APSDEP/Japan Regional Meeting on Workplace-Based Skills Recognition and Training, OVTA, Chiba, Japan, 7-10 March, p. 19.

Ashton, D. and Sung, J. (2001). *Lessons from Abroad,* Report for the PIU Project on Workforce Development, UK Cabinet Office.

Ashton, D.; Davies, B.; Felstead, A. and Green, F. (1998). *Work Skills in Britain*, Oxford and Warwick Universities, ESRC Centre on Skills, Knowledge and Organisational Performance.

Ashton, D.; Green, F.; James, D. and Sung, J. (1999). *Education and Training for Development in East Asia: The Political Economy of Skill Formation in East Asian Newly Industrialised Economies*, London, Routledge.

Ashton, D.; Sung, J. and Turbin, J. (2000). "*Towards a Framework for the Comparative Analysis of National Systems of Skill Formation*" in International Journal of Training and Development, (4)1, pp. 8-25.

Ashton, D.; Sung, J.; Raddon, A. and Powell, M. (2001). *National Frameworks for Workplace Learning*, Paper Delivered to the CIPD Seminar on Workplace Learning, London, 1-2 April.

Ashworth, G.J. and Dietvorst, A.G.J. (eds.) (1995). *'Tourism and Spatial Transformations: Implications for Policy and Planning'*, CAB International: UK.

Ashworth, G.J. and Voogd, H. (1990). *'Selling the City'*, Wiley: UK.

ASTD (1996). "Training Industry Trends 1996" in *Training and Development*, Nov., Alexandria, VA, ASTD.

ASTD (2000). Mary McCain, *High Performance Workforce Investment Systems for the New Economy*, talk Prepared for the CLMS Conference: Implementing High Performance Work Practices, Dublin, 6 Sept., 2000.

ASTD (2000a). *State of the Industry Report*, 2000, Alexandria: ASTD.

Astroff, Milton T. (1998). *Convention Sales and Services*. Cranbury: Waterbury Press.

Atkinson, H. Berry, A. and Jarvis, R. (1995). *'Business Accounting for Hospitality and Tourism'*, ITBP: UK.

Augustine, Grace Melvina and Mary Bryan (1935). *Some Aspects of Management of College Residence Halls for Women*. New York: F.S. Crofts & Co.

Axtell, Roger E. (1990). *The Do's and Taboos of Hosting International Visitors*. New York: Wiley.

Bacchus and Cordon bleu (School: Paris France) (1885). *New Guide for the Hotel, bar, Restaurant, Butler, and Chef: Being a Handbook for the Management of Hotel and American bars, and the Manufacture of the Principal New and Fashionable Drinks: Hotel & Restaurant Cookery, as Now Practised, with the Newest Entrees and Dishes*. London: Nicholson.

Bacon, N. and Blyton, P. (2000). "*Industrial Relations and the Diffusion of Teamworking: Survey Evidence from the UK Steel Industry*", in The International Journal of Operations and Production Management, 20(8), pp. 911-31.

Bailey, T. (1993). *Organizational Innovation in the Apparel Industry*, in Industrial Relations, 32, pp. 30-48.

Baker, Reginald Owen (1947). *The Query Book for Hotelmen and Caterers.* London: Practical Press.

Baker, S. Bradley, P. Huyton, J. (1994). *Principles of Hotel Front Office Operations*, Cassell: UK.

Baldacchino, G. (1997). *Global Tourism and Informal Labour Relations: The Small-Scale Syndrome at Work*, Mansell: UK.

Baldacchino, G. (1997). *Global Tourism and Informal Labour Relations: The Small-scale Syndrome at Work*, Mansell: UK.

Baldry, C.; Bain, P. and Taylor, P. (1998). "*Bright Satanic Offices: Intensification, Control and Team Taylorism*", in Thompson, P. and Warhurst, C. (eds.) *Workplaces of the Future*, London, Macmillan Business, pp. 163-83.

Barke, M. Towner, J. and Newton, M. (eds.) (1995). '*Tourism in Spain*', CAB: UK.

Barnard, M.E. and Rogers, R.A. (2000). "*How are Internally Oriented HRM Policies Related to High Performance Work Practices? Evidence from Singapore*", in International Journal of Human Resource Management, 11(6), pp. 1017-46.

Baucom, Alfred H. (1994). *Hospitality Design for the Graying Generation: Meeting the Needs of a Growing Market.* New York: Wiley, 1996.

Baum, T. (1993). *Human Resource Issues in International Tourism*, Butterworth Heinemann: UK.

Baum, T. (1995). *Managing Human Resources in the European Hospitality and Tourism Industry: A Strategic Approach*, Chapman and Hall.

Baum, T. (1995). *Managing Human Resources in the European Tourism and Hospitality Industry: A Strategic Approach*, ITBP: UK.

Baum, T. (1997), '*Making or Breaking the Tourist Experience: The Role of Human Resource Management*', in C. Ryan (ed.) *The Tourist Experience: A New Introduction*, Cassell, 92-111.

Baum, T. (1999), *Human Resource Issues in International Tourism*, Butterworth-Heinemann.

Beale, Joseph Henry (1906). *The Law of Innkeepers and Hotels: Including Other Public Houses, Theatres, Sleeping Cars.* Boston: William J. Nagel.

Beardwell, I. and Holden, L. HRM, (1997), *A Contemporary Perspective*, Pitman.

Beaver, A. (1993), *Mind Your Own Travel Business: A Manual of Retail Travel Practice (3 Volume Set)*, A. Beaver: UK.

Becker, B.E.; Huselid, M.A.; Pickus, P.S. and Spratt, M. (1997). *"HR as a Source Of Shareholder Value: Research and Recommendations"* in Human Resource Management, 36, pp. 39-47.

Becker, B.E.; Huselid, M.A.; Pickus, P.S. and Spratt, M. (1998). *"High Performance Work Systems and Firm Performance: A Synthesis of Research and Managerial Implications"*, in Research in Personnel and Human Resource Management, Vol. 16, Stamford, JAI Press, Stamford, CT., pp. 53-101.

Beer, M. (1997). *The Transformation of the Human Resource Function: Resolving the Tension between a Traditional Administrative and A New Strategic Role*, in Human Resource Management, 36, pp. 49-56.

Bellucci, Elio C. (, 1994). *The Hospitality Law Desk Reference.* Miami: Southern Beverage Journal.

Belous, R.S. and Appelbaum, E. (1988). *Human Resource Flexibility and Older Workers: Management and Labour Views.* Paper presented at the Forty-first Annual Meeting of the Industrial Relations Research Association, New York.

Berg, P.; Applebaum, E.; Bailey, T. and Kalleberg, A.L. (2000). *"Modular Production: Improving Performance in the Apparel Industry"* in Ichniowski, I.; Levine, D.I.; Olson C. and Strauss, G., *The American Workplace: Skills, Compensation and Employee Involvement*, Cambridge, Cambridge University Press.

Bertrand, O. and Noyelle, T. (1988). *Human Resources and Corporate Strategy: Technological Change in Banks and Insurance Companies*, Paris, OECD.

Betcherman, G. (1997). *Changing Workplace Strategies: Achieving Better Outcomes for Enterprises, Workers and Society*, Government of Canada and OECD.

Betcherman, G.; Leckie, N. and McMullen, K. (1997). *Developing Skills in the Canadian Workplace*, Ottawa, Canadian Policy Research Networks, Inc.

Black, Wendy. *Elegant Hotels of Europe*. Glen Cove: PBC International, 1994.

Blackwell, J., and Stear, L. (ed), (1989). *Case-Histories of Tourism and Hospitality*, Australian-international Magazine Services Sydney.

Bodi, A., Lees, K., Bell, M., Benson, J., Worland, D., Jureidini, R., Bray, M., (1992). *Progress at the Workplace (Private Sector Services): Workplace Reform and Award Restructuring*, National Key Centre in Industrial Relations (Monash University), Melbourne.

Boella, M.J. (1996). *Human Resource Management in the Hospitality Industry'*, Stanley Thornes: UK.

Boella, Michael John. (1999). *Principles of Hospitality Law*. London: Cassell.

Boissevain, J. (ed.) (1996), *Coping with Tourists: European Reactions to Mass Tourism*, Berghahn Books: UK.

Boni, G. de and Frederick Francis Sharles (1926). *Hotel Organization, Management and Accountancy*. Hotel Organization and Management. London New York: Sir I. Pitman.

Boni, G. de and Frederick Francis Sharles (1931). *Hotel Organization, Management and Accountancy*. London; New York: Sir I. Pitman.

Boni, G. de. (1939). *Hotel Organization, Management and Accountancy*. London: Pitman.

Boniface, B.G. and Cooper, C. (1994), *Geography of Travel and Tourism*, Butterworth Heinemann: UK.

Boniface, P. (1995). *Managing Quality Cultural Tourism*, Routledge: UK.

Boomer, Lucius Messenger (1931). *Hotel Management; Principles and Practice*. New York: Harper.

Boomer, Lucius Messenger (1938). *Hotel Management; Principles and Practice*. New York: Harper.

Borocz, J. (1996). *Leisure Migration: A Sociological Study on Tourism*, Pergamon Press: UK.

Bowen, D.E., (1986). *"Managing Customers as Human Resources in Service Organisations"*, HRM, Fall, pp. 371-84.

Bowes, Anna De Planter (1989). *Bowes and Church's Food Values of Portions Commonly Used*. New York: Perennial Library.

Bowes, Anna De Planter (1994). *Bowes and Church's Food Values of Portions Commonly Used*. Philadelphia: J.B. Lippincott.

Bowey, A. and Thorpe, R. (1986). *Payment Systems and Productivity*, Basingstoke, Macmillan.

Boxall, P. and Purcell, J. (2000). *'Strategic Human Resource Management: Where have We Come from and Where should We be Going?'*, International Journal of Management Reviews, 2(2): 183-203.

Bradley, Alice (1922). *Cooking for Profit; Catering and Food Service Management*. Chicago: American School of Home Economics.

Bradley, Alice (1925). *Cooking for Profit; Catering and Food Service Management*. Chicago: American School of Home Economics.

Bradley, Alice (1933). *Cooking for Profit; Catering and Food Service Management*. Chicago: American School of Home Economics.

Bramham, P., Henry, I., Mommaas, H. and Van der Poel, H. (eds.) (1993). *Leisure Policies in Europe*, CAB International: UK.

Braverman, H. (1974). *Labour and Monopoly Capital*, New York, New Left Books.

Brennen, Jennifer (1984). *The Cuisines of Asia: Nine Great Oriental Cuisines by Technique*. New York: St. Martin's.

Briggs, S. (1997). *Successful Tourism Marketing*, Kogan Page: UK.

Briguglio, L. Butler, R. Harrison, D. Filho, W. (eds.) (1996) *Sustainable Tourism in Islands and Small States: Case Studies*, Pinter: UK, HB, 1855673711 £45.00.

Briguglio, L., Archer, B., Jafari, J. and Wall, G. (eds.) (1996). *Sustainable Tourism in Islands and Small States: Issues and Policies*, Pinter: UK.

Brody, Marjorie (1994). *Business Etiquette*. Burr Ridge: Mirror Press.

Brookes, J.C. *The Cellarman's Handbook and Barman's Guide: a Practical Guide to the Management of Public House Hotel Bars and Cellars; Valuable Information and Hints to all Barmen and Cellarmen Engaged in the Licensed Trade, Club Stewards, Hotel Cellarmen, etc.* London: J.C. Brookes.

Brown, Douglas Robert (1991). *The Restaurant Managers Handbook: How to Set Up, Operate, and Manage a Financially Successful Restaurant*. Lauderhill, Atlantic Pub..

Brown, Edward Fisher. *Lunches for School Children. Necessity and Outgrowth of Economic Destitution—Free Lunches Versus Lunches at Cost—School Feeding and Education—the American Tendency—the New York Movement—Economy of Central Kitchen—Medical Inspection of Handlers—The Cost—The Profit in Citizenship*. New York, 1914.

Brown, F. (1998). *Tourism: Blight or Blessing?*, Butterworth Heinemann: UK.

Brown, P. and Lauder, H. (2001). *Capitalism and Social Progress: The Future of Society in a Global Economy*, Basingstoke and New York, Palgrave.

Brown, P.; Green, A. and Lauder, H. (2001). *High Skills: Globalization, Competitiveness and Skill Formation*, Oxford, Oxford University Press.

Bruce Jackman's Restaurateur. Restaurant Training Systems. (1997).

Brunt, P. (1997). *Market Research in Travel & Tourism*, Butterworth Heinemann: UK.

Bryan, Mary and Alice M. Zabriskie (1940). *The School Cafeteria*. New York.: F.S. Crofts & Co..

Bryan, Mary and Etta Howes Handy (1933). *Furnishings and Equipment for Residence Halls*. New York city: Teachers college Columbia university.

Bryan, Mary De Garmo and Alice M. Zabriskie (1946). *The School Cafeteria*. New York: F.S. Crofts.

Bryman, A. (1995). *Disney and his Worlds*, Routledge: UK.

Bryson, McDowell (1992). *Concierge: Key to Hospitality: A Training Manual*. New York: Wiley.

Buckner, Robert W. (1998). *Site Selection: New Advancements in Methods and Technology*. New York: Lebhar-Friedman Books.

Buhalis, D. Tjoa, A.M. and Jafari, J. (eds.) (1998). *Information and Communication Technologies in Tourism: Enter 98*, Springer Verlag: Vienna.

Bull, A. (1995). *The Economics of Travel and Tourism*, Longman: UK.

Bunce, M. (1997). *The Countryside Ideal: Anglo-American Images of Landscape*, Routledge: UK.

Bureau of Tourism Research, (1989). *International Visitor Survey*, AGPS, Canberra.

Bureau of Tourism Research, (1990). *Hospitality Industry Labour Force Survey*, AGPS, Canberra.

Burns, P. and Holden, A. (1995). *Tourism: A New Perspective*, Prentice Hall: UK.

Burton, J. and Burton, L. (1994). *Interpersonal Skills for Travel and Tourism*, Longman: UK.

Burton, R. (1995). *Travel Geography*, Longman: UK.

Business Decisions Limited (2000). *"Government Support Programmes for New Forms of Work Organisation"*, Report for DG Employment and Social Affairs, Jan.

Butler, R. and Hinch, T. (eds.) (1996). *Tourism and Indigenous Peoples*, ITBP: UK.

Butler, R., Hall, R. and Jenkins, M. (eds.) (1998). *Tourism and Recreation in Rural Areas*, Wiley: UK.

Buttle, F. (1986). *Hotel and Food Service Marketing: A Managerial Approach*, Cassell: UK.

Byrnes, W.J. (1993). *Management and the Arts*, Focal Press: UK.

Cahill, Dennis J. (1997). *How Consumers Pick a Hotel: Strategic Segmentation and Target Marketing*. New York: Haworth Press.

Callus, R., Morehead, A., Cufly, M., Buchanan, J. (1991). *Industrial Relations at Work: The Australian Workplace Industrial Relations Survey*, Commonwealth Department of Industrial Relations, Canberra.

Canny, A. (2002). *'Flexible Labour? The Growth of Student Employment in the UK'*, Journal of Education and Work, 15(3), 277-301.

Cappelli, P. (1996). *Technology and Skill Requirements: Implications for Establishment of Wage Structures*, in New England Economic Review, May-June, pp. 139-54.

Cappelli, P. (1998). *Technology, Work Organisation and Wage Structures*, The Wharton School, Quoted in OECD, 1999.

Cappelli, P. and Rogobsky, N. (1994). *"New Work Systems and Skill Requirements"*, in International Labour Review, No. 2, pp. 205-20.

Carlzon, J. (1987). *Moments of Truth*, Ballinger.

Carmouche, Rita (1995). *Behavioural Studies in Hospitality Management*. New York: Chapman & Hall.

Carter, W.J., (1988). *"Developing a Service Management Philosophy in the Australian Hospitality Industry"*. Research Report, Graduate School of Management, University of Melbourne, Melbourne.

Carver, Ethel C. (1933). *Practical Catering: A Manual of Applied Dietetics for Schools, Institutions and Families*. London: Methuen.

Casado, Matt A. (1994). *Food and Beverage Service Manual*. New York: Wiley.

Case Study Guide for Use with the Incentive Travel Case Study Book. New York; The Society, 1991.

Cater, E. and Lowman, G. (1994). *Ecotourism: A Sustainable Option*, Wiley: UK.

Cheng, A. and Brown, A. (1998). *'HRM Strategies and Labour Turnover in the Hotel Industry: A Comparative Study of Australia and Singapore'*, International Journal of Human Resource Management, 9(1), 136-154.

Chesser, Gerald (1992). *Art and Science of Culinary Preparation: A Culinarian's Manual.* St. Augustine: Educational Institute of the American Culinary.

Chew, LK.H, Teo, A.C.Y., (1991). *"Human Resource Practice in Singapore: A Survey of Local Firms and MNCs"*, Asia Pacific HRM, Autumn, pp. 430-38.

Chmelynski, Carol Ann Caprione (2000). *Opportunities in Food Service Careers.* Lincolnwood: VGM Career Horizons.

Cichy, Ronald F. (1994). *Quality Sanitation Management.* East Lansing: Educational Institute of the American Hotel & Motel Association.

Cichy, Ronald F. (1998). *Managing Service in Food and Beverage Operations.* Lansing: Educational Institute of the American Hotel and Motel Association.

CIPD (2001). *"Training and Development 2001"*, Survey Report, London, Chartered Institute of Personnel and Development.

Clarenbach, Ernst. (1930). *Clarenbach's Hotel Accounting.* Chicago, Ill.: Hotel Monthly Press.

Clark, M. (1995). *Interpersonal Skills for Hospitality Management,* ITBP: UK.

Clark, M., Riley, M., Wilkie, E. and Wood, R.C. (1998). *Researching and Writing Dissertations in Hospitality and Tourism,* ITBP: UK.

Clark, Mona (1995). *Interpersonal Skills for Hospitality Managers.* London: Chapman Hill.

Clift, S. and Grabowski, P. (eds.) (1997). *Tourism and Health: Risks, Research and Responses,* Pinter: UK.

Coccossis, H. and Nijkamp, P. (eds.) (1995). *Sustainable Tourism Development,* Ashgate: UK.

Cole, G.A. (1996), *Management Theory and Practice,* D.P. Publications.

Coleman, S. and Keep, E. (2001). *Background Literature Review for Performance and Innovation Unit Project on Workforce Development,* UK Cabinet Office.

Collin, P.H. (1994). *Dictionary of Hotels, Tourism and Catering Management,* Peter Collin: UK.

Collins, M.F. and Cooper, I.S. (eds.) (1997). *Leisure Management: Issues and Applications,* CAB International: UK.

Collins, R.R., (1987). "The Strategic Contributios of the Human Resource Function", *HRM Australia,* November, pp. 5-20.

Columbia University (1913). Teachers College. School of Practical Arts. *Opportunities in Household and Institutional Administration*. New York.

Columbus (1997). *World Travel Health Guide*, Columbus Press: UK.

Columbus (1998). *World Ski and Snowboarding Guide*, Columbus Press: UK.

Columbus (1998). *World Travel Atlas*, Columbus Press: UK.

Columbus (1998). *World Travel Sales Guide*, Columbus Press: UK.

Conlin, M. and Baum, T. (eds.) (1995), *Island Tourism: Management Principles and Practice*, Wiley: UK.

Contemporary Club Management. East Lansing: Educational Institute, American Hotel and Motel Association, 1997.

Convention Liaison Council Manual: A Working Guide for Effective Meetings and Conventions. Washington, D.C.: Convention Liaison Council, 1994.

Cooke, A. (1994). *Economics of Leisure and Sport*, ITBP: UK.

Cooper, Ann. (1998). *A Woman's Place is in the Kitchen": The Evolution of Women Chefs*. Van Nostrand Reinhold.

Cooper, C. and Wanhill, S. (eds.) (1997). *Tourism Development: Environmental and Community Issues*, Wiley: UK.

Cooper, C., Fletcher, J., Gilbert, D., Wanhill, S. and Shepherd, R. (1998). *Tourism: Principles and Practice*, Longman: UK.

Cooper, C.P. (1989). *Progress in Tourism, Recreation and Hospitality Management*, Vol. 1, Belhaven Press: UK.

Cooper, C.P. and Lockwood, A. (1992). *Progress in Tourism, Recreation and Hospitality Management*, Vol. 4, Belhaven Press: UK.

Cordery, J. (2001). Negative Items (Telephone Conversation).

Corke, J. (1993). *Tourism Law*, Elm: UK.

Cosh, A.; Hughes, A. and Weeks, M. (2000). *The Relationship between, Training and Employment Growth in Small and Medium-Sized Enterprises*, Nottingham. DfEE Publications.

Cote, Raymond (1997). *Understanding Hospitality Accounting I*. East Lansing: Educational Institute of the American Hotel and Motel Association.

Cote, Raymond (1997). *Understanding Hospitality Accounting II*. East Lansing: Educational Institute of the American Hotel and Motel Association.

Coupland, D. (1993). *Generation X: Tales for an Accelerated Culture*, Abacus.

Cournoyer, Norman G. (1993). *Hotel, Restaurant, and Travel Law: A Preventive Approach*. Albany: Delmar Publishers.

Cracknell, H.L. (1979). *Escoffier: The Complete Guide to the Art of Modern Cookery*. New York: John Wiley.

Croall, J. (1995). *Preserve or Destroy?: Tourism and the Environment*, Caloust Gulbenkian Foundation: UK.

Crockett, Albert Stevens, Waldorf-Astoria Hotel (New York N.Y.: 1897-1929), and Herndon/Vehling Collection. *The Old Waldorf-astoria Bar Book; with Amendments Due to Repeal of the xviiith; Giving the Correct Recipes for Five Hundred Cocktails and Mixed Drinks known and served at the world's most famous brass rail before prohibition, together with more than one hundred established formulas for cocktails and other beverages, originated while prohibition was in effect; the whole flavored with dashes of history mixed in a shaker of anecdote and served with a chaser of illuminative information*. New York: A.S. Crockett, 1935.

Crossley, John C. (1997). *Introduction to Commercial and Entrepreneurial Recreation*. Champaign: Sagamore Publishing.

Crouch, C.; Finegold, D. and Sako, M. (1999). *Are Skills the Answer?*, Oxford, Oxford University Press.

Crysdale, S. (ed.) (1998). *Youth's Stormy Launching from Home and School to Work in the Information Age*, McGill-Queens University Press.

Cullen, P. (1997). *Economics for Hospitality Management*; ITBP: UK.

Cully, M.; O'Reilly, A.; Woodland, S. and Dix, G. (1999). *Britain at Work: As Depicted by the 1998 Workplace Employee Relations Survey*, London, Routledge.

Curtis, S. and Lucas, R. (2001). 'A Coincidence of Needs? Employers and Full-time Students', *Employee Relations*, 23(1), 38-54.

Cushman, G., Veal, A.J. and Zuzanek, J. (eds.) (1996). *World Leisure Participation: Free Time in the Global Village*, CAB International: UK.

Cushman, G., Veal, A.J. and Zuzanek, J. (eds.) (1996). *World Leisure Participation: Free Time in the Global Village*, CAB International: UK.

D'Annunzio-Green, N., Maxwell, G. and Watson, S. (2002). *Human Resource Management: International Perspectives in Hospitality and Tourism*, Continuum.

Daboval, J.M. (1998). *A Comparison between Baby Boomer and Generation X Employees' Bases and Foci of Commitment.*

Dissertation Abstracts International, University Microfilms No. AAT 98-23312.

Dahl, Crete M. (1931). *Housekeeping Management in Hotels and Institutions; Purchasing, Upkeep, and Administration.* New York London,: Harper & Brothers.

Dahl, Crete M. (1933). *The Efficient Maid in Hotels and Clubs.* Stamford Conn.: Dahl.

Dahl, Crete M. (1939). *Housekeeping Management and Organization for Hotels and Institutions. A Reference Book for Executives in Hotels, Hospitals, Clubs, Institutions, and Departments of Hotel Administration and Institution Management in Schools and Colleges.* Stamford, Conn.: The Dahls.

Dahl, Crete M. (1945). *Housekeeping Management & Organization for Hotels & Institutions. Reference Book for Executives in Hotels, Hospitals, Clubs, Institutions, and Departments of Institution Management in Schools and Colleges.* Stamford Conn: The Dahls.

Dahl, Crete M. and Grace H. Woolley (1949). *Housekeepers' Guide to Selecting and Training Employees.* Stamford Conn: Dahl Pub. Co.

Dahl, J.O. (1927). *Restaurant Management, Principles and Practice.* New York: Harper & Brothers.

Dahl, J.O. (1929). *Selling Public Hospitality: A Handbook of Advertising and Publicity for Hotels, Restaurants and Apartment Houses.* New York: Harper & Brothers.

Dahl, J.O. (1930). *Profitable Restaurant Advertising.* S l: s.n.

Dahl, J.O. (1933). *Dining Room Management for Head Waitresses and Hostesses.* New York: J.O. Dahl.

Dahl, J.O. (1933). *Planning Profitable Restaurant Advertising.* New York: J.O. Dahl.

Dahl, J.O. (1935). ***Dictionary** of 1001 Menu Terms, Foods, Wines, Spirits, **Cocktails**.* Stamford Conn: J.O. Dahl.

Dahl, J.O. (1935). *The Efficient Waitress Manual.* Stamford Conn: J.O. Dahl.

Dahl, J.O. (1936). *Dictionary of 1001 Menu Terms, Foods, Wines, Spirits, Cocktails,* Stamford Conn: J.O. Dahl.

Dahl, J.O. (1936). *Dining Room Management for the Head Waitress and Hostess.* Stamford Conn: Hospitality Guild.

Dahl, J.O. (1939). *Tea Room Profits.* Stamford, Conn: The Dahls.

Dahl, J.O. (1939). *Advertising and Promotion for Hotels and Restaurants; A Reference Book for Hotel and Restaurant Executives,*

Sales Managers; Advertising and Publicity Directors, Advertising Agencies, Publishers and Students. Stamford Conn: The Dahls.

Dahl, J.O. (1939). *Food Standards Handbook for Quantity Cookery; Buying Guide, Portion Sizes, Weights-Measures.* Stamford Conn: The Dahls.

Dahl, J.O. (1941). *200 Ways to Control Food Costs in Quantity Cookery.* Stamford Conn: The Dahls.

Dahl, J.O. (1942). *Restaurant Profits and Management Methods.* Stamford, Conn.: The Dahls.

Dahl, J.O. (1945). *Soda Fountain and Luncheonette Management.* Stamford, Conn: Dahl Pub. Co.

Dahl, J.O. (1945). *Storeroom Management and Control for Quantity Cookery Profits.* Stamford Conn: The Dahls.

Dahl, J.O. (1945). *The Efficient Waitress Manual.* Stamford Conn: The Dahls.

Dahl, J.O. and J.H. Breland (1945). *Food Standards Handbook for Quantity Cookery.* Stamford Conn: Whitlock Press.

Dahl, Joseph Oliver (1928). *Kitchen Management, Construction, Planning, Administration.* New York, London: Harper & Brothers.

Dahl, Joseph Oliver (1930). *Soda Fountain and Luncheonette Management.* New York London: Harper & brothers.

Dahl, Joseph Oliver (1944). *Restaurant Management, Principles and Practice.* New York, London: Harper & brothers.

Dana, Arthur W. (1949). *Kitchen Planning for Quality Food Service.* New York: Harper.

Dann, G.M.S. (1996). *Language of Tourism: A Sociolinguistic Perspective,* CAB International: UK.

Dann, G.M.S. (1996). *Language of Tourism: A Sociolinguistic Perspective,* CAB International: UK.

Darrah, C.N. (1996). *Learning and Work: An Exploration in Industrial Ethnography,* New York, Garland.

Davidoff, Donald M. (1994). *Contact: Customer Service in the Hospitality and Tourism Industry.* Englewood Cliffs: Prentice Hall.

Davidson, R. (1993). *Tourism,* Longman: UK.

Davidson, R. (1994). *Business Travel,* Longman: UK.

Davidson, R. (1998). *Tourism in Europe,* 2nd ed., Longman: UK.

Davidson, R. and Maitland, R. (1997). *Tourism Destinations,* Hodder and Stoughton, UK.

Debrah, Y.A., "Recruitment and Retention Practices in a Labour Scarce Economy: An Examination of the Hotel Industry in Singapore", *Working Paper Series No.2-92*, Sabre Centre, Nanyang Technological University, Singapore.

Deegan, J. and Dineen, D.A. (1997). *Tourism Policy and Performance: The Irish Experience*, ITBP: UK.

Dehnbostel, P. and Molzberger, G. (2001). "*Combination of Formal Learning and Learning by Experience in Industrial Enterprises*", in Streumer, Jan. N. (ed.) *Perspectives on Learning at the Workspace*, Proceedings of the Second Conference on HRD Research and Practice across Europe 20001, University of Twente Enschede, the Netherlands, 26-27 Jan. 2001, pp. 77-88.

Delery, J.E.; Gupta, N.; Shaw, J.D. (1997). *Human Resource Management and Firm Performance: A Systems Perspective*, Paper Presented to the 1997 Southern Management Association Meeting, Fayetteville, Department of Management, University of Arkansas, quoted in Applebaum *et al.* (2000).

Dench, S.; Perryman, S. and Giles, L. (1998). *Employers' Perceptions of Key Skills*, University of Sussex, Institute of Employment Studies.

Denmark Government (2000). *Adult Education and Continuing Training in Denmark.*

Department for Education and Employment (2000). *Employers Skill Survey: Case Study Hospitality Sector*, DfEE.

Department for Education and Employment (DfEE) (1998). "The Role of Employee Development Schemes in Increasing Learning at Work", *Research Report No. 73*, Aug.

Department for Education and Employment (DfEE) (2000). *A Second Evaluation of the Union Learning Fund*, Research Brief, No. 208, York Consulting, July.

Department for Education and Employment (DfEE) (2000). *Individual Learning Accounts Newsletter*, Feb.

Department of the Environment (1990). *Tourism and the Inner City*, DOE: UK.

Dickinson, B. and Vladimir, A. (1996). *Selling the Sea: Inside Look at the Cruise Industry*, Wiley: UK.

Dicksee, Lawrence Robert (1905). *Hotel Accounts.* London: Gee & Co.

Dix, C. and Baird, C. (1998). *Front Office Operations*, Longman: UK.

Doganis, R. (1991). *Flying Off Course: The Economics of International Airlines*, Routledge: UK.

Doganis, R. (1992). *The Airport Business*, Routledge: UK.

Donovan, Frances R. (1920). *The Woman Who Waits.* Boston: R.G. Badger.

Dore, R. (1973). *British Factory Japanese Factory: The Origins of National Diversity in Industrial Relations*, London, George Allen and Unwin.

Dore, R. (2000). *Stock Market Capitalism: Welfare Capitalism—Japan and Germany versus the Anglo-Saxons*, Oxford, Oxford University Press.

Dornenburg, Andrew (1995). *Becoming a Chef: With Recipes and Reflections from America's Leading Chefs*. New York: Van Nostrand Reinhold.

Dornenburg, Andrew (1996). *Culinary Artistry*. New York: John Wiley & Sons.

Doswell, R. (1997). *Tourism: How Effective Management Makes the Difference*, Butterworth Heinemann: UK.

Downes, J. and Paton, T. (1993). *Travel Agency Law*, Longman: UK.

Drago, R. (1988). "*Quality Circle Survival: An Exploratory Analysis*, in Industrial Relations 27, pp. 336-51.

Drinkers, Drivers, and Bartenders: Balancing Private Choices and Public Accountability. Chicago: University of Chicago Press, 2000.

Dunlop, J.T. and Weil, D. (2000). "Diffusion and Performance of Modular Production in the US Apparel Industry, in Ichniowski, C.; Levine, D.I.; Olson, C. and Strauss, G., *The American Workplace: Skills, Compensation and Employee Involvement*, Cambridge, Cambridge University Press, pp. 38-61.

Dunning, Frances (1941). *Standards for Cafeteria Service*. Minneapolis: Burgess Pub. Co.

Dybowski, G. (1998). New Technologies and Work Organisation: Impact on Vocational Education and Training, in Tessaring, M., (ed.): Vocational Education and Training—The European Research Field. *Background Report 1998*, Vol. 1, Thessaloniki, CEDEFOP.

Earle, Alice Morse (1901). *Stage-coach and Tavern Days.* New York, London: Macmillan & Co.

Earle, Alice Morse (1912). *Stage-coach and Tavern Days.* New York: Macmillan.

Earle, Alice Morse (1938). *Stage-coach and Tavern Days.* New York, London: The Macmillan Company; Macmillan & Co. Ltd.

Easton, G.S.; Jarrell, S.L. (2000). "The Effects of Total Quality

Management on Corporate Performance: An Empirical Investigation, 172-233 in Ichniowski, C.; Levine, D.I.; Olson, C.; Strauss G.: *The American Workplace: Skills, Compensation and Employee Involvement*, Cambridge, Cambridge University Press.

Eaton, B. (1996). *European Leisure Business: Strategies for the Future*, Elm: UK.

Eaton, J. (2001). *Globalization and Human Resource Management in the Airline Industry*, Ashgate.

Eberts, Marjorie (1997). *Careers in Travel, Tourism, and Hospitality*. Lincolnwood: VGM Career Horizons.

Eckel, Peter J. (1985). *College & University Foodservice Management Standards*. Westport: AVI Pub. Company.

Eckert, Fred William and Howard L. Dayton (1947). *The Hotel Lease; A Study of the Business Elements and Principles Involved in Making Leases that are Equitable to Both Lessee and Lessor.* Chicago: Hotel Monthly Press.

Economic Research: Economic Impact of Travel and Tourism. Travel Industry Association of America, 2004.

Elias, N. (1978). *What is Sociology?*, London, Hutchinson.

Elliot, J. (1997). *Tourism: Politics and Public Sector Management*, Routledge: UK.

Elliot, Virginia (1933). *Quiet Drinking: A Book of Beer, Wines & Cocktails and What to Serve with Them.* New York: Harcourt.

Elliott, R.N. (1926). *Tea Room and Cafeteria Management*. Boston: Little Brown and Co.

Elliott, R.N. (1927). *Tea Room and Cafeteria Management*. Boston: Little Brown and Company.

Ellis, Raymond C. (1995). *Security and Loss Prevention Management*. East Lansing: Educational Institute of the American Hotel & Motel Association.

Emery, W.H. (1947). *A Handbook of Industrial and Institutional Catering by W.H. Emery.* London Bailliere Tindall and Cox.

Emery, William H. (1988). *The Chef's Guide to Practical Restaurant Cookery*. New York: Van Nostrand Reinhold.

Encyclopaedia Britannica. "Personnel Administration is also Frequently Called Personnel Management, Industrial Relations, Employee Relations" *Encyclopædia Britannica.*

Engestrom, Y. (1993). *"Developmental Studies of Work as A Testbench of Activity Theory: The Case of Primary Care Medical Services"* in

Chaiklin, S. and Lave, J. (eds.): Understanding Practise: Perspectives on Activity and Context, Cambridge, Cambridge University Press.

Engestrom, Y. (1996). *Innovative Learning in Work Teams: Analysing Cycles of Knowledge Creation in Practice*, San Diego.

Eraut, M.; Alderton, J.; Cole, G. and Senker, P. (1998). Learning from Other People at Work, in Coffield, F. (ed.): *Learning at Work*, Bristol, Policy Press.

Escoffier, Auguste (1969). *Escoffier Cook Book: A Guide to the Fine Art Cookery*. New York: Crown.

Ethics in Hospitality Management: A Book of Readings. Lansing: Educational Institute of the American Hotel and Motel Association, 1992.

Evans, K. and Heinz, W.R. (1991). "Career Trajectories in Britain and Germany", in Bynner, J. and Roberts, K. (1991): *Youth and Work: Transition to Employment in England and Germany*, London, Anglo-German Foundation, pp. 205-28.

Evans, M.J., Moutinho, L. and Van Raaij, W.F. (1996). *Applied Consumer Behaviour*, Addison Wesley Longman: UK.

Evans, M.J., Moutinho, L. and Van Raaij, W.F. (1996). *Applied Consumer Behaviour*, Addison Wesley Longman: UK.

Fellows, Charles (1900). *A Selection of Dishes and the Chef's Reminder*. Chicago: American Hotel Register Co.

Fellows, Charles (1909). *A Selection of Dishes and the Chef's Reminder*. Chicago: Hotel Monthly Press.

Fellows, Charles (1910). *The Menu Maker; Suggestions for Selecting and Arranging Menus for Hotels and Restaurants, with Object of Changing from Day to Day to Give Continuous Variety of Foods in Season*. Chicago: The Hotel Monthly Press.

Fellows, Charles (1919). *A Selection of Dishes and the Chef's Reminder; A High Class Culinary Text Book*. Chicago: The Hotel Monthly.

Fellows, Charles (1920). *The Menu Maker: Suggestions for Selecting and Arranging Menus for Hotels and Resturants, with Object of Changing from Day to Day to Give Continuous Variety of Foods in Season*. Chicago II: The Hotel Monthly.

Fellows, Charles (1920). *The Menu Maker; Suggestions for Selecting and Arranging Menus for Hotels and Restaurants, with Object of Changing from Day to Day to Give Continuous Variety of Foods in Season*. Chicago: The Hotel Monthly Press.

Fellows, Charles. (1924). *Fellows' Menu Maker. Appendix...Menus and Bills of Fare.* Chicago: Hotel Monthly.

Fellows, Charles (1944). *A Selection of Dishes and the Chef's Reminder: A High Class Culinary Text book.* Evanston II: John Wiley.

Fellows, Charles and Katherine Golden Bitting Collection on Gastronomy (Library of Congress) (1896). *A Selection of Dishes.* Pittsburgh PA: Rawsthorne Engraving and Print.

Felstead, A. and Ashton, D. (2000). *Tracing the Link: Organisational Structures and Skill Demands,* in Human Resource Management Journal, Vol. 10, No. 3, Nov., pp. 3-21.

Felstead, A.; Ashton, D. (2000) and Green, F. (2000). "*Are Britain's Workplace Skills Becoming More Unequal?*", in Cambridge Journal of Economics, (24) 6, pp.709-727.

Financial Times 9.10.2000, p. XII, report by Robert Taylor based on the Task Force on Reconstructing America's Labour Market Institutions, Institute for Work and Employment Research, Massachusetts Institute of Technology.

Finegold, D. (1999). "*Creating Self-sustaining, High-skills Ecosystems*", in Oxford Review of Economic Policy, 15(1), pp. 60-81.

Finegold, D. and Soskice, D. (1988). "*The Failure of Training in Britain: Analysis and Prescription*", in Oxford Review of Economic Policy, 4(3), pp. 21-53.

Finegold, D. and Wagner, K. (1998). "*The Search for Flexibility: Skills and Workplace Innovation in the German Pump Industry*", in British Journal of Industrial Relations, 36(3), pp. 469-87.

Finkelstein, L.M., Gonnerman, M.E.J. and Johnson, B.A. (1999). *The Development of Measures of Age and Generation Identity.* Paper presented at the Poster Session Presented at the 14th Annual Meeting of the Society for Industrial and Organizational Psychology, Atlanta, GA.

Fisk, Warren Wells (1947). *Evidence of Needs of Hotel Managers in Regard to Training and Education.*

Fitzgibbon, M. and Kelly, A. (1997), *From Maestro to Manager: Critical Issues in Arts and Culture Management,* Oaktree Press: UK.

Fleischman, Ernest M. (1947). *The Modern Luncheonette; Planning, Layout, Construction, Operation. A Practical Guide to Success in the Luncheonette and Restaurant Business.* Stamford, Conn.: Dahl Pub. Co.

Fleming, D. and Soborg, H. (2001). *Proactive Human Resource Development Policies in Malaysia,* paper presented at the Conference on Global Change, Global Governance and National Economic Restructuring, Oct., Arresodal Conference Centre, Denmark.

Flor, Bill (1996). *No Vacancy: A Tried and True Guide to Get More Business!* Jacksonville: No Vacancy.

Foley, M., Lennon, J. and Maxwell, G. (eds.) (1997). *Hospitality, Tourism and Leisure Management: Issues in Strategy and Culture,* Cassell: UK.

Foodservice Standards in Resorts. New York: Van Nostrand Reinhold, 1987.

Forrest, Lewis C. (1996). *Training for the Hospitality Industry.* East Lansing: Educational Institute of the American Hotel and Motel Association.

Forteza, J.A., and Prieto, J.M. (1994). *Aging and Work Behaviour.* in H.C. Triandis, D. Dunnette, & L.M. Hough (Eds.), Handbook of Industrial and Organizational Psychology. (2nd ed., Vol. 4, 447-483). Palo Alto, CA: Consulting Psychologists Press.

Foster, D.L. (1991). *Sales and Marketing for the Travel Professional,* Glencoe/McGraw Hill: UK.

Foster, John S. III. (1990-1999). *Book 1, the Law of Meetings, Conventions, and Trade Shows: Selected Articles on Meeting & Facility Contracts.* Atlanta: John S. Foster Esq..

Foster, John S. III. (1990-1999). *Book 3, the Law of Meetings, Conventions, and Trade Shows: Selected Articles on Independent Meeting Planners & the Law.* Atlanta: John S. Foster Esq..

Foster, John S. III. (1990-1999). *Book 4, the Law of Meetings, Conventions, and Trade Shows: What Hoteliers Need to Know About Legal Affairs Management.* Atlanta: John S. Foster Esq..

France, L. (ed.) (1997). *Earthscan Reader in Sustainable Tourism,* Earthscan: UK.

Frazis, H.; Gittleman, M.; Horrigan, M. and Joyce, M. (1997). *"Formal and Informal Training: Evidence from a Matched Employee-Employer Survey"*, in Libecap, G.D. (ed.). *"Advances in the Study of Entrepreneurship, Innovation and Economic Growth"*, Greenwich, JAI Press.

Frechtling, D.C. (1996). *Practical Tourism Forecasting*, Butterworth Heinemann: UK.

Friberg, Bo. (1996). *Professional Pastry Chef*. New York: Van Nostrand Reinhold.

Fridgen, Joseph. (1996). *Dimensions of Tourism*. East Lansing: Educational Institute, American Hotel and Motel Association.

Frooman, Abraham Arthur. *Five Steps to Effective Institutional Food Buying*. Chicago, 1948.

Froud, J.; Haslam, C.; Johal, S. and Williams, K. (2000). *"Restructuring for Shareholder Value and the Implications for Labour"*, in Cambridge Journal of Economics, 24, pp. 771-97.

Furlong, A. and Cartmel, F. (1997). *Young People and Social Change*, Buckingham, Open University Press.

Gabriel, Y., (1988). *Working Lives in Catering*, Routledge, London.

Gardner, Liese. (1997). *The Art of Event Design*. Malibu: Miramar Communications.

Gayle, D. (ed.) (1993). *Tourism Marketing and Management in the Caribbean*, Routledge: UK.

Gee, C.Y., Makens, J.C. and Choy, D.J.L. (1997). *The Travel Industry*, Van Nostrand Reinhold: UK.

Gee, Chuck Y. (1994). *International Hotels: Development and Management*. East Lansing: Educational Institute of the American Hotel & Motel Association.

Gee, Chuck Y. (1996). *Resort Development and Management*. East Lansing: Educational Institute of the American Hotel & Motel Association.

Gee, CY. (ed.) (1997). *International Tourism: A Global Perspective*, World Tourism Organisation: Spain.

Gephart, M.A. and Van Buren, M.E. (1998). *Building Synergy: The Power of High Performance Work Systems*, Alexandria, ASTD.

Getz, D. (1997). *Event Management and Event Tourism*, Cognizant Communications: USA.

Gibson, J., MacIntyre, E., Wood, I., Kemp, K. and Pearson, S. (1997). *Leisure and Recreation Optional Units: Advanced GNVQ*, Longman: UK.

Gill, C. and Krieger, H. (1999). *"Direct and representative participation in Europe: Recent survey evidence"*, in The International Journal of Human Resource Management, 10(4), pp. 572-91.

Gill, Winifred Ethel. *Business Affairs for Institutional Management*. London: Evans.

Gisslen, Wayne (1999). *Professional Cooking*. New York: Wiley.
Glasson, J. Godfrey, K. and Goodey, B. (1995). *Towards Visitor Impact Management*, Avebury: UK.
Glossary of Hospitality Terms. East Lansing: The Institute, 1995.
Glyptis, S. (ed.) (1993). *Leisure and the Environment: Essays in Honour of Professor J.A.Patmore*, Belhaven Press: UK.
Go, F.M. and Pine, R. (1995). *Globalization Strategy in the Hotel Industry*, Routledge: UK.
Go, F.M., Monachello, M.L. and Baum, T. (1996). *Human Resource Management in the Hospitality Industry*, Wiley: UK.
Goins, John B. (1914). *The American Waiter*; Instructions in American and European Plan Service, Banquet and Private Party Work. Chicago: The Hotel Monthly.
Gold, J.R. and Ward, S.V. (eds.) (1994). *Place Promotion: The Use of Publicity and Public Relations to Sell Cities and Regions*, Wiley: UK.
Goldberg, James M. (1996). *The Meeting Planner's Legal Handbook*. Washington, D.C.: Goldberg & Associates.
Goldblatt, Joe Jeff. (1997). *Special Events: Best Practices in Modern Event Management*. New York: Van Nostrand Reinhold.
Goldfeld, Abraham (1938). *The Diary of a Housing Manager*. Chicago: National Association of Housing Officials.
Goldsmith, A., Nickson, D., Sloan, D. and Wood, R.C. (1997). *Human Resource Management for Hospitality Services*, ITBP: UK.
Goodall, B. and Ashworth, G. (eds.) (1988). *Marketing in the Tourism Industry: The Promotion of Destination Regions*, ITBP: UK.
Graham, B. (1995). *Geography and Air Transport*, Wiley: UK.
Grainger-Jones, B. (1998). *Managing Leisure*, Butterworth Heinemann: UK.
Gray, Madeline and Vass De Lo Padua (1946). *How to be a Success in the Restaurant Business*. New York: Greenberg.
Gray, Madeline and Vass De Lo Padua (1947). *How to Cook for Profit; A Complete Guide to Food in Quantity, from Order Pad to Diner's Table*. New York: Greenberg.
Gray, Madeline and Vass De Lo Padua (1948). *How to be a Success in the Restaurant Business*. Chicago: Nelson-Hall.
Gray, R., (1992), *"Communicating the Customer Service Mission to Employees—A Case Study on the Ritz-Carlton, Sydney"*, Conference, May, Sydney.

Green, F.; Ashton, D. and Felstead, A. (2001). *Estimating the Determinants and Supply of Computing, Problem-Solving, Communication, Social and Teamworking Skills*, in Oxford Review of Economic Policy, 53(3), pp. 406-33.

Green, John Dismukes (1925). *The Back of the House.* New York: Gehring.

Greenstein, Lou. (1992). *A La Carte: A Tour of Dining History*. Glen Cove: PBC International.

Grohusko, J.A. (1908). *Jack's Manual; A Treatise on the Care and Handling of Wines and Liquors, Storing, Binning, and Serving; Recipes for Fancy Mixed Drinks and when and How to Serve.* New York: Printed by E.V. Brokaw & bro.

Grohusko, J.A. (1910). *Jack's Manual on the Vintage and Production, Care and Handling of Wines, Liquors, etc.: A Handbook of Information for Home, Club, or Hotel: Recipes for Fancy Mixed Drinks and when and How to Serve.* New York: McClunn & Co.

Grohusko, J.A. (1933). *Jack's Manual on the Vintage and Production, Care and Handling of Wines, Liquors, etc.; A Handbook of Information for Homes, Clubs, Hotels and Restaurants.* New York: A.A. Knopf.

Grugulis, I. and Wilkinson, A. (2002). *'Managing Culture at British Airways: Hype, Hope and Reality'*, Long Range Planning 35(2), 179-194.

Guemier, I., and Lockwood, A., (1989). *"Core and Peripheral Employees in Hotel Operations"*, Personnel Review, 18, pp. 9-15.

Guest, D.E. (1997). *Human Resource Management and Performance: A Review and Research Agenda*, in International Journal of Human Resource Management, 8(3), pp. 263-90.

Guest, D.E. (1999). *Human Resource Management—The Workers' Verdict*, in Human Resource Management Journal, 9(3), pp. 5-25.

Guest, D.E. (2000). *"HR and the Bottom Line: Has the Penny Dropped?"*, in People Management, 20 July, 2000, pp. 26-31.

Guest, D.E. and Hoque, K. (1994). *"The Good, the Bad and the Ugly: Human Resource Management in New Non-Union Establishments*, in Human Resource Management Journal, 5(1), pp. 1-14.

Guest, D.E.; Michie, J.; Sheenan, M.; Conway, N. and Wetochi, M. (2000). *Effective People Management: Initial Findings of the Future of Work Study*, CIPD Plymouth Distributors.

Gunn, C.A. (1994). *Tourism Planning: Basics, Concepts and Cases*, Taylor and Francis: UK.

Gunn, C.A. (1997). *Vacationscape: Developing Tourist Areas*, Taylor and Francis: UK.

Guthrie, J.P. (2001). *High Involvement Work Practices, Turnover, and Productivity: Evidence from New Zealand*, in Academy of Management Journal, (44)1, pp. 180-90.

Hackman, J.R.; Wageman, R.; Ruddy, T.M. and Charles, L.R. (2000). "*Team Effectiveness in Theory and Practice*", in Cary, L.; Cooper and Locke, E., *Industrial and Organizational Psychology*, Oxford, Blackwell.

Hall, C.M. (1992). *Hallmark Tourist Events: Impacts, Management and Planning*, Wiley: UK.

Hall, C.M. (1994). *Tourism and Politics: Policy, Power and Place*, Wiley: UK.

Hall, C.M. (1997). *Tourism in the Pacific Rim: Development Impacts and Markets*, 2nd ed., Longman: Australia.

Hall, C.M. and Jenkins, J.M. (1995). *Tourism and Public Policy*, ITBP: UK.

Hall, C.M. and Lew, A. (eds.) (1998). *Sustainable Tourism: A Geographical Perspective*, Addison Wesley Longman: UK.

Hall, C.M. and Macarthur, S. (eds.) (1998). *Integrated Heritage Management*, Stationery Office: UK.

Hall, C.M. and Page, S.J. (1996). *Tourism in the Pacific: Issues and Cases*, ITBP: UK.

Hall, M. (ed.) (1998). *Sustainable Tourism: A Geographical Perspective*, Longman: UK.

Halvorsen, Francine (1998). *Eating Around the World in Your Neighborhood*. New York: Wiley.

Hamilton, Francis Frazee (1947). *Hotel Front Desk Management, a Treatise on the Best Methods and Procedures in Use in Small Hotels*. Miami, Fla.: Francis Frazee Hamilton.

Hamilton, W.I. (1930). *Promoting New Hotels: When does it Pay?* New York: Harper.

Handy, C. (1998), *Understanding Organisations*, Penguin Books.

Hanlon, P. (1996). *Global Airlines: Competition in a Transnational Industry*, Butterworth Heinemann: UK.

Harris, P. (1995). *Accounting and Finance for the International Hospitality Industry*, Butterworth Heinemann: UK.

Harris, R. and Leiper, N. (1995). *Sustainable Tourism: An Australian Perspective*, Butterworth Heinemann: UK.

Harris, R., Heath, E., Toepper, L. and Williams, P. (1998). *Sustainable Tourism: A Global Perspective*, Butterworth Heinemann: UK.

Harrison, D. (1992). *Tourism and the Less Developed Countries*, Wiley: UK.

Harrison, L.C. and Husbands, W. (1996). *Practising Responsible Tourism*, Wiley: UK.

Harrison, R. (1994). *Manual of Heritage Management*, Butterworth Heinemann: UK.

Harrison, R. (2000). *"Learning Knowledge Productivity and Strategic Progress"*, in International Journal of Training and Development, 4(4), pp. 244-58.

Hartmann, L.C. (1998). *The Impact of Trends in Labour-Force Participation in Australia*, in M. Patrickson and L. Hartmann (Eds.), Managing an Ageing Workforce (3-25). Warriewood, Australia: Woodslane Pty Limited.

Hayes, Harriet (1932). *et al. College-Operated Residence Halls for Women Students in 125 Colleges and Universities.* New York city: Teachers college Columbia University.

Hayes, Harriet (1932). *Planning Residence Halls for Undergraduate Students in American Colleges and Universities; A Handbook for the Use of College Officers and Members of Building Committees.* New York city: Teachers college Columbia University.

Hays, Judi Radice (1994). *Restaurant & Food Graphics*. Glen Cove: PBC International.

Haywood, L. and Butcher (1994). *Community Leisure and Recreation: Theory and Practice*, Focal Press: UK.

Heath, E. and Wall, G. (1992). *Marketing Tourism Destinations*, Wiley: UK.

Heckscher, C. and Schurman, S. (1997). *Towards Jobs and Justice: Can Labour-Management Cooperation Deliver Jobs and Justice?* in *Industrial Relations Journal*, 28(4), pp. 323-30.

Heery, E. and Noon, M. (2001). *A Dictionary of Human Resource Management*, Oxford University Press.

Heinz, W.R. (1999). *"Job-Entry Patterns in A Life—Course Perspective"*, in From Education to Work: Cross-National Perspectives, Cambridge, Cambridge University Press, pp. 214-31.

Heinze, Stella E. (1945). *The Hospital Housekeeper's Handbook.* Winston-Salem, N C: The Author.

Heinze, Stella E. (1949). *The Hospital Housekeeper's Handbook.* Winston-Salem, NC.

Heldenbrand, Howard Van Woert (1930). *Front Office Psychology.* Chicago: The Hotel Monthly Press.

Heldenbrand, Howard Van Woert (1944). *Front Office Psychology.* Chicago II: The Hotel Monthly Press.

Hendricks, K.B. and Singhal, V.R. (2000). "*Implementing Effective Total Quality Management Programmes and Financial Performance: A Synthesis of Evidence from the Quality Award Winners*, in Ichniowski, C.; Levine, D.I.; Olson, C. and Strauss, G., *The American Workplace: Skills, Compensation and Employee Involvement*, Cambridge, Cambridge University Press, pp. 234-72.

Herbert, D.T. (1995). *Heritage, Tourism and Society*, Pinter: UK.

Herman, A.M. (1999). "*Future Work: Trends and Challenges for Work in the 21st Century*", Report of the US Department of Labour.

Heskett, J.L. "*Lessons in the Service Sector*, HBR. March-April 1987, pp. 118-26.

Heskett, J.L., Sasser, W. E. Jn., Hart, Christopher, W.L., (1990). *Service Breakthroughs: Changing the Rules of the Game*, The Free Press, New York.

Hewstone, M., and Brown, R. (Eds.) (1986). *Contact and Conflict in Intergroup Encounters*. Oxford: Basil Blackwell Ltd.

Hildreth, Richard A. (1990). *Essentials of Meeting Management.* Englewood Cliffs: Prentice Hall.

Hill, E., O'Sullivan, C. and O'Sullivan, T. (1995). *Creative Arts Marketing*, Butterworth Heinemann: UK.

Hill, Janet McKenzie (1914). *The Up-to-Date Waitress.* Boston: Little Brown and Co.

Hill, Janet McKenzie and M. Miller (1908). *The Up-to-Date waitress.* Boston: Little Brown and Company.

Hill, S. (1991). "*Why Quality Circles Failed but Total Quality Might Succeed*, in British Journal of Industrial Relations, 29(4), pp. 541-68.

Hill, S.; Wilkinson, A. (1995). *In search of TQM.*, in Employee Relations, 17(3), pp. 8-25.

Hinkin, Timothy R. (1995). *Cases in Hospitality Management: A Critical Incident Approach*. New York: Wiley.

Hirschhorn, L. (1984). *Beyond mechanisation: Work and Technology in a Postindustrial Age*, Cambridge, Mass., MIT Press.

Hitz, Ralph and National Hotel Management Co. (1936). *Standard Practice Manuals for Hotel Operation.* New York: Harper.

Hoke, Ann. (1940). *Restaurant Menu Planning.* New York, London: Harper & Brothers.

Holloway, C.J. (1998). *The Business of Tourism*, Longman: UK.

Holloway, C.J. and Robinson, C. (1995). *Marketing for Tourism*, 3rd ed., Longman: UK.

Holmes, F.H. (1937). *Hotel Training Course.* Chicago: F.H. Holmes.

Hoque, K. (2000). *Human Resource Management in the Hotel Industry*, Routledge.

Horner, P. (1996). *Travel Agency Practice*, Longman: UK.

Horner, S. and Swarbrooke, J. (1996). *Marketing Tourism Hospitality and Leisure in Europe*, ITBP: UK.

Hornsby, John Allan and Richard Ernest Schmidt (1913). *The Modern Hospital; Its Inspiration: Its Architecture: Its Equipment: Its Operation.* Philadelphia and London: W.B. Saunders Company.

Horwath & Horwath and Patterson Publishing Co. (1927). *Questions and Answers Illustrating Restaurant Operating Costs.* Chicago: Patterson Pub. Co.

Horwath, Ernest B. and Louis Toth (1928). *Hotel Accounting, Including Departmental Control, Food Costing, and Auditing.* New York: The Ronald Press Company.

Hospitality 101: Tools of the Trade. Hospitality Innovators, 1995.

Hospitality Training Foundation (2003). *Labour Market Review 2003*, HtF.

Hospitality: The Journal of the Hotel & Catering International Management Association. London: HCIMA.

Hotel and Travel Index. Secaucus: News America Publishing Inc., Winter 1998-99.

Hotel and Travel Index. Secaucus: Reed Travel Group, 1997.

Hotel Management Clipping Bureau of Good Ideas. New York: Ahrens Pub. Co.

How to be the Perfect Waiter or Waitress:...and Earn Great Tips! Beverly Hills: LAPS, Inc., 1996.

Hubbell, Erma and Roxanna Allen (1930). *The Hostess and Social Executive, a Guide to Women who Desire to Enter this Fascinating*

Field of Endeavor. Los Angeles: Huron & Stanton Printing Company.

Huczynski, A. and Buchanan, D. (1997), *Organisational Behaviour an Introductory Text,* Prentice Hall.

Hunter, L.W. (1999). *Transforming Retail Banking,* in Cappelli, P. (ed.): *Employment Practices and Business Strategies,* New York, Oxford, pp. 153-194.

Huselid, M. (1995). *The Impact of Human Resource Management Practices on Turnover, Productivity, and Corporate Financial Performance,* in Academy of Management Journal, 38, pp. 972-91.

Huselid, M.; Becker, B. (2000). *Methodological Issues in Cross-sectional and Panel Estimates of the Link between Human Resource Strategies and Firm Performance,* in Ichniowski, C.; Levine, D.I.; Olson, C.; Strauss, G., The American Workplace: Skills, Compensation and Employee Involvement, Cambridge, Cambridge University Press, pp. 111-136.

Huseman, R.C.; Goodman, J.P. (1999). *Leading with Knowledge: The Nature of Competition in the 21st Century,* London, Sage.

Ichniowski, C. (1990). *Human Resource Management Systems and the Performance of US Manufacturing Businesses,* National Bureau of Economic Research Working Paper No. 3449, Washington, DC.

Ichniowski, C. (1992). *Human Resource Practices and Productive Labour-Management Relations,* in Lewin, D.; Mitchell, O.; Sherer, P. (eds.): Research frontiers in industrial relations and human resources. Madison, WI, Industrial Relations Research Association.

Ichniowski, C.; Kochan, T.A.; Levine, D.I.; Olson, C.; Strauss, G. (2000). *What Works at Work: Overview and Assessment,* in Ichniowski, C.; Levine, D.I.; Olson, C.; Strauss, G., The American Workplace: Skills, Compensation and Employee Involvement, Cambridge, Cambridge University Press, pp. 1-37.

Ichniowski, C.; Shaw, K,; Prenushi, G. (1997). *The Effects of Human Resource Practices on Productivity: A Study of Steel Finishing Lines,* in *American Economic Review,* 87(3), pp. 291-313.

Ichniowski, C.; Shaw, K. (1995). *Old Dogs and New Tricks: Determinants of the Adoption of Productivity-enhancing Work Practices,* Brookings Papers on Economic Activity: Microeconomics, Spring, pp. 1-65.

ILO (1998). *World Employment Report: Employability in the Global Economy: How Training Matters*, 1998-99, Geneva, International Labour Office.

ILO (2001). *World Employment Report: Life at Work in the Information Economy*, Geneva, International Labour Office.

Inkpen, G. (1998). *Information Technology for Travel and Tourism*, 2nd Longman: UK.

Inskeep, E. (1994). *National and Regional Tourism Planning: Methodologies and Case Studies*, ITBP: UK.

Inskeep, E. (1997). *Tourism Planning*, Van Nostrand Reinhold: UK.

Institute on Design Construction and New Equipment for Food Service in Hospitals (1947). 1st Chicago 1946. *Lectures and Discussions Presented at American Hospital Association Institute on Design, Construction and New Equipment for Food Service in Hospitals.* Chicago.

International Association of Scientific Experts in Tourism.

International Labour Organization (2001). *Human Resource Development, Employment and Globalization in the Hotel Catering and Tourism Sector*, ILO.

International Meeting Industry Glossary. Champaign: International Association of Convention & Visitor Bureaus.

International Transport Workers Federation (ITF) (2004). *'The Cuts don't Work'*, Available at http://www. itfglobal.org/transport-international/ti10cuts.cfm (accessed 2 July 2006).

Introduction to Hospitality Operations. London: Cassell, 1996.

Ioannides, D. and Debbage, K.G. (eds.) (1998). *The Economic Geography of the Tourist Industry: A Supply-Side Analysis*, Routledge: UK.

IPD (1998). *Changing Role of the Trainer*, IPD Internal Draft Report.

IPD (1999). *Training and Development in Britain 1999*, IPD Survey Report, Institute of Personnel and Development, London.

Irons, K. (1993). *Managing Service Companies: Strategies for Success*, Addison Welsey Longman: UK.

Irons, K. (1997). *The World of Super Service: Creating Profit through a Passion for Customer Service*, Addison Welsey Longman: UK.

Jafar, J. (1998). *Encyclopaedia of Tourism*, Routledge.

Jensen, Clayne R. (2000). *Opportunities in Recreation and Leisure Careers*. Lincolnwood: VGM Career Horizons.

Johnson, Harry (1934). *The New and Improved Illustrated Bartenders' Manual; or, How to Mix Drinks of the Present Style, Containing*

Valuable Instructions and Hints by the Author in Reference to the Management of A Bar, A Hotel and A Restaurant. Newark N J: C.E. Graham & Co.

Johnson, P. and Thomas, B. (eds.) (1992). *Choice and Demand in Tourism,* Mansell: UK.

Johnson, P. and Thomas, B. (eds.) (1992). *Perspectives on Tourism Policy,* Mansell: UK.

Jollife, L. and Farnsworth, R. (2003). *'Seasonality in Tourism Employment: Human Resources Challenges'*, International Journal of Contemporary Hospitality Management, 15(6), 312-16.

Jones, C. and Jowett, V. (1998). *Managing Facilities,* Butterworth Heinemann: UK.

Jones, P. (1996). *Introduction to Hospitality Operations: An Indispensable Guide to the Industry,* Cassell: UK.

Jones, P. and Kipps, M. (1995). *Flight Catering,* Longman: UK.

Jones, P. and Lockwood, A. (1989). *The Management of Hotel Operations: An Innovative Approach to the Study of Hotel Management,* Cassell: UK.

Jones, P. and Merricks, P., (1996). *The Management of Foodservice Operations,* Cassell: UK.

Jones, P. and Pizam, A. (1993). *The International Hospitality Industry: Organisational and Operational Issues,* Longman: UK.

Jordan, Debra J. (1996). *Leadership in Leisure Services: Making a Difference.* State College: Venture Pub..

Kaercher, K. (1997). *Reinventing the Package Holiday Business,* Deutscher Universitats Verlag: Germany.

Kaiser, Clifford A. (1939). *Group Feeding.* United States: s.n.

Kaiser, Clifford A. (1940). *Group Feeding.* Seattle: Frayn printing co.

Kaiser, Clifford A. (1946). *Group Feeding.* New York London: McGraw-Hill Book Company inc.

Kappa, Margaret M. (1997). *Managing Housekeeping Operations.* East Lansing: Educational Institute, American Hotel & Motel Association.

Kärcher, K. (1997). *Reinventing the Package Holiday Business.*

Karousos, George. (1993). *American Regional Cooking for 8 or 50.* New York: Wiley.

Kasavana, Michael L. (1995). *Managing Front Office Operations.* Lansing: Educational Institute of the American Hotel and Motel Association.

Kasavana, Michael L. (1997). *Managing Computers in the Hospitality Industry*. East Lansing: Educational Institute, the American Hotel and Motel Association.

Kasavana, Michael L. (1998). *Managing Front Office Operations*. Lansing: Educational Institute of the American Hotel and Motel Association.

Katsigris, Costas (1999). *Design and Equipment for Restaurants and Foodservice: A Management View*. New York: Wiley.

Katz, H.C.; Kochan, T.A.; Keefe, J.H. (1987). *Industrial Relations and Productivity in the US Automobile Industry*, Brookings Papers on Economic Activity, 3, pp. 688-715.

Katz, Jeff B. (1997). *Restaurant Planning, Design, and Construction: A Survival Manual for Owners, Operators, and Developers*. New York: John Wiley.

Kavanaugh, Raphael R. (1995). *Supervision in the Hospitality Industry*. East Lansing: Educational Institute of the American Hotel & Motel Association.

Kawakami, K. and Dovidio, J.F. (2001). *The Reliability of Implicit Stereotyping*. Personality and Social Psychology Bulletin, 27(2), 212-225.

Kazarian, Edward A. (1989). *Foodservice Facilities Planning*. New York: Van Nostrand Reinhold.

Kearns, P.; Papadopoulos, G. (2000). *Building a Learning and Training Culture: The Experience of Five OECD Countries*, NCVER (The National Centre for Vocational Education Research), Leabrook, South Australia.

Keep, E. and Mayhew, K. (1999). *The Leisure Sector (Skills Task Force Research Paper 6)*, DfEE.

Keep, E.; (2000). *Creating a Knowledge Driven Economy—Definitions, Challenges and Opportunities*, SKOPE Policy Paper No. 2, Sept., ESRC Centre on Skills, Knowledge and Organisational Performance, University of Warwick.

Keep, E.; Mayhew, K. (1998). Was Ratner Right?—Product Market and Competitive Strategies and their Links with Skills and Knowledge, *Employment Policy Institute Economic Report*, 12(3).

Kelley, M.R. (1989). *Alternative Forms of Work Organization under Programmable Automation*, in S. Wood (ed.) The Transformation of Work, London, Unwin Hyman, pp. 235-246.

Kelliher, C. and Johnson, K. (1997). 'Personnel Management in Hotels—An Update: A Move to Human Resource

Management?', *Progress in Tourism and Hospitality Research*, 3, 321-331.

Kelliher, C. and Perrett, G. (2001). 'Business Strategy and Approaches to HRM—A Case Study of New Developments in the United Kingdom Restaurant Industry', *Personnel Review*, 30(4), 421-437.

Kelly, J. (1978). A Reappraisal of Socio-technical Work Systems and Firm Performance, *Monthly Labour Review*, May, pp. 1069-99.

Kemp, K. and Pearson, S. (1996). *Intermediate GNVQ Leisure and Tourism-Optional Units*, Addison Wesley Longman: UK.

Kemp, K. and Pearson, S. (1997). *Leisure and Tourism: GNVQ Intermediate*, Addison Wesley Longman: UK.

Kerley, N. (1949). *The Milner Story*. n.p.: Milner Hotels Management Co.

Kessels, J. (1996). *Knowledge Productivity and the Corporate Curriculum*, in Schreinemakers, J.F. (ed.), *Knowledge Management: Organization, Competence and Methodology*, Proceedings of the Fourth International ISMICK (International Symposium on the Management of Industrial and Corporate Knowledge) Symposium, 21-22 Oct., Rotterdam, Wurzburg, ERGON Verl.

Kim, Il-Sun Yang (1992). *Inventory Control Systems in Foodservice Organizations: Programmed Study Guide*. Ames: Iowa State University Press.

King, B. (1998). *Creating Island Resorts*, Routledge: UK.

Kinnaird, V. (1994). *Tourism: A Gender Analysis*, Wiley: UK.

Kirby, David (September 27, 1998). *The Tourist Trap; with all Those Visitors Trampling the Welcome Mat, can New York be the Host with the Most for Everyone*? (Web). *News Article. The New York Times*. Retrieved on March 21, 2007.

Kirkman, B.L.; Lowe, K,; Young, D.P. (1999). *High-performance Work Organizations: Definitions, Practices, and an Annotated Bibliography*, Greensboro, North Carolina, Center for Creative Leadership.

Klein, S., Schmid, B., Tjoa, A.M. and Werthner, H. (eds.) (1996). *Information and Communication Technologies in Tourism: Enter 96*, Springer Verlag: Vienna.

Kling, J. (1995). *High Performance Work Systems and Firm Performance*, *Monthly Labour Review*, May, pp. 29-36.

Knowles, T. (1996). *Corporate Strategy for Hospitality*, Longman: UK.

Knowles, T. (1998). *Hospitality Management: An Introduction*, 2nd ed., Longman: UK.

Kohn, M.L.; Schooler, C. (1983). *Work and Personality: an Inquiry into the Impact of Social Stratification*, Norwood, NJ, Ablex.

Kohn, M.L.; Slomczynski, K.M. (1990). *Social Structure and Self-Direction: A Comparative Analysis of the United States and Poland*, Oxford, Blackwell.

Koike, K. (1995). *The Economics of Work in Japan*, Tokyo, LTCB International Library Foundation.

Koike, K. (1997). *Human Resource Development*, Tokyo, Japan Institute of Labour.

Koike, K. (2000). *Workers' Skills on the Shop Floor and Government Role*, Paper presented to ILO Tripartite Regional Meeting, Bangkok, 12-14, Dec., p. 18.

Koike, K.; Inoki, T. (eds.) (1990). *Skill Formation in Japan and Southeast Asia*, Tokyo, University of Tokyo Press.

Kotas, R. and Conlan, M. (1997). *Hospitality Accounting*, ITBP: UK.

Kotas, R., Teare, R., Logie, J., Jayawardena, C. and Bowen, J. (eds.) (1996). *The International Hospitality Business*, Cassell: UK.

Kotler, P., Bowen and Makens (1998). *Marketing for Hospitality and Tourism*, Prentice Hall: UK.

Kotschevar, Lendal H. (1996). *Managing Bar and Beverage Operations*. East Lansing: Educational Institute of the American Hotel and Motel Association.

Krahn, H.J.; Lowe, G.S. (1993). *Work, Industry and Canadian Society*, Scarborough, Nelson, Canada.

Kring, Robin (1993). *Party Creations: Book of Theme Event Design*. Denver: Clear Creek Pub..

Krippendorf, J. (1989). *The Holiday Makers: Understanding the Impact of Leisure and Travel*, Butterworth Heinemann: UK.

Krogt, F.; Warmerdam, J. (1997). *Training in Different Types of Organizations: Differences and Dynamics in the Organization of Learning at Work*, in International Journal of Human Resource Management, 8(1), pp. 87-105.

Kudrle, Albert E. (1995). *Public Relations for Hospitality Managers: Communicating for Greater Profits*. New York: Wiley.

Kuhn, Max. (1905). *All Happy; A Hint from Mr. Max Kuhn, Chief*

Controller of The Waldorf-astoria, Concerning A Method of Keeping Everybody Happy Who is Engaged in the Conduct of A Hotel, Café or Restaurant. New York: Wynkoop Hallenbeck Crawford Co.

Kurlantzick, Joshua (2005). *The True Meaning of the Tourist Trap (Web). News Article*. The Washington Post. Retrieved on March 21, 2007.

Lafferty, G., McMillan, J., (1989). "Labouring Leisure, Work and Industrial Relations in the Tourism Industry: Case-studies of Casinos", *Labour and Industry*. 2, 1, pp. 32-59.

Larousse, David Paul. (1993). *Sauce Bible: Guide to the Saucier's Craft*. New York: Wiley.

Larousse, David Paul. (1996). *Professional Gardẽ Manager: A Guide to the Art of the Buffet*. New York: Wiley.

Lashley, C. and Taylor, S. (1998). *'Hospitality Retail Operations Types and Styles in the Management of Human Resources'*, Journal of Retailing and Consumer Services, 5(3), 153-165.

Lattin, Gerald W. (1995). *Lodging and Food Service Industry*. East Lansing: Educational Institute of the American Hotel & Motel Association.

Lauder, H. (1999). *Competitiveness and the Problem of Low Skill Equilibria: A Comparative Analysis*, in Journal of Education and Work: (123), pp. 281-294.

Lave, J.; Wenger, E. (1991). *Situated Learning: Legitimate Peripheral Participation*, Cambridge, Cambridge University Press.

Lavery, P. (1996). *Travel and Tourism*, Elm: UK.

Lavery, P. and Van Doren, C. (1990). *Travel and Tourism: A North-American-European Perspective*, Elm: UK.

Law, C.M. (1994). *Urban Tourism: Attracting Visitors to Large Cities*, Mansell: UK.

Law, C.M. (ed.) (1996). *Tourism in Major Cities*, ITBP: UK.

Lawler, E. (1986). *High-involvement Management*, San Francisco, Jossey-Bass.

Lawler, E.; Mohrman, S.A. (1987). *Quality Circles: After the Honeymoon*, in *Organizational Dynamics*, 15(4), pp. 42-55.

Lawler, E.; Mohrman, S.A.; Ledford, G.E. (1998). *Strategies for High Performance Organizations*, CEO Report, San Francisco, Jossey-Bass.

Laws, E. (1991). *Tourism Marketing: Service and Quality Management Perspectives*, Stanley Thornes: UK.

Laws, E. (1995). *Tourist Destination Management: Issues, Analysis and Policies*, ITBP: UK.

Laws, E. (1997). *Managing Packaged Tourism: Relationships, Responsibilities and Service Quality in the Inclusive Holiday Industry*, ITBP: UK.

Laws, E. (1997). *The ATTT Tourism Education Handbook*, Tourism Society: UK.

Laws, E., Moscardo, G. and Faulkner, B. (eds.) (1998). *Embracing and Managing Change in Tourism*, Routledge: UK.

Lawson, F. (1995). *Hotels and Resorts: Planning, Design and Refurbishment*, Architectural Press: UK.

Lawson, F. (1998). *Tourism and Recreation Development*, Focal Press: UK.

Lazer, William (1999). *Contemporary Hospitality Marketing: A Service Management Approach*. Lansing: Educational Institute of the American Hotel and Motel Association.

Lea, J. (1998). *Tourism and Development in the Third World*, Routledge: UK.

Lee, W.K., Ghosh, B.C., Oliga, J., (1990). *"Strategies for Hotels in Singapore"*, Endec Practice Monograph 2, Nanyang Technological University, Singapore.

Leelaratne, P.M. (2000). *Work-Based Skills Training and Recognition in Sri Lanka*, paper delivered to the ILO/ASPDEP Conference on Workplace-Based Skills Recognition and Training, OVTA, Japan, March 2000.

Legge, K. (2001). *Silver Bullet or Spent Round? Assessing the Meaning of the High Commitment Management/Performance Relationship*, in J. Storey (ed.): *Human Resource Management: A Critical Text*, second edition, London, Thomson Learning, pp. 21-36.

Legge, Karen (2004). *Human Resource Management: Rhetorics and Realities*, Anniversary Edition, Basingstoke: Palgrave Macmillan.

Leiper, N. (1995). *Tourism Management*, RMIT Press: Australia.

Lentz, Edith M. (1947). *The Tremont Hotel Study, 1945-46: An Operational Report*. Chicago: Committee on Human Relations in Industry University of Chicago.

Leshin, Cynthia B. (1997). *Internet Investigations in Hospitality, Travel, and Tourism*. Upper Saddle River: Prentice Hall.

Levine, D. (1998). *Working in the 21st century: Government Policies to Promote Opportunity, Learning and Productivity*, Armonk, NY, Sharpe.

Levine, D. (2000). *Public Policy Implications* in Ichniowski, C.; Levine, D.I.; Olson, C.; Strauss, G., The American Workplace: Skills, Compensation and Employee Involvement, Cambridge, Cambridge University Press, pp. 273-82.

Lewis, Clifford Morgan and Lewis Hotel Training Schools (Washington D.C.) (1938). *Lewis Hotel Training Course.* Washington, D.C.: Lewis Hotel Training Schools.

Lewis, K.; Lytton, S. (1997). *How to Transform Your Company and Enjoy it*, Chalford, Management Books.

Lewis, Robert C. (1995). *Marketing Leadership in Hospitality: Foundations and Practices*. New York: Van Nostrand Reinhold.

Lewis, Robert C. (1997). *Cases in Hospitality Marketing and Management*. New York: John Wiley.

Lickorish, L. and Jenkins, K. (1997). *An Introduction to Tourism*, Focal Press: UK.

Lickorish, L.J., with Jefferson, A., Bodlender, J. and Jenkins, C.L. (1991). *Developing Tourism Destinations: Policies and Perspectives*, FT Management: UK.

Lindsay, C. and McQuaid, R.W. (2004). *'Avoiding the "Mcjobs": Unemployed Job Seekers and Attitudes to Service Work'*, Work, Employment and Society, 18(2), 297-319.

Livingstone, Helen. (1950). *Food Service; for Restaurant, Coffee Shop, Hotel, Cafeteria, Home.* Blooming II: McKnight and McKnight Pub. Co.

Lloyd, C. (2000). *High Involvement Work Systems: The Only Option for UK High Skill Sectors?*, SKOPE Research Paper No. 11, Winter, University of Warwick.

Lockhart, D.G. and Drakakis-Smith, D. (1996). *Island Tourism: Trends and Prospects*, Pinter: UK.

Lockwood, A. and Jones, P. (1984). *People and the Hotel and Catering Industry: An Introduction to Behavioural Studies and Human Relations*, Cassell: UK.

Lockwood, A. Baker, M. Ghillyer, A. (1996). *Quality Management in Hospitality*, Cassell, UK.

Loken, Joan K. (1995). *The HACCP Food Safety Manual*. New York: Wiley.

Long-term Prospects: Tourism 2020 Vision. World Tourism (2004).

Lowe, G.S. (2000). *The Quality of Work: A People-centred Agenda*, Don Mills, Ontario, Oxford.

Lucas, R. (1995). *Managing Employee Relations in the Hotel and Catering Industry*, Cassell: UK.

Lucas, R. (2004). *Employment Relations in the Hospitality and Tourism Industries*, Routledge.

Lucas, Rosemary E. (1995). *Managing Employee Relations in the Hotel and Catering Industry*. London: Cassell.

Lumsdon, L. (1997). *Tourism Marketing*, ITBP: UK.

Lundberg, D. Stavenga, M Krishnamoorthy, M. (1995). *Tourism Economics*, Wiley: USA.

Lundberg, Donald E. (1985). *The Tourist Business*. Van Nostrand Reinhold.

Lyford, Carrie A. (1932). *The School Dormitory, Administrative and Educational Problems*. Boston: M. Barrows & company.

Lynch, L.M.; Black, S.E. (1998). *Beyond the Incidence of Employer-Provided Training*, in Industrial and Labour Relations Review, No. 1, pp. 6-31.

MacDonald, C. and Sirianni, C. (1996). *Working in the Service Society*, Temple University Press.

MacDuffie, J.P. (1995). *Human Resource Bundles and Manufacturing Performance: Organizational Logic and Flexible Production Systems in the World Auto Industry*, in *Industrial and Labour Relations Review*, 48, pp. 197-221.

MacDuffie, J.P.; Frits, K.; Pil, F.K. (2000). *The Adoption of High-Involvement Work Practices*, in Ichniowski, C, Kochan, T.A., Levine, D, I., Olson, C. and Strauss, G., 2000: *What Works at Work: Overview and Assessment*, pp. 1-37, in Ichniowski, C.; Levine, D.I.; Olson, C.; Strauss, G., *The American Workplace: Skills, Compensation and Employee Involvement*, Cambridge, Cambridge University Press, pp. 137-171.

MacDuffie, J.P.; Kochan, T.A. (1995). *Do US Firms Invest Less in Human Resources? Training in the World Auto Industry*, in *Industrial Relations* 34(2), pp. 147-168.

MacEachern, Malcolm Thomas (1940). *Hospital Organization and Management*. Chicago: Physicians' record co.

MacEachern, Malcolm Thomas and L. Margueriete Prime (1946). *Hospital Organization and Management*. Chicago: Physicians' record co.

MacEachern, Malcolm Thomas and L. Margueriete Prime. (1947). *Hospital Organization and Management.* Chicago: Physicians' record co.

MacEachern, Malcolm Thomas. (1935). *Hospital Organization and Management.* Chicago: Physicians' record co.

MacLellan, R. and Smith, R. (eds.) (1998). *Tourism in Scotland,* ITBP: UK.

Madden, Clarence. (1935). *The Advertising of Hotels; An inquiry and Some Suggestive Considerations; Written for the Hotel Executive Who Needs Well-founded Opinions About the Profit-possibilities of Advertising in His Own Operation.* Chicago: Hotel Monthly Press.

Management Refresher, Course, England London, and Hotels and Restaurants Association of Great Britain. (1948). *Management Lectures: Being an introduction and Ten Lectures Given to the Members of the Hotels and Restaurants Association of Great Britain, Attending the First Management Refresher Course in London, January 1948.* London: The Association.

March, C.A. (1950). *Building Operation and Maintenance.* New York: McGraw-Hill.

Marchant, Eleanor. *Serving and Waiting; Modern Methods of Table Preparation.* New York: F.A. Stokes Company, 1905.

Marchington, M. and Grugulis, I. (2000). *'Best Practice' Human Resource Management: Perfect Opportunity or Dangerous Illusion?",* International Journal of Human Resource Management, 11(6), 1104-1124.

Marston, Kathryne S. (1945). *Cafeteria Supervision.* Stamford Conn: C. Dahl.

Martyn, Charles (1903). *The Financial Side of Hotel Keeping.* New York: The Caterer Pub. Co.

Martyn, Charles and Frank W. Doolittle (1904). *"Fables" of the Hotel Profession and Poems of "Good Cheer".* New York: The Caterer Pub. Co.

Marvin, Bill (1997). *Guest-Based Marketing: How to Increase Restaurant Sales Without Breaking Your Budget.* New York: John Wiley.

Mason, Dexter and H.M. Metcalf (1930). *The Art of Drinking; or, What to Make with What You Have, Together with Divers Succulent Canapés Suitable to Each Occasion.* New York: Farrar & Rinehart.

Mason, G. (1999). *Product Strategies, Work Force Skills, and 'High-Involvement' Work Practices,* in P. Cappelli (ed.): *Employment Practices and Business Strategies,* New York, Oxford, pp. 193-216.

Mathieson, A. and Wall, G. (1992). *Tourism: Economic, Physical and Social Impacts,* Longman: UK.

Matlay, H. (1999). Employers' Perceptions and Implementation of S/NVQs in Britain: A Critical Overview, in *International Journal of Training and Development,* Vol. 3. No. 2, pp. 132-141.

Maury, Sarah Webb and Lena L. Tachau. (1915). *A Penny Lunch, Its Equipment, Menus and Management.* Louisville Ky: The Standard Printing Co. Incorporated.

Mazanec, J.A. with Grabler, K., Maier, G., Mazanec, J.A. and Wober, K. (1997). *International City Tourism,* Pinter: UK.

McComb, David J. (1907). *Remco's Manual of Apartment House Service.* New York: The McClure Company.

McCormack, F. (1994). *Water Based Recreation: Managing Water Resources for Leisure.*

McDonnell, Jane (1994). *Step By Step Art of Table Decorating.* New York: Crescent Books.

McGovern, John. (1910). *Hospitality; Mine Host, from the Time of Babylon to the Age of the Aeroplane.* Chicago: The Hotel Monthly.

McGunnigle, P. and Jameson, S. (2000). *'HRM in UK Hotels: A Focus on Commitment'*, Employee Relations, 22(4), 403-422.

McIntosh, R.W., Goeldner, C.R. and Ritchie, J.R.B. (1995). *Tourism: Principles, Practices, Philosophies,* Wiley: UK.

McKenney, Ella Clark (1923). *Cooking problems of the Community Group and Formulas Standardized for Quantity work; Breads.* Boston: Whitcomb & Barrows.

McMillan, J., Lafferty, G., (1989). *"The Tourism Workforce: Service or Servility"*, in Carroll, P. *et al.* (eds), *Tourism in Australia,* Harcourt Brace Jovanovich, Sydney, pp. 82-96.

McMurrer; Van Buren, M.; Woodwell, W.H. (2000). *The 2000 ASTD State of the Industry Report,* Alexandria, VA, ASTD.

McNeill, L. (1997). *Travel In the Digital Age,* Bowerdean Publishing: UK.

McSwane, David Zachary. (2000). *Essentials of Food Safety and Sanitation.* Upper Saddle River: Prentice Hall.

Medlik, S. (1994). *The Business of Hotels,* Butterworth Heinemann: UK.

Medlik, S. (1995). *Managing Tourism*, Butterworth Heinemann: UK.

Medlik, S. (1996). *Dictionary of Travel, Tourism and Hospitality*, Butterworth Heinemann: UK.

Medlik, S. (1997). *Understanding Tourism*, Butterworth Heinemann: UK.

Meek, Howard Bagnall. (1938). *Theory of Hotel Room Rates.* Ithaca N Y: Cornell University.

Meeting Co-ordinator: Standards. Mississauga: Meeting Professionals International, Canadian Council, 1994.

Meeting Manager: Standards. Mississauga: Meeting Professionals International, Canadian Council, 1994.

Middleton, V.T.C. (1994). *Marketing in Travel and Tourism*, Butterworth Heinemann: UK.

Middleton, V.T.C. with Hawkins, R. (1998). *Sustainable Tourism: A Marketing Perspective*, Butterworth Heinemann: UK.

Mill, R.C. (1992). *The Tourism System: An Introductory Text*, Prentice Hall: UK.

Mill, R.C. and Morrison, A.M., (1998). *The Tourism System*, 3rd ed., Kendall/Hunt Publishing 4050 Westmark Drive, Dubuque, Iowa 52002.

Mills, Irving J. (1989). *Tabletop Presentations: A Guide for the Foodservice Professional.* New York: Van Nostrand Reinhold.

Mommaas, H., Van der Poel, H., Bramham, P. and Henry, I.P. (eds.) (1996). *Leisure Research in Europe: Methods and Traditions*, CAB International: UK.

Montanari, A. and Williams, A.M. (1995). *European Tourism: Regions, Spaces and Restructuring*, Wiley: UK.

Morrison, A.M. (1996). *Hospitality and Travel Marketing*, Delmar: UK.

Mowforth, M. and Munt, I. (1998). *Tourism and Sustainability: New Tourism in the Third World*, Routledge: UK.

Mullins, L.J. (1996), *Management and Organisational Behaviour*, Pitman, 4th ed.

Mullins, L.J. (1998). *Managing People in the Hospitality Industry*, Longman: UK.

Murphy, P.E. (1985). *Tourism: A Community Approach*, ITBP: UK.

Murphy, P.E. (ed.) (1997). *Quality Management in Urban Tourism* Wiley: UK.

Nam, Inja. (1993). *Art of Garnishing*. New York: Van Nostrand Reinhold.

Nankervis, A.R., (1990). *"Servants or Service: Perspectives of the Australian Hotel Industry"*, Working Paper No. 73, August, School of Business, University of Western Sydney (Nepean), Sydney.

Nankervis, A.R., (1991). *"Human Resource Management in the Australian Hotel Industry"*, Working Paper No. 79, September, Faculty of Commerce, University of Western Sydney (Nepean), Sydney.

Nash, D. (1996). *Anthropology of Tourism*, Pergamon Press: UK.

Nation's Restaurant News: The Weekly Newspaper of the Food Service Industry. New York: Lebhar-Friedman.

National Food Reform Association. (1910). *The Feeding of Nurses. Report of The Proceedings at A Conference of Matrons of Hospitals and Similar Institutions Held at Caxton Hall, Westminster, November 5th, 1910*. Westminster S W.

New Professional Chef. New York: Wiley, 1996.

New York State Restaurant Association and Elsabelle Curtis, and Crete M. Dahl (1945). *How to Get and Keep Restaurant Employees: The Association Reference Book*. New York: New York State Restaurant Association.

New York State Restaurant Association and Elsabelle Curtis (1949). *How to Cut Labour Costs*. New York: New York State Restaurant Association.

New York State Restaurant Association., Max J. Kleiner, and Samuel A. Coleman (1948). *The Sanitation Manual, A Guide for Management*. New York: New York State Restaurant Association, .

New Yorker Hotel (1931). *Front Office Manual, New Yorker Hotel*. S l: s.n.

Newspaper Item—Author Unknown.

Nicholls, Henry (2006). *The Tourist Trap* (*The Galapagos Islands are The World's Prime Eco-tourism Destination. Now the Sheer Number of Visitors is Endangering Their Future*) (Web). *News Article*. Guardian. Retrieved on March 21, 2007.

Nickson, D. and Wood, R.C. (2000). 'HRM in the Hotel Industry: A Comment and Response', *Human Resource Management Journal*, 10(4), 88-90.

Nickson, D., Baum, T., Losekoot, E. *et al.* (2002). *Skills, Organizational Performance and Economic Activity in the Hospitality Industry: A Literature Review*, Universities of Oxford and Warwick: SKOPE.

Ninemeier, Jack D. (1995). *Management of Food and Beverage Operations*. East Lansing: Educational Institute of the American Hotel and Motel Association.

Ninemeier, Jack D. (1998). *Planning and Control for Food and Beverage Operations*. Orlando: Educational Institute.

Notarius, Barbara (1996). *Open Your Own Bed & Breakfast*. New York: John Wiley & Sons, Inc..

Nykiel, Ronald A. (1997). *Marketing in the Hospitality Industry*. East Lansing: Educational Institute of the American Hotel and Motel Association.

O'Brien, Daniel J. and Charles Bennington Couchman. (1927). *Hotel Administration, Accounts and Control*. New York: McGraw-Hill Book Company Inc.

O'Connor, P. (1996). *Using Computers in Hospitality*, Cassell: UK.

O'Reilly, J. (1992). *Where do You Draw the Line? Functional Flexibility, Training and Skill in Britain and France*, in *Work Employment and Society*, 6(3), pp. 369-396.

Odell, Margaret K. and Earl Poe Strong (1947). *Records Management and Filing Operations*. New York: McGraw-Hill Book Co.

OECD (1996). *Technology, Productivity and Job Creation: Best Policy Practices*, Paris, OECD.

OECD (1999). *Employment Outlook*, June 1999, Paris, OECD.

OECD (2000). *Is There a New Economy?*, First Report on the OECD Growth Project, Paris, OECD.

OECD (2000a). *Thematic Review on Adult Learning, Norway*, Background Report, Paris, OECD, June.

OECD (2001). *Science, Technology and Industry Scoreboard 2001*, Paris, OECD.

Ogden, Henry N. and Henry Burdett Cleveland (1912). *Practical Methods of Sewage Disposal for Residences, Hotels and Institutions*. New York: J. Wiley.

Ohio Dietetic Association (1946). *Manual for School and Institutional Lunchrooms*. Cleveland.

Online Article (access date is shown in square parentheses).

Only the Best on Customer Service. Tulsa: Win Publications, 1996.

Onstenk, J. (1997). *Innovation, Work Teams and Learning On-the-Job*, Paper for EU Seminar on Knowledge and Work, Amsterdam, cited in Stern and Sommerlad: Workplace learning, culture and performance, IPD/IFTDO, London, IPD, 1999.

Oppermann, M. (ed.) (1997). *Pacific Rim Tourism*, CAB International: UK.

Oppermann, M. and Chon, K.S. (1997). *Tourism in Developing Countries*, ITBP: UK.

Osterman, P. (1994). *How Common is Workplace Transformation and Who Adopts It?*, in *Industrial and Labour Relations Review*, 47(2), pp. 173-188.

Osterman, P. (1995). *Skill, Training and Work Organisation in American Establishments*, in *Industrial Relations*, Vol. 34. No. 2, April, pp. 125-146.

Osterman, P. (1998). *Work Reorganization in an Era of Restructuring: Trends in Diffusion and Impacts on Employee Welfare*, Sloan School, The MIT Press, mimeo, quoted in OECD, 1999.

Osterman, P. (1998a). *Changing Work Organisation in America: What has Happened and Who has Benefited?* in Transfer, 2, pp. 246-263.

Otterbourg, Robert K. (1999). *Success Without College. Careers in the Food Service Industry*. Hauppauge: Barron's Educational Series.

Owen, G. (1998). *Accounting for Hospitality, Tourism and Leisure*, Longman: UK.

Page, S. (1994). *Transport for Tourism*, ITBP: UK.

Page, S. (1995). *Urban Tourism*, ITBP: UK.

Page, S. and Hall, C. (1998). *The geography of recreation and tourism*, Routledge: UK.

Page, S.J. and Getz, D. (eds.) (1997). *The Business of Rural Tourism: International Perspectives*, ITBP: UK.

Palmer, Mary E. (1908). *Guide to Hotel Housekeeping*. Charleston W Va: The Tribune Printing Co.

Pannett, A. and Boella, M. (1996). *Principles of Hospitality Law*, Cassell: UK.

Patterson, M.G.; West, M.A.; Lawthorn, R.; Nickells, S. (1997). *The Impact of People Management Practices on Business Performance*, in IPD Issues in People Management, No. 22, London.

Pattullo, P. (1996). *Last Resorts: The Cost of Tourism in the Caribbean*, Cassell: UK.

Payne, C.; Lloyd, C (2001). *Towards a Political Economy of Skill?*, paper presented at the Labour Process Conference, London, Royal Holloway, March.

Peacock, M. (1995). *Information Technology in the Hospitality Industry*, Cassell: UK.

Pearce, D. (1989). *Tourist Development*, Longman: UK.

Pearce, D. (1992). *Tourist Organisations*, Longman: UK.

Pearce, D. (1995). *Tourism Today: A Geographical Analysis*, Longman: UK.

Pearce, P., Morrison, A. and Rutledge, J. (1998). *Tourism: Bridges Across Continents*, Irwin McGraw-Hill Australia.

Pearce, P.L., Moscardo, G. Ross, G. (1997). *Tourism Community Relationships*, Pergamon Press: UK.

Pender, Lesley (1999). *Marketing Management for Travel and Tourism*. Cheltenham: Stanley Thornes Publishers.

People 1st (2006). *Skills Needs Assessment*, People 1st.

Pepitone, J.S. (1995). *Future Training,: A Roadmap for Restructuring the Training Function*, Dallas, Advantage Learning Press.

Perego, Grace (1934). *Apartment House Ownership and Management; Purchasing, Leasing and Managing*. Rochester N.Y.: Rochester alliance press inc.

Personnel management (2005). *The Columbia Encyclopedia* (Sixth Edition). Columbia University Press. Retrieved on 2007-10-17. "personnel management—see industrial management."

Peters, T.J., Waterman, R.H., (1982). *In Search of Excellence: Lessons from America's Best Run Companies*, Harper & Row, London.

Peterson, James. (1998). *Sauces: Classical and Contemporary Sauce Making*. New York: Van Nostrand Reinhold.

Pfeffer, J. (1998). *The Human Equation: Building Profits by Putting People First*, Boston, Harvard Business School Press.

Pigors, Paul John William and Charles Andrew Myers (1947). *Personnel Administration, a Point of View and a Method*. New York: McGraw-Hill Book Co.

Pil, F.K.; MacDuffie, J.P. (1999). *Organizational and Environmental Factors Influencing the Use and Diffusion of High Involvement Work Practices*, in Cappelli, P.: Employment practices and business strategy, Oxford, Oxford University Press, pp. 81-106.

Pil, F.K.; MacDuffie, J.P. (2000). *The Adoption of High-Involvement Work Practices*, in Ichniowski, C.; Kochan, T.A.; Levine, D.I.; Olson, C.; Strauss, G. (2000): *What Works at Work: Overview and Assessment*, in Ichniowski, C.; Levine, D.I.; Olson, C.; Strauss, G., The American Workplace: Skills, Compensation and Employee Involvement, Cambridge, Cambridge University Press, pp. 1-37.

Pixley, Francis William (1914). *Clubs and Their Management*. New York: Sir I. Pitman.

Pixley, Francis W. (1927). *Clubs and Their Management*. London New York etc: Sir I. Pitman & Sons Ltd.

Pizam, A. and Mansfield (eds.) (1995). *Tourism, Crime and International Security Issues*, Wiley: UK.

Plante, Ellen M. (1995). *The American Kitchen: 1700 to the Present*. New York: Facts On File.

Pocket Guide to the ADA: Americans with Disabilities Act Accessibility Guidelines for Buildings and Facilities. New York: John Wiley and Sons, 1997.

Pollard, S. (1965). *The Genesis of Modern Management*, Harmondsworth, Penguin.

Pompl, W. and Lavery, P. (eds.) (1995). *Tourism in Europe: Structures and Developments*, CAB International: UK.

Poon, A. (1993). *Tourism, Technology and Competitive Strategies*, CAB: UK.

Porter, M. (1985). *Competitive Advantage*, New York, Free Press.

Powell, Fred. (1971). *Bartender's Standard Manual*. New York: Wings Book.

Powers, T. (1997). *Marketing Hospitality*, Wiley: UK.

Powers, Thomas F. (1995). *Introduction to Management in the Hospitality Industry*. New York: Wiley.

Powers, Thomas F. (1995). *Introduction to the Hospitality Industry*. New York: Wiley.

Powers, Thomas F. (1997). *Marketing Hospitality*. New York: Wiley.

Poynter, J. (1993). *How to Research and Write a Thesis in Hospitality and Tourism: A Step by Step Guide for College Students*, Wiley: UK.

Practical, Man (1850). *The Innkeeper and Public Brewer: Containing Hints for Managing Spirits and Wines*. London: G. Biggs.

Prais, S.J., Jarvis, V., Wagner, K., (1989). *"Productivity and Vocational Skills in Services in Britain and Germany: Hotels"*, National Institute Economic Review (U.K.), November, pp. 52-72.

Price, L. (1994). *'Poor Personnel Practice in the Hotel and Catering*

Industry—Does It Matter?', Human Resource Management Journal, 4(4), 44-62.

Price, M.F. (ed.) (1996). *People and Tourism in Fragile Environments,* Wiley: UK.

Priestley, G.K., Edwards, J.A. and Coccossis, H. (eds.) (1996). *Sustainable Tourism?: European Experiences,* CAB International: UK, HB.

Professional Chef's Techniques of Healthy Cooking. New York: John Wiley & Sons, 1993.

Professional Meeting Management. Birmingham: Professional Convention Management, 1996.

Promoting Tourism in Rural America. USDA, National Agricultural Library, Rural Information Center, 2004.

Proskauer, Julien J. (1933). *What'll You Have ?: A Not Too Dry Text Book About Cocktails...And What to Serve with Them.* New York: A.L. Burt Co.

Purcell, J. (1999). *Best Practice and Best Fit: chimera or cul-de-sac,* in *Human Resource Management Journal,* 9(3), pp. 26-41.

Radell, Neva Henrietta (1935). *Accounting and Food Control for Home Economics Students.* New York: F.S. Crofts & Co.

Ramage, Edward D. (1931). *A Study of Minor Operated Departments: Based on the Operating Statements of one Hundred Eighty Hotels.* Ithaca, N.Y.: [E. Ramage?].

Rande, Wallace L. (1996). *Introduction to Professional Foodservice.* New York: Wiley.

Raper, P.; Ashton, D.; Felstead, A.; Storey, J. (1997). *Towards the Learning Organisation? Explaining Current Trends in Training Practice in the UK,* in *International Journal of Training and Development,* Vol. 1, No. 1, pp. 9-21.

Ravenscroft, N. (1992). *Recreation Planning and Development,* Macmillan: UK.

Redman, T. and Matthews, B. (1998). *'Service Quality and Human Resource Management: A Review and Research Agenda',* Personnel Review, 27(1), 57-77.

Reed, Lewis. (1993). *Specs: The Comprehensive Foodservice Purchasing and Specification Manual.* Van Nostrand Reinhold.

Reeve, Archie Frederick (1935). *Club Economies; "Suggestions for Membership Clubs and How to Operate Within Their Budget".* New York: Cleveland Publishing Co.

Thompson, P.; Wallace, T.; Flecker, G.; Ahlstrand, R. (1995). *It Ain't What You Do, It's The Way That You Do It: Production Organisation and Skill Utilisation in Commercial Vehicle*, in *Work, Employment and Society*, 9(4), pp. 719-42.

Timo, N., (1992). *"Employment Relations of the Labour Market in Tourism"*, Journal of Employment Relations, 1, 1, November.

Tjoa, A.M. (1997). *Information and Communication Technologies in Tourism: Enter 97*, Springer Verlag: Vienna.

Ton, My. (1996). *Greening Your Property*. Washington, D.C.: Green Seal.

Torkildsen, G. (1992). *Leisure and Recreation Management*, Spon: UK.

Towers, David. *Human Resource Management Essays*. Retrieved on 2007-10-17.

Travel and Tourism: An Overlooked Industry in the U.S. and Tenth DistrictPDF (595 KiB). By Chad Wilkerson. *Economic Review*, Third Quarter 2003. Federal Reserve Board in Kansas.

Tribe, J. (1995). *The Economics of Leisure and Tourism: Environments, Markets and Impacts*, Butterworth Heinemann: UK.

Tribe, J. (1997). *Corporate Strategy for Tourism*, ITBP: UK.

Tunbride, J.E. and Ashworth, G.J. (1995). *Dissonant Heritage: The Management of the Past as a Resource in Conflict*, Wiley: UK.

Tung-Chun Huang (1997). *The Effect of Participative Management on Organizational Performance: The Case of Taiwan*, in *International Journal of Human Resource Management*, 8(5), pp. 677-689.

Turbin, J. (2001). *Policy Borrowing: Lessons from European Attempts to Transfer Training Practices* in *International Journal of Education and Training*, forthcoming, June 2001.

Turner, E. (1949). *A Catering Business of Your Own; Teashop, Cafe & Restaurant Management*. London: Practical Press Ltd.

Ulm, Robert A. (1994). *How Much to Buy: A Foodservice Purchasing Workbook*. New York: Macmillan Pub. Company.

Ulrich, Dave (1996). *Human Resource Champions: The Next Agenda for Adding Value and Delivering Results*. Boston, Mass.: Harvard Business School Press.

United Hotels Company of America (1928). *Administrative Control: A Manual for Managers*. New York: United Hotels Co. of America.

Unwin, L. (2000). *Delivering Key Skills Effectively*, London, Department for Education and Employment.

UNWTO World Tourism Barometer. World Tourism Organization, (2007).

Urry, J. (1995). *Consuming Places*, Routledge: UK.

Van Buren, M. (1999). *A Yardstick for Knowledge Management*, Alexandria, ASTD.

Van Buren, M.; King, S.B. (2000). *The 2000 ASTD International Comparisons Report*, Alexandria, ASTD.

Van den Berg, L. Van der Borg, J. Van der Meer, J. (1995). *Urban Tourism: Performance and Strategies in Eight European Cities*, Avebury: UK.

Van Hoof, Hubert B. (1996). *A Host of Opportunities: An Introduction to Hospitality Management*. Chicago: Irwin.

Vaughan, E. (1994). *'The Trail between Sense and Sentiment: A Reflection on the Language of HRM'*, Journal of General Management, 19(3), 20-32.

Veal, A.J. (1997). *Research Methods for Leisure and Tourism: A Practical Guide*, FT Management: UK.

Vehling, Joseph Dommers *et al.* (1854). *Cooking, or, Practical and Economical Training for Those Who are to be Servants, Wives, and Mothers: Management of The Kitchen, Plain Cooking, Bread-making, Baking, Brewing, Pickling, etc.* London: J. Masters.

Vellas, F. and Becherel, L. (1995). *International Tourism*, Macmillan: UK.

Venison, P. (1983). *Managing Hotels*, Butterworth Heinemann: UK.

Verma, A.; Kochan, T.A.; Landsbury, R.D. (1995). *Employment Relations in the Growing Asian Economies*, London, Routledge.

Virts, William B. (1996). *Purchasing for Hospitality Operations*. East Lansing: Educational Institute of the American Hotel and Motel Association.

VNR's Encyclopaedia of Hospitality and Tourism. New York: Van Nostrand Reinhold, 1993.

Vukonic, B. (1996) *Tourism and Religion*, Pergamon Press: UK.

Wadhams, Caroline Reed (1917). *Simple Directions for the Waitress or Parlor Maid.* New York: Longmans Green and Co..

Wahab, S. and Pigram, J.J. (eds.) (1997) *Tourism, Development and Growth: The Challenge of Sustainability*, Routledge: UK.

Waldren, J. (1996). *Insiders and Outsiders: Paradise and Reality in Mallorca*, Berghahn Books: UK.

Walker, John R. (1996). *Introduction to Hospitality*. Upper Saddle River: Prentice Hall.

Waller, Keith (1996). *Improving Food and Beverage Performance.* Oxford: Butterworth-Heinemann.

Walsh, Joseph F. (1935). *Sound Spending, With Special Reference to the Operating Cost of Institutions, Schools, Colleges, Hospitals, Orphanages, Convents, Monasteries, etc., Seminaries, Parishes.* Cleveland: Seminary Press.

Walsh, Margaret M. and Welfare Federation of Cleveland (1950). *Food and Nutrition Manual for Institutions.* Cleveland: Welfare Federation of Cleveland.

Walter, B., (1987). *"Smile Until it Hurts"*, Australian Business, November, pp. 66-69.

Wan Seman Bin Wan Ahmad (1999). *Country Paper: Malaysia,* delivered to the ILO Asian and Pacific Tripartite Consultative Meeting on Human Resource Development and Training, Singapore, 30 June-2 July.

Wang Xiaojun (2000). *Profile of Chinese Enterprise Training and Intra-enterprise Appraisal,* paper delivered to the ILO/ASPDEP Conference on Workplace-Based Skills Recognition and Training, OVTA, Japan, March 2000.

Ware, Richard (1991). *How to Open Your Own Restaurant: A Guide for Entrepreneurs*. New York: Penguin Books.

Water Resources for Lodging Operations. East Lansing: Educational Institute of the American Hotel & Motel Association, 1995.

Watt, D. (1998). *Event Management in Leisure and Tourism*, Longman: UK.

Wearne, N. and Morrison, A. (1996). *Hospitality Marketing,* Focal Press: UK.

Weaver, D. (1998). *Ecotourism in the Less Developed World,* CAB International: UK.

Weinstein, M.; Kochan, T. (1995). *The Limits of Diffusion: Recent Developments in Industrial Relations and Human Resource Practices in the United States,* in Locke, R.; Kochan, T. and Piore, M. (eds.): *Employment Relations in a Changing Economy,* Cambridge, MA, MIT Press.

Wells, A.T. (1993). *Air Transportation,* ITBP: UK.

Wendehack, Clifford Charles (1929). *Golf and Country Clubs; A Survey of the Requirement of Planning Construction and Equipment of the Modern Club House.* New York: W. Helburn inc.

Wenzel, G.L. (1948). *Handbook of Restaurant Costs: How to Maintain a 40 per cent Food Cost and a 25 per cent Payroll.* Austin, Texas: G. Wenzel.

Wenzel, G.L. (1948). *Portion Control and Food Cost Manual,* New York, N.Y.: Paper Cup and Container Institute.

Werner Hunziker and Kurt (1941). *Grundriss der Allgemeinen Fremdenverkehrslehre.* OCLC.

West, Bessie Brooks and LeVelle Wood (1938). *Food Service in Institutions.* New York; London: J. Wiley & Sons Inc; Chapman & Hall Limited.

West, Bessie Brooks and LeVelle Wood (1945). *Food Service in Institutions.* New York: Wiley.

Western Australia Police Service (1999). *Western Australia Police Service Annual Report 1999.* Perth, Western Australia.

Wheatcroft, S. (1994), *Aviation and Tourism Policies: Balancing the Benefits,* ITBP: UK.

Whitaker, Alma Fullford (1933). *Bacchus Behave! The Lost Art of Polite Drinking.* New York: F.A. Stokes, .

Whitehead, Jessup (1889). *The Steward's Handbook and Guide to Party Catering.* Chicago: J. Anderson & Co. printers.

Whitehead, Jessup *et al.* (1903). *The Steward's Handbook and Guide to Party Catering.* Chicago: J. Whitehead & Co.

Whitfield, K. (2000). *High-performance Workplaces, Training, and the Distribution of Skills,* in Industrial Relations, 39(1), pp. 1-25.

Whitley, R. (1999). *Divergent Capitalisms: The Social Structuring and Change of Business Systems,* Oxford, Oxford University Press.

Wickens, P. (1999). *Energise Your Enterprise,* London, Macmillan.

Wigger, G. Eugene (1997). *Themes, Dreams, and Schemes: Banquet Menu Ideas, Concepts, and Thematic Experiences.* New York: John Wiley.

Wilkinson, A. (1988). *"Empowerment: Theory and Practice".* Personnel Review 27(1): 40-56. Retrieved on 2007-10-17.

Wilkinson, Jule (1981). *Complete Book of Cooking Equipment.* Boston: CBI Pub. Company.

Wilkinson, P. (1997). *Tourism Policy and Planning: Case Studies form the Commonwealth Caribbean,* Cognizant Communications: USA.

Williams, A.M. and Shaw, G. (1991). *Tourism and Economic Development: Western European Experiences,* Wiley: UK.

Williamson, Jefferson and Herndon/Vehling Collection (1930). *The American Hotel; An Anecdotal History.* New York: A.A. Knopf.

Winfield, P., *et al.* (2000), *Core Management for HR Students and Practitioners,* Butterworth-Heinemann.

Witt, S.F. and Moutinho, L. (1995). *Tourism Marketing and Management Handbook: Student Edition*, Prentice Hall: UK.

Witt, S.F. and Witt, C.A. (1992). *Modelling and Forecasting Demand in Tourism*, Academic Press: UK.

Witt, S.F., Brooke, M.Z. and Buckley, P.J. (1995). *The Management of International Tourism*, ITBP: UK.

Wolff, M.P. and H.R. (1884). Haweis. *Food for the Million: A Plan for Starting Public Kitchens: With Statistical Tables, Calculations of The Prices of Thirty-six Dishes, Statement of the Starting Expense, the Yearly Current Expenditure, the Gross and Net Profits of A Public Kitchen, and A Ground-plan.* London: Sampson Low Marston Searle and Rivington.

Womack, J.P.; Jones, D.T.; Roos, D. (1990). *The Machine that Changed the World*, New York, Rawson Associates.

Women of Taste: Recipes and Profiles of Famous Women Chefs. New York: Wiley, 1997.

Wood, R.C. (1994). *Organizational Behaviour for Hospitality Management*, Butterworth Heinemann: UK.

Wood, R.C. (1997), *Working in Hotels and Catering*, International Thomson Press, 2nd edition.

Wood, S. (1999). *Human Resource Management and Performance*, in International Journal of Management Review, I (4), pp. 367-413.

Wood, S.; with de Menezes, L.; Lasaosa, A. (2001): *High Involvement Management and Performance*, Paper Delivered at CLMS, University of Leicester, May 2001.

Woods, Robert H. (1996). *Quality Leadership and Management in the Hospitality Industry*. East Lansing: Educational Institute of the American Hotel & Motel Association.

Woods, Robert H. (1997). *Managing Hospitality Human Resources*. East Lansing: Educational Institute of the American Hotel & Motel Association.

World Bank (1994). *Averting the Old Age Crisis: Policies to Protect the Old and Promote Growth*. Washington DC: World Bank and Oxford University Press.

World Travel and Tourism Council (WTTC) (2006). *Travel and Tourism Climbing New Heights: The 2006 Travel and Tourism Economic Research*, at http://www.wttc.org/2006TSA/pdf/Executive%20Summary%202006.pdf.

Worthington, May. *Sally, Army Dietitian* (1944). New York: Dodd Mead.

WTO (1990). *Integration of Tourism in Europe*, World Tourism Organisation Madrid.

WTO (1991). *Tourism to the Year 2000: Qualitative Aspects Affecting Global Growth*, World Tourism Organisation Madrid.

WTO (1992). *An Integrated Approach to Resort Development*.

WTO (1992). *Guidelines: Development of National Parks and Protected Areas for Tourism*, World Tourism Organisation Madrid.

WTO (1992). *World Directory of Tourism Education and Training Institutions*, World Tourism Organisation Madrid.

WTO (1993). *Investments and Financing in the Tourism Industry*, World Tourism Organisation Madrid.

WTO (1993). *Sustainable Tourism Development: Guide for Local Planners*, World Tourism Organisation Madrid.

WTO (1993). *Tourism Development and Responsibility of the State*, World Tourism Organisation Madrid.

WTO (1994). *GATS Implications for Tourism*, World Tourism Organisation Madrid.

WTO (1994). *Global Tourism Forecasts 'Africa'*, World Tourism Organisation Madrid.

WTO (1994). *Global Tourism Forecasts 'Americas'*, World Tourism Organisation Madrid.

WTO (1994). *Global Tourism Forecasts 'East Asia and the Pacific'*, World Tourism Organisation Madrid.

WTO (1994). *Global Tourism Forecasts 'Europe' World*, Tourism Organisation Madrid.

WTO (1994). *Global Tourism Forecasts 'Middle East'*, World Tourism Organisation Madrid.

WTO (1994). *Global Tourism Forecasts 'South Asia'*, World Tourism Organisation Madrid.

WTO (1994). *Global Tourism Forecasts the World*, World Tourism Organisation Madrid.

WTO (1994). *Tourism Statistics in the Central and Eastern European Countries*, World Tourism Organisation Madrid.

WTO (1994). *WTO Basic Documents*, World Tourism Organisation, Madrid.

WTO (1995). *Collection and Compilation of Tourism Statistics: Technical Manual No. 4*, World Tourism Organisation Madrid.

WTO (1995). *Collection of Domestic Tourism Statistics: Technical Manual No. 3*, World Tourism Organisation Madrid.

WTO (1995). *Collection of Tourism Expenditure Statistics: Technical Manual No. 2*, World Tourism Organisation Madrid.

WTO (1995). *Concepts, Definitions, and Classifications for Tourism Statistics: Technical Manual No. 1*, World Tourism Organisation Madrid.

WTO (1995). *Educating The Educators in Tourism*, World Tourism Organisation Madrid.

WTO (1995). *Implications of the WTO/UN Tourism Definitions*, World Tourism Organisation Madrid.

WTO (1995). *Shining in the Media Spotlight*, World Tourism Organisation Madrid.

WTO (1996). *Awards for Improving the Coastal Environment: The Example of the Blue Flag*, World Tourism Organisation Madrid.

WTO (1996). *Budgets of National Tourism Administration*, World Tourism Organisation Madrid.

WTO (1996). *Educating the Educators: A Manual of Tourism and Hospitality Education*, World Tourism Organization: UK.

WTO (1996). *Recommendations on Tourism Statistics*, World Tourism Organisation Madrid.

WTO (1996). *Timeshare: The New Force in Tourism*, World Tourism Organisation Madrid.

WTO (1996). *Tourism and Environmental Protection*, World Tourism Organisation Madrid.

WTO (1996). *Tourism and New Information Technologies*, World Tourism Organisation Madrid.

WTO (1996). *Tourist Safety and Security: Practical Measures for Destinations*, World Tourism Organisation Madrid.

WTO (1996). *What Tourism Managers Need to Know*, World Tourism Organisation Madrid.

WTO (1997). *'Africa' Tourism Market Trends 1997 Series*, World Tourism Organisation Madrid.

WTO (1997). *Agenda 21 for the Travel and Tourism Industry*, World Tourism Organisation Madrid.

WTO (1997). *'Americas' Tourism Market Trends 1997 Series*, World Tourism Organisation Madrid.

WTO (1997). *Asia Tourism—Towards New Horizons*, World Tourism Organisation Madrid.

WTO (1997). *Compendium of Tourism Statistics,* World Tourism Organisation Madrid.

WTO (1997). *'Europe' Tourism Market Trends 1997 Series,* World Tourism Organisation Madrid.

WTO (1997). *'Middle East' Tourism Market Trends 1997 Series,* World Tourism Organisation Madrid.

WTO (1997). *East Asia and the Pacific,* Tourism Market Trends 1997 Series, World Tourism Organisation Madrid.

WTO (1997). *Marketing the Mediterranean as a Region,* World Tourism Organisation Madrid.

WTO (1997). *Multilateral and Bilateral Sources of Financing for Tourism Development,* World Tourism Organisation Madrid.

WTO (1997). *Quality—A Challenge for Tourism,* World Tourism Organisation Madrid.

WTO (1997). *Rural Tourism: A Solution for Employment, Local Development, and Environment,* World Tourism Organisation Madrid.

WTO (1997). *Senior Tourism,* World Tourism Organisation Madrid.

WTO (1997). *South Asia Tourism Market Trends 1997 Series,* World Tourism Organisation Madrid.

WTO (1997). *Yearbook of Tourism Statistics,* World Tourism Organisation Madrid.

Yale, P. (1992). *Tourism in the UK,* Elm: UK.

Yale, P. (1995). *The Business of Tour Operations,* Longman: UK.

Yale, P. (1998). *From Tourist Attractions to Heritage Tourism,* Elm: UK.

Yaqub, Z. and Bedford (1997). *European Travel Law,* Wiley: UK.

Yeoman, I. and Ingold, A. (1997). *Yield Management: Strategies for the Service Industries,* Cassell: UK.

Youell, R. (1995). *Leisure and Tourism: Advanced GNVQ,* Longman: UK.

Youell, R. (1996). *The Complete A-Z Leisure, Travel and Tourism Handbook,* Hodder and Stoughton: UK.

Youell, R. (1996). *Travel and Tourism Optional Units: Advanced GNVQ,* Longman: UK.

Youell, R. (1998). *Tourism: An Introduction,* Longman: UK.

Youndt, M.; Snell, S.A.; Dean, J.W. Lepak, D.P. (1996). *Human Resource Management, Manufacturing Strategy, and Firm Performance,* in Academy of Management Journal, 39(4), pp. 836-866.

Young Women's Christian Association of the U.S.A. National Board., Jeanette Dutchess, and Emma H. Phinney (1930). *Housing for Girls; the Y.W.C.A. Residence and Its Management.* New York: Woman's Press.

Zaccarelli, Herman E. (1991). *Food Service Management by Checklist: A Handbook of Control Techniques*. New York: Wiley.

Zahler, Karen Gantz (1996). *Superchefs: Signature Recipes From America's New Royalty*. New York: John Wiley & Sons.

Zeithami, A., Parasuraman, A., Berry, L., (1990). *Delivering Quality Service: Balancing Customer Perceptions and Expectations,* The Free Press, New York.

Journals and Other Reading

It is recommended that students also read widely from magazines produced by the professional bodies such as the Institute of Personnel and Development, as well as publications like the Employment Gazette, International Human Resource Management Journal, Harvard Business Review and Management Today.

Index